CIDER

hard and sweet

2ND edition

HISTORY, TRADITIONS, AND MAKING YOUR OWN

Ben Watson

The Countryman Press • *Woodstock, Vermont*

Library of Congress Cataloging-in-Publication Data
Watson, Ben, 1961–
 Cider, hard and sweet : history, traditions, and making your own / Ben Watson.
— 2nd ed.
     p. cm.
 Includes bibliographical references and index.
 ISBN 978-0-88150-819-2 (alk. paper)
 1. Cider. I. Title.
 TP563.W38 2008
 641.3'411—dc22

                         2008028918

Book design and composition by Melanie Jolicoeur
Title page photo: Cidermaking at Log Cabin Farm in Dummerston, Vermont, in the early 1900s, courtesy of Frances Manix
Illustrations on pages 58 and 70 © by Jill Shaffer
Illustrations on pages 3, 5, 8, 11, 14, 15, 17, 29, 30, 33, 42, 46, 49, 51, 54, 61, 66, 73, 79, 87, 92, 97, 99, 105, 109, 111, 116, 119, 124, 129, 138, 144, 147, 154, 158, and 161 © by Melanie Jolicoeur

Published by The Countryman Press, P.O. Box 748, Woodstock, VT 05091

Distributed by W. W. Norton & Company, Inc., 500 Fifth Avenue, New York, NY 10110

Printed in the United States of America

10 9 8 7 6 5 4 3 2 1

In memory of Dan Chaffee (1946–2007)
and Elisabeth Swain (1941–2008)

CONTENTS

ACKNOWLEDGMENTS

Many cidermakers and apple growers provided either material or moral support during the course of this project. Special thanks go to Judith and Terry Maloney of West County Winery in Colrain, Massachusetts, and Stephen Wood and Louisa Spencer of Farnum Hill Ciders in Lebanon, New Hampshire, for being so generous over the years with both their time and their excellent ciders. Also to Rich Stadnik, my friend, grafting partner, and sounding board at Pup's Cider, Greenfield, New Hampshire.

I am deeply indebted to two gentlemen in particular for sharing with me their years of wisdom and experience. Dr. Andrew Lea of Oxfordshire, England, is a food scientist who formerly worked at the Long Ashton Research Station in Bristol. On matters biological, chemical, and historical, his advice and insights have proved invaluable to myself and many other cidermakers, both amateur and professional. Likewise, my friend Tom Burford, a seventh-generation Virginia orchardist, has been my trusted guide to the history and practice of fruit growing.

Additional thanks go to Ouida Young, Trish Wesley-Umbrell, Hannah Proctor, Roger Swain, and Jason Martel; the Shelton family of Vintage Virginia Apples, North Garden, Virginia; Homer Dunn, Alyson's Orchard, Walpole, New Hampshire; Diane Flynt, Foggy Ridge Cider, Dugspur, Virginia; John Bunker, Fedco Trees, Waterville, Maine; Dick Dunn and the many generous and knowledgeable contributors to The Cider Digest e-group, especially Gary Awdey, Terry Bradshaw, John Howard, Claude Jolicoeur, and Bill Rhyne; Charles McGonegal, AeppelTreow Winery, Burlington, Wisconsin; Charles Crawford, Domaine Pinnacle, Frelighsburg, Quebec; Christie Higginbottom, Old Sturbridge Village, Sturbridge, Massachusetts; and Christian Drouin, Domaine Coeur de Lion, Choudray Rabut, Normandy. To the extent that this book succeeds, it truly stands on the shoulders on these and many other experts and enthusiasts.

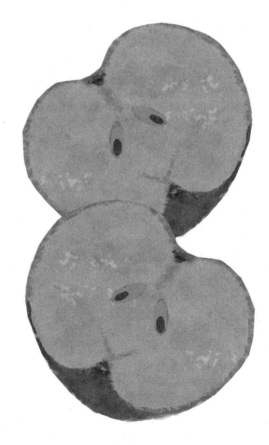

PREFACE TO THE SECOND EDITION

The French scientist/philosopher Pascal once wrote that no man differs more from another than he does from himself at another time in his life. So it comes as something of a surprise to me that, almost a decade after the original publication of *Cider, Hard and Sweet*, I should find myself more engaged than ever in the culture of cider in America.

Over these past few years I have had the pleasure of meeting many more cider producers and apple growers, and through my travels I've even become something of a cider evangelist. Every year I host tastings of heritage apple varieties and present pairings of farmstead cheeses with artisanal hard ciders, in venues ranging from the old churches and meetinghouses of rural New England to large convention centers in San Francisco, and from a charter school in Chattanooga, Tennessee, to a market town in northern Italy.

Everywhere I've visited I have been impressed with the growing passion for real food, food that is well grown or well made by small-scale farmers and craft producers. The desire for local, sustainable food systems is becoming even more widespread and firmly rooted in these times of rising food and energy prices. People are demanding quality, to be sure, but also "traceability," an understanding of where their food comes from, how it is grown, and by whom. The explosion in the number of local farmers' markets in recent years is a good indicator of this trend, but so too is the concept of community supported agriculture (CSA) farms, and the popularity of organizations like Slow Food and many grassroots "localvore" groups, which encourage people to think globally and eat locally. For everyone who cares about the quality and diversity of the food we eat, these are exciting times—full of opportunity, adventure, and discovery.

Recent changes in the American cider culture and landscape have been dramatic, and mostly positive. In 1999, when the first edition of *Cider, Hard and Sweet*, appeared, most people thought of "hard cider" only as the mass-marketed six-pack product located next to the wine coolers. And while that image still persists, the makers of quality craft ciders have also received regular attention from food and wine writers, who are realizing, albeit very slowly, that well-made cider not only pairs beautifully with a wide range of foods, but at its best can be as complex and interesting as many wines.

Not so long ago there were only a handful of artisanal cidermakers, mainly clustered in the Northeast and Pacific Northwest. Today, however, there are many new producers making good cider in different areas of the country. The Upper Midwest/Great Lakes region and the Piedmont South in Virginia and North Carolina are two such centers: the first one a well-established fruit-growing and -processing area, the second one rich in history, with a core group of very sophisticated orchardists and producers. In the years to come, this spread in cider culture will help more Americans to rediscover the pleasures of this wonderful beverage. Just as importantly, these new cidermakers are helping to define and develop uniquely regional styles, using apple varieties adapted to local climates and soils and connected to local tastes and traditions.

Another thing I've noticed in the past few years is the vast improvement in the quality of American ciders.

Both new and long-established producers are selling cider that is more consistent and far more drinkable than was the case when I first wrote this book. New producers have learned from existing ones, and the knowledge of the cidermaking process is much more readily available in this country today than it ever has been. I also believe that American cider has benefited from the recent development of objective standards and style guidelines, which provide a common vocabulary for evaluating and discussing different products.

Unfortunately, the prospects for real (raw) sweet cider are not so rosy. State and federal regulatory agencies continue to strongly discourage the production of unpasteurized juice, due to stated health concerns. As a result, many small local orchards have stopped pressing cider altogether, breaking a decades-old fall tradition. Although the legality of direct sales of raw cider vary from state to state, with a strong but largely "underground" demand for real sweet cider the result, it is becoming clearer with each passing year that the best defense against the permanent loss of real cider is to learn how to press it yourself. And that remains one of the principal aims of this book.

With nine more seasons of experience behind me in terms of my own cidermaking, I hope to offer some additional insights and updates in the pages that follow.

In addition, I have added two entirely new chapters to the book. Chapter 7 on "Perry, or Pear Cider" deals with that little-known but historic beverage made from pears, which is so analogous to apple cider, yet unique and special in its own right. Chapter 10 deals with "Cidermaking: Beyond the Basics," a subject that readers have frequently requested I address, once they have made their initial batches of hard cider at home. In addition, there is new information on cooking with cider, cider styles and traditions, and other material.

Cider, Hard and Sweet was never designed to be a complete guide for budding commercial producers of cider, but rather a history, a celebration, and an entry point for individuals who either want to try their hand at making their own hard or sweet cider, or who simply enjoy and appreciate it. Fortunately, for people who are serious about going further in their cidermaking studies, there are lots of excellent resources, both in print and online, that will provide you with mountains of information and help to feed a lifetime hobby.

So, with a mixture of goodwill and humility, I wish you, dear reader, all the pleasures of the orchard and the cider house. Wassail!

Francestown, New Hampshire
May 2008

> The noblest of fruits is the apple. Let the most beautiful or swiftest have it.
>
> —Henry David Thoreau, *Journal*, October 31, 1851

INTRODUCTION

DRIVE OUT INTO THE COUNTRY on some crisp, clear day in the fall, to an orchard that presses its own apples to make unpasteurized, preservative-free cider. If it is well made, from a select blend of apple varieties, the cider will have a rich, dark color, as complex and opaque as dark beer or good gumbo. Now take a long drink. It will have a deep, refreshing taste with a balanced sweetness and acidity and complex flavor notes. It will also feel alive in your mouth, with an ineffable but unmistakable quality that stimulates the palate and makes you want to take another drink. This, in short, is the genuine article—real cider made by a person who knows something about apples and who cares about quality. Even to the uninitiated, the difference between this beverage and the insipid, store-bought juice that masquerades under the name of cider is immediately clear.

My greatest fear, however, is that a new generation of Americans may be growing up without *ever* having known or tasted real cider—not to mention many of the other traditional and natural delicacies that represent our collective food heritage. All too often, our tastes become circumscribed and defined by the kinds of boring, denatured foods we are offered at the supermarket. Then, when we are presented with products like heat-treated and preservative-laden cider, we tend to settle for them if we have known nothing else (or nothing better). And in time that inferior quality becomes the new standard for excellence. That was one of my reasons for writing this book: to help define what real cider is, and to argue for it; to encourage you to seek out quality and demand more of your food and the people who supply it.

And so it happened that, over the course of several harvest seasons, I found myself traveling extensively, interviewing apple growers and master cidermakers wherever I went. In every orchard and cider mill, I met people who were passionate about good cider and knowledgeable in the time-honored ways of how to make it. I also met many of their customers, who still possessed the kind of sensual memory and sophisticated taste buds that could distinguish between a cider or an apple that was merely good and one that was truly extraordinary. Most importantly, these people were passing on their discerning taste to their children, which makes me confident that the days of honest farm-fresh cider are far from being over.

Another encouraging sign has been the ongoing revival of alcoholic or "hard" cider in America and its growing popularity both here and abroad, even in the traditional cider-making countries of Europe. Following close on the heels of the microbrew revolution of the 1980s, the renaissance of hard cider—once so integral to the rural life and economy of America—was perhaps inevitable. Devotees of fine food and drink are demanding more variety and distinction in their daily wines or brews, and many people seem to want a lighter, and arguably healthier, alternative to beers and ales. As a result, many of the country's major breweries and wineries, as well as some smaller independents, are now producing hard cider, which is marketed, like beer, in six-packs and on draft from kegs.

The appearance of these "draft ciders" in stores nationwide, and the rapid expansion of the market for hard cider, is beginning to create a stronger demand for more interesting and traditional styles of hard cider. Don't get me wrong: Draft ciders are fine, uncomplicated brews, very light and refreshing on a hot summer's day. But the dictates of mass production and distribution mean that they are fermented rapidly, watered down, often excessively carbonated, and contain additives like juice concentrates and preservatives. This means that these industrial brews will never exhibit the same complexity that you will find in a well-made local or homemade hard cider, with its delicate bouquet and naturally sparkling effervescence. The good news is that more and more people today are supporting, or establishing, small regional cideries, and at the same time rediscovering classic old American apples like the Baldwin and Roxbury Russet, which can be made into excellent varietal and blended hard ciders, in a wide range of styles.

Which brings me to another reason for writing this book: my hope that more people will try making their own cider (sweet and hard) at home. After all, the apple has always been the quintessential homestead fruit. From the time of the first European settlements to the early years of the twentieth century, most Americans grew and used apples for myriad purposes: for fresh eating, as we do today; in cooking and in baking; preserved, either by drying slices or in classic receipts like apple butter and boiled cider; or turned into hard cider, applejack, and cider vinegar. Even the spent pomace left over from the cider press was used as a livestock feed, all-natural weed killer, and compost material, or buried in nursery rows to develop potentially new and improved native seedling varieties.

Today our farm population is a fraction of what it was in colonial times, or even a hundred years ago. Yet the pendulum is once again swinging back to the land, as it does every few years. Now, though, there is for the first time the technology of the personal computer and the Internet to consider, both of which have helped to spark the burgeoning work-at-home movement. Not so many years ago, country squirehood meant either dropping out of corporate life altogether or enduring a lengthy commute from the sticks to the city. This is much less true today; so perhaps the prospects for a home orchard revival are not so farfetched. And importantly, in these times of lightning-fast broadband speeds and instant gratification, planting apple varieties that have been grafted onto dwarf or semidwarf rootstocks means that you are no longer putting in trees whose fruits only your children will enjoy.

Whether you choose to make your own fresh cider using a small hand-screw press or take your apples to a local mill for custom grinding and pressing, you can and should experiment with different varieties and blends until you find the ones that you like best. Even if you decide to forgo your own home orchard and to support your local cider mill, there's no excuse for not having a try at making your own hard cider at home. The specter of federal agents pounding on your door will never materialize: The government says it's perfectly legal to make up to two hundred gallons of hard cider a year for your own household use. What's more, cidermaking is ridiculously easy for beginners—much simpler and cheaper than brewing beer. And as you gain confidence and experience, you may find that you are making hard cider that is every bit as good as—maybe even better than—anything you can buy at the liquor store.

This book is intended for people who, like me, are apple enthusiasts, and who would like to learn what constitutes good cider as well as the basics of how to make it. The word connoisseur sounds pretentious, but all it really signifies is someone who has acquired a specialized

Introduction

knowledge of a given art or subject, or has developed an informed or discriminating taste. And though the term *wine snob* is well established in our lexicon, I rarely hear anyone use the term *cider snob* to describe me or any of my fellow aficionados. Maybe it's cider's humble origins and the rustic image of cider drinkers—rural swains sitting around an oaken barrel in the apple barn—that explains its refreshing lack of pretension. Certainly my own experience with cidermakers, amateur and professional, has been without exception delightful, filled with bonhomie and a great generosity of spirit. I remember one sticky summer afternoon that I spent at a cider orchard in western New Hampshire. The air smelled like ozone, so muggy and thick you could cut it with a knife. Every few minutes another passing thunderstorm would dump a torrential shower upon the apple trees. During one of these tropical downpours my host, a master cidermaker, and I got stuck way out among the trees, and we ran like kids for the shelter of the cider house. Soon we were laughing, soaked to the skin and now shivering in the fifty-degree chill of his fermenting room. "Would you like to sample this barrel?" he asked, and a few minutes later we were splitting a bottle of his best stuff, chatting like old friends who had just been reunited. Cider people are like that.

By the time you finish this book, I hope you will be closer to becoming a "cider person" in your own right, and that you will be inspired to strike out on your own, to discover new and interesting styles of cider, or to create them yourself at home. Here's to you!

Cider, Hard and Sweet

> "What you have told us is all very good. It is indeed bad to eat apples. It is better to make them all into cider."
>
> —Benjamin Franklin in *Remarks Concerning the Savages of North America*, reporting an American Indian's response to hearing the story of Adam and Eve

1. THE HISTORY OF CIDER

NO ONE KNOWS FOR CERTAIN who discovered cider, or exactly where in the world it was first made and consumed. In part this is because of cider's sheer antiquity, its origins lost, like so many early human developments, in the mists of prehistory. In part it is also due to the widespread distribution of apples throughout the world's temperate growing regions. And because there would be no cider without apples, to really understand the history and development of cider and cidermaking, it is essential to know a little about where the apple comes from and how it has evolved.

Of all the fruits of this earth, few have been more celebrated than the apple, few have been cultivated more widely, and few have had a longer history of use and enjoyment, especially among the great civilizations of Europe and Asia. In recent centuries, as conquerors and colonists migrated from the Eurasian continent to the four corners of the globe, the apple invariably went along for the ride—either in the form of seeds, which spawned new and unique varieties, or as grafted trees or scions (cuttings) taken from old and valued parent strains.

The species that we now know as the cultivated apple *(Malus pumila,* or *M. domestica)* probably arose in the valleys and rugged foothills of the Tien Shan Mountains, in the border country between northwest China and the former Soviet republics of Kazakhstan and Kirghizstan. In fact, the Kazakh capital's name, Alma-Ata, means literally "father of apples." From this mountainous region to the shores of the Caspian Sea, plant researchers have discovered wild groves of the domestic apple's main ancestor, *M. sieversii.* The trees and fruits of this one species are incredibly diverse, in many respects similar to the wide range of today's cultivated apple varieties. Scientists are still debating how much or how little other wild species of apples might have contributed to the genetic makeup of our modern apple. These include the bitter-fruited *M. orientalis,* which hails from the Caucasus region, and the European crab apple, *M. sylvestris,* whose native range stretches from the British Isles to Turkey.

In September 2005, I had the opportunity to tour the Central Asian apple collection at the USDA's Plant Genetics Research Unit in Geneva, New York, which for more than a century has been the center of apple research in America. My guide was Dr. Phil Forsline, who had traveled to the former Soviet Central Asian republics beginning in the late 1980s and had brought back seeds and cuttings of wild apple trees from a variety of locations and climates, from mountains to deserts. To see these mature trees in fruit today is a wonderful experience, and it illustrates dramatically just how diverse *M. sieversii* can be. Although the majority of apples were small, yellow, and often quite bitter or astringent (great for cidermaking!), there were also a few "elite" varieties that could just as easily have been brought to the market and sold for eating out of hand, with little or no improvement needed. The fact that some wild apples

could be so large and tasty was a revelation to me, and demonstrated just how efficiently natural selection can work over thousands of years, even in remote regions where humans haven't been living or farming. In a recent book, authors Barrie Juniper and David Mabberley suggest that bears and horses, not humans, were chiefly responsible for the selection, improvement, and dispersion of the wild apple.[1] Today the goal, at Geneva and elsewhere, is to revisit the genetic roots of the apple, and to use the ancestral *M. sieversii* to breed greater disease resistance into our cultivated apples, creating new varieties that will require far less spraying, chemical or otherwise.

Even before the modern apple became widely known in Europe and Asia, there is evidence to suggest that various indigenous peoples were already making extensive use of wild apples. Wild apples were depicted in Paleolithic cave art that dates from between 35,000 and 8000 B.C.E., and archeologists have found the carbonized remains of apples in Anatolia dating back to 6500 B.C.E., and at the sites of Neolithic lake settlements in what is now Switzerland and Italy, which were occupied between 2000 and 1600 B.C.E.

How these ancient peoples used apples is more a matter of conjecture than scientific fact. It seems likely, however, that they would have sampled fruit from all kinds of apple trees, selecting those apples that tasted sweetest and most palatable. And it isn't much more of a stretch to imagine how these earliest orchardists first discovered cider, as wild yeasts that are found everywhere (in the air, on the ground, and on the skins and flesh of apples) will go to work on apples naturally and begin the process of fermentation. They would have found, as the naturalist Henry David Thoreau did in his rambles around Walden Pond, that even the sharpest apples mellow nicely with age—especially after the first winter frosts:

Those which a month ago were sour, crabbed, and quite unpalatable to the civilized taste, such at least as were frozen while sound, let a warmer sun come to thaw them—for they are extremely sensitive to its rays—are found to be filled with a rich, sweet cider, better than any bottled cider that I know of, and with which I am better acquainted than with wine. All apples are good in this state, and your jaws are the cider-press. . . . It is a way to keep cider sweet without boiling. Let the frost come to freeze them first, solid as stones, and then the rain or a warm winter day to thaw them, and they will seem to have borrowed a flavor from heaven through the medium of the air in which they hang.[2]

Prehistoric peoples doubtless would have tasted this kind of natural cider. But we can also imagine other scenarios that might have led them to an understanding and appreciation of alcoholic or "hard" cider. Perhaps some band of hunter-gatherers drank a bit of the clear liquid that pooled in the hollow of a tree beneath a heap of partially crushed apples. We can only guess what that first sip must have tasted like to them: Did they hear the angels sing, or did they spit out the fizzy, tangy stuff? Regardless, it seems reasonable to assume that cider was probably discovered many times over, by many indigenous peoples, in almost every region of the world where apple trees were growing wild.

Around eight thousand years ago, with the development of agriculture and the rise of the first great cities and civilizations, apples began to appear both as an article of trade and as a cultivated crop in the ancient world. While the climates of Egypt and the Tigris-Euphrates Valley were probably not cool enough to grow apple trees successfully (at least on any large scale), there is ample evidence that apples were imported by caravan along the long-distance trade routes that wound all the way from India and China to the eastern Mediterranean. These silk and spice roads passed directly through the apple's Central Asian homeland, and before long the virtues of the fruit had led to its cultivation in many lands, including Persia, Asia Minor, and northern Mesopotamia.

Apples were celebrated by the earliest writers, both popular and agricultural. Homer mentions them in the *Odyssey*, when the wandering hero Odysseus sees them growing in the gardens of Alkinöos, king of Phaiakia. The fruit was also said to have been a favorite dessert of Philip of Macedon and of his son, Alexander the Great. It was a custom they probably picked up from the Persians, who regularly served apples along with other fruits as a final course at their banquets. In fact, by imperial Roman times, apples had become such a common fixture at meals that they gave rise to the proverbial Latin expression *ova ad malum* ("from the egg to the apple"), which implied the whole progression of a meal or, by extension, the whole scope of any event. Today we would say "from soup to nuts" to convey the same idea, but back then eggs were customarily served as the first course at a Roman meal, and apples as dessert.

Cider in Roman History

The first recorded references to cider also date back to Roman times. In 55 B.C.E. Julius Caesar began his conquest of Britain, where his soldiers found the Celtic inhabitants fermenting the juice of the native crab apples to make an alcoholic beverage. The Roman legionnaires and administrators who subsequently settled in portions of Gaul (present-day France) and Britain are credited with having introduced several cultivated varieties of apples, at least one of which has traditionally thought to have survived to modern times: the Court Pendu Plat, also known as the Wise Apple because it blossoms very late, thus "wisely" avoiding early spring frosts. (Another very old Breton variety, the *Pomme d'Api*, or Lady apple, was long associated with the Appia variety of Roman times, though modern European authorities doubt there is any connection).[3] Even more importantly, though, the Romans brought with them their horticultural knowledge, and introduced orcharding techniques like grafting and pruning, which they in turn had picked up from the Greeks and the Syrians.

By the second and third centuries A.D., Roman authorities reported that various European peoples were making a number of more or less ciderlike drinks *(pomorum)*, created from different types of fruit, that were reportedly similar to grape wines and in some cases superior to them. In the fourth century, Palladius wrote that the Romans themselves were making perry, or pear wine, and Columella listed thirty-eight different varieties of pears and twenty-four varieties of apples. Around the same time, Saint Jerome used the term *sicera* to describe fermented apple juice, from which we derive the word *cider. Sikera* was actually a Greek word meaning simply "intoxicating beverage," and it comes in turn from the Hebrew word *sekar* (which some people also believe to be the root of the slang term *schnockered*.)

Cider in Western Europe

With the collapse of the Western Roman Empire in the fifth century A.D., the horticultural arts entered a period of decline in many parts of Europe. Fortunately, along with other fields of knowledge, the skills of grafting, pruning, and fruit-growing were preserved during the Dark Ages by the Christian monastic orders. Monastery gardens featured many types of edible and useful plants, and the rise and spread of the Church's influence encouraged the large-scale planting of fruit trees and vines on abbey lands.

At the same time, the Islamic Moors, who ruled much of Spain until the late fifteenth century, established impressive botanic gardens and built on the knowledge of classical authors, developing new varieties and techniques that greatly influenced those gardeners who followed them. In fact, we probably have the Moors to thank for developing many of the classic bitter, high-tannin apples that still make the richest, most distinctive ciders. And although most cider drinkers in North America, through cultural familiarity, consider French and English hard ciders the finest in the world, the people of northern Spain were making *sidra,* or cider, long before the birth of Christ. With a moderate climate similar to that of our Pacific Northwest—one where apple orchards mingle with orange groves—the coastal regions of Asturias and the Euskadi, or Basque country of Spain, represent perhaps the oldest apple-growing lands in Europe.

Many of the apples grown at this time were seedlings. Yet cultivated apple varieties rarely, if ever, resemble their parents when grown from seed. Seedlings from large apples may produce small fruit; seedlings of red apples may have green or yellow fruit; and seedlings of sour apples may bear much sweeter fruit. For this reason, apple varieties that were considered especially valuable for eating or culinary use would usually have been propagated vegetatively by grafting, while less choice or less palatable fruit from seedling trees would have been pressed into cider.

Given this fact, it is somewhat curious that a strong cider-drinking culture developed only gradually in northwestern Europe, over a period of several centuries. It is true that the emperor Charlemagne issued an edict stating that brewers, including cider- and perry makers, should be encouraged to develop their trade. Yet even in Normandy, which would become one of the world's most celebrated cidermaking regions, cider was widely consumed before the twelfth century only in years when there was a shortage of beer or other drinks brewed from grains and herbs, which were the most common beverages at the time. Not until the fourteenth century did cider become as popular and available as beer and wine in Normandy. By 1371, however, almost as much cider was being sold at Caen as wine, and some of it was being shipped up the Seine to the Paris market.

Cider in Normandy was subject to heavy taxation during the disastrous Hundred Years War between England and France (1337–1453), but in the century following the wars its popularity spread greatly. In 1532 Francois I toured Normandy and ordered several barrels of cider made from the Pomme d'Espice apple for himself. At Val-de-Seine in the Contentin region, a gentleman named Guillaume Dursus began studying the different kinds of cider apples and assembled a collection of those he considered the best varieties, taking the grafts from his home in northern Spain. And in 1588 Charles IX's physician, a man from Normandy named Julien le Paulmier, published a treatise entitled *De Vino et Pomaceo,* in which he listed some eighty-two varieties of cider apples. Paulmier's work helped to increase the popularity of cider over a much broader area of France and encouraged its sale.

During the sixteenth and seventeenth centuries, the production of cider spread from Normandy to other parts of France: Brittany, Maine, Picardy, Île-de-France, and Orléans. In the eighteenth century agricultural societies were formed that encouraged the production of cider and cider apples by sponsoring prizes and competitions. Beginning in 1863, grapevines in French vineyards suffered extensive damage from phylloxera, an insect related to aphids. By the time the destruction had run its course, and the great vineyards were replanting European wine grapes grafted onto insect-resistant American rootstocks, the French interest in cider was beginning to grow. Eventually, by the end of the nineteenth century, the French government estimated that more than one million persons were engaged in cider-making; by 1902 the nation was producing around 647 millions gallons commercially (that is, not counting what farmers were making and drinking themselves).

Cider in England

On their arrival in Britain the Romans found the inhabitants making cider from the European crab apple *(Malus sylvestris),* which had been growing wild there since Neolithic times. Evidence at the Windmill Hill archaeological site in Wiltshire suggests that the ancient Britons used apples for food, though they seem to have relied mainly on wild trees rather than planting them to any great extent. However, the Roman introduction of cultivated apples and horticultural know-how soon led to the first orchards being established in England.

This situation changed drastically with the fall of Rome, and orchards were abandoned as a succession of invaders—Jutes, Saxons, and Danes—attacked British towns and settlements. As in the rest of Europe, though, the spread of Christianity helped to keep both knowledge and useful arts alive in the monasteries. The monastery at Ely in Cambridgeshire was especially famous for its orchards and vineyards, and a twelfth-century plan of the Christ Church monastery in Canterbury shows its *pomerium* or apple garden, where apples and pears were grown for both eating and pressing into cider and perry.

The Norman Conquest in 1066 sparked a new interest in cider in England. The Normans introduced many apple varieties, including the Pearmain, a long, pear-shaped apple that was the first named variety recorded in Britain. Cider soon became the most popular drink after ale, and it began to be widely used as a means of exchange to pay tithes and rents. A deed of 1204 stipulated that the tenancy of the manor of Runham in

Norfolk would bring in an annual rent of "200 Pearmaines and four hogsheads of Pear-maine cyder," payable to the Exchequer every Michaelmas (September 29) by Robert de Evermore, the lord of the manor. A hundred years later, seventy-four of the eighty parishes in West Sussex were paying their church tithes in cider.

As early as the reign of Henry III in the thirteenth century, the borough of Worcester had already become famous for its fruit trees and cider orchards. By the end of that century, a number of choice apple varieties had been collected in the royal gardens at Westminster, Charing, and the Tower, as well as in the gardens of English noblemen. In the main apple-growing counties of the time—Kent, Somerset, and Hampshire—most manors had their own cider mills and were pressing their own cider.

In the early sixteenth century, cider lost some of its popularity in relation to ale when hops were first intro-

This "Ingenio" mill, used for grinding apples before pressing, was invented by Englishman John Worlidge and depicted in his 1676 book, *Vinetum Britannicum*.

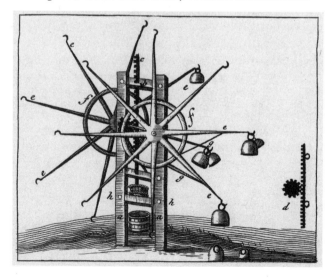

Cider, Hard and Sweet

duced to England from Flanders. Hops greatly improved the flavor, as well as the keeping qualities, of British ale. Yet around the same time Richard Harris—fruiterer to Henry VIII—advanced the cause of British apple-growing when he reportedly "fetched out of France a great store of grafts, especially pippins [a dessert apple also suitable for cidermaking], before which there were no pippins in England." These trees, along with other fruits, were planted in an orchard of about 140 acres at Teynham in Kent.

The famous cider orchards of England's West Country became increasingly well established during the sixteenth and seventeenth centuries, particularly in the counties of Herefordshire, Gloucestershire, and Worcestershire. By the end of the seventeenth century, cider was being produced throughout much of southern England, including the West Country, West Midlands, Devon, Somerset, Shropshire, and the Welsh border counties. This century has been called the Golden Age of Apples in England, and the county of Herefordshire in particular was described at this time by John Evelyn as having "become in a manner but one entire orchard."

Adding to the growing fame of Herefordshire's cider was the celebrated Redstreak apple, which, it is said, grew from a seed planted by Charles I's ambassador to France, Lord Scudamore, on his estate at Holme Lacy. Scudamore was one of the many Royalist nobles and gentlemen who had retired to their country homes after fighting in the English Civil War, and who spent the years of the Protectorate cultivating their gardens and identifying new and interesting varieties of fruit—all in all, a very productive and civilized way to pass the time during a period of social upheaval and internal exile.

The keen interest in identifying and improving cider apple varieties in the seventeenth century led to both technological advancements and a marked improvement in the quality of cider. John Worlidge, in his *Vinetum Britannicum* (1676), listed useful cider apples, and other amateur cidermakers also kept careful records about the relative merits of single-variety ciders and blends. Lord Scudamore is credited with having bottled cider as early as the 1640s at Holme Lacy, at a time when almost all cider was stored in wooden barrels and drawn off "on draft" as needed. Scudamore made use of the new, stronger, coke-fired English glass bottles that had been recently introduced. The slight fermentation that took place in the bottles released carbon dioxide gas, which produced a sparkling drink and helped preserve the cider better than could half-emptied wooden casks or barrels, where aerobic organisms came in contact with the cider and often spoiled it.

The rich soils and the mild, moist climate of England's West Country made this region an ideal place to grow apple or pear trees, and cidermaking in general fit extremely well into Britain's farm economy of the seventeenth century. Productive, low-maintenance, and long-lived, apple trees were set out widely spaced in the field or orchard, with either crops or sod grown among them, the latter for pasturing dairy herds. Most cider apples didn't need to be picked until October or later, by which time other crops had been harvested and the farmer had a bit of leisure. Once pressed into cider, the leftover apple pomace could be soaked with water and pressed again to make a weak "water-cider" or "ciderkin," then finally used as a feed for livestock. Farmworkers received a cider allowance as part of their wages, typically two quarts a day for a man and one for a boy. This practice dates back to at least the thirteenth century, when workers in monastery orchards were paid in cider, and it continued for nearly five hundred years, until it was finally declared illegal in 1878.

Two other factors that encouraged cider production

John Worlidge's design for a continuous cider press, from *Vinetum Britannicum* (1676).

in England at this time were the shortage of burnable wood and international trade restrictions. To brew ale required fuel for heat, both to malt the barley and to boil the wort before fermentation; the cidermaking process, on the other hand, didn't require heat. Wood in England was in very short supply, so planting fruit trees made doubly good sense: There were apples and pears for making cider and perry, plus wood from old trees for fuel and other uses. Add to this the shaky international relations between England and other European nations, particularly wine-producing countries like France and Germany, and it's easy to see why hard cider came to be seen not only as a refreshing and wholesome draught, but even as a patriotic national beverage.

By the eighteenth century, the English thirst for cider had become prodigious. According to the novelist Daniel Defoe, some ten to twenty thousand hogsheads of cider (between one and two million gallons) were exported from the area around the port of Exeter during the 1720s, and the construction of canals enabled mer-

Chapter 1: The History of Cider

chants to transport cider in bottles to London and other markets.

Ironically, the very popularity of cider in England helped contribute to its decline during the middle part of the eighteenth century. Up until this time, cidermaking had largely been a rural practice engaged in by farmers, who produced a rough cider for home use and local sale, and by landed gentlemen, who had the leisure and resources necessary to experiment with different apple varieties and production techniques, in an attempt to match or even surpass the quality of imported wines. But with the initial stirrings of the Industrial Revolution and the movement of workers off the farms and into the cities and factories, the quality of English cider began to drop, even as demand remained strong. Unscrupulous cider merchants began buying large volumes of sweet, unfermented juice and producing adulterated or watered-down beverages that resembled real cider in name only. The "Devonshire colic," a palsy-like sickness

Phil Forline, curator of the apple collection at USDA's Plant Genetic Resources Unit in Geneva, New York, discusses apple trees grown from seeds collected in Central Asia (background), with a group of visitors, September 2005. *Ben Watson*

caused by lead leaching into cider from the joints and pipes of manufacturing equipment, further damaged cider's reputation, as did the rough drink known as scrumpy, which might be made from rotten fruit, other fruit juices, surplus vegetables, sugars—just about anything that would ferment. The new British ales like Whitbread, Bass, and Guinness were seen, quite rightly, as being more healthful than these degraded ciders, which came to be considered a beverage of the urban lower classes and as a cheap, quick way to get drunk.

The first attempt to revive the popularity and good name of English cider occurred near the end of the eighteenth century, when the famous plant breeder Thomas Andrew Knight published his *Treatise on Cider,* and then, in 1811, the *Pomona Herefordiensis,* which included information on all of the cider apples and perry pears grown in the county of Hereford. Around this time many English apple varieties, particularly the Golden Pippin, were seriously afflicted with diseases such as apple canker. Knight began to make intentional crosses between different varieties in an attempt to create new apples and halt the decline, and this sparked a new wave of interest in fruit breeding during the nineteenth century, encouraged by the activities of the Royal Horticultural Society and other groups.

In the late nineteenth century, the character of English cider began to change, as small regional cidermaking gave way to a more centralized, industrial system of production. Between 1870 and 1900, more than a dozen cider factories opened around Herefordshire, including H. P. Bulmer Ltd., which was founded in 1887 by Percy Bulmer and is now the largest cidermaker in the world, marketing no fewer than seventeen brands and accounting for more than half the cider consumed in Britain.

Cider, Hard and Sweet

The Apple Comes to America

Not surprisingly, the apple was one the first crops introduced to American shores by colonists from England and western Europe. Although a few species of small wild apples are native to North America, such as the garland or sweet crab *(Malus coronaria),* the prairie crab *(M. ioensis),* and the southern crab *(M. angustifolia),* it is not clear to what extent they were used by the Native Americans. However, the first cultivated apple trees were planted in Boston (at that time known by its Indian name of Shawmut) as early as 1623 by William Blackstone (or Blaxton), a dissident Church of England clergyman and a minister to the settlers at Plymouth.

Tradition has it that Blackstone was something of an eccentric character and that he once saddle-trained a bull, which he rode around the countryside, distributing apples and flowers to his friends. Like so many free spirits of the time, Blackstone apparently ran afoul of the British colonial authorities, so in 1635 he moved to Rhode Island, planting his first orchard there and introducing what, by some accounts, was America's first native apple variety, Blaxton's Yellow Sweeting. Others bestow this honor on Roxbury Russet, a greenish yellow apple with a rough skin (another common name is Leathercoat) whose original tree was discovered sometime before 1649 on a hill in Roxbury, Massachusetts, near Boston. More than 350 years later, it's still grown and is still a fine multipurpose apple.

To the settlers of this new country, the apple represented the perfect homestead fruit. An apple tree, once it began to bear, would dependably produce bushels of fruit that could be used immediately for eating or cooking. Some varieties, like Roxbury Russet, could be stored in a cold cellar and kept all winter long, while others, like the old Hightop Sweet apple reputedly grown at

Apple trees grown in Geneva, New York, from seeds collected in Central Asia. *Ben Watson*

Plymouth Plantation, could be sliced and dried for later use. But cider played the most crucial role in America's rural economy, as pressing and fermenting the fresh juice of the apple was the easiest way for farmers to preserve the enormous harvest that came from even a modest orchard. Cider was also the basis for many other products, such as applejack, apple brandy, and cider vinegar,

Chapter 1: The History of Cider

which was used to preserve other fresh foods and for myriad other purposes around the home.

Americans planted apples wherever the climate allowed, from the New England colonies to the mountains of northern Georgia. In 1647 apples were being grafted onto wild native rootstocks in Virginia, and in the same year the first grafted tree arrived from Europe—a variety imported from Holland known as the Summer Bonchretien, which was planted by Gov. Peter Stuyvesant in New Amsterdam. Stuyvesant's farm was located in the Bouwerij (Bowery) district, and the trunk of this historic apple tree remained standing on the corner of Third Avenue and 13th Street in New York City until 1866, when it was broken off by a cart.

While well-to-do planters and colonial officials could afford to import grafted stock from Europe, much of the apple's spread in America was by seed, which could be easily carried and planted by settlers pushing inland and westward. Many farmers spread pomace (the seeds and skins left over from pressing cider) onto their fields, then took grafts from any seedlings that sprang up and bore good fruit.

The American folk hero Johnny Appleseed became a symbol of the apple's spread as it followed western settlement in the years after the Revolutionary War. Born in Leominster, Massachusetts, in 1774, the historical Appleseed's real name was John Chapman. In the first half of the nineteenth century, Chapman did operate an extensive frontier nursery in the Susquehanna Valley of Pennsylvania, from which he traveled as far afield as Ohio and Indiana, preaching, planting apple seeds, and selling seedling trees to settlers, who were eager to install such familiar and useful domestic plants, and to demonstrate that they were improving their homestead land grants.

Because these seedling trees produced fruits that were unlike the apples they came from, new types of American apples quickly emerged, many of them unnamed varieties and unique to a particular farm or estate. By the early 1800s, American nurserymen were already offering around one hundred named varieties of apples for sale; by 1850, more than five hundred widely recognized varieties were being cultivated; and in 1872 Charles Downing's *Fruit and Fruit Trees of America* listed close to eleven hundred different kinds of apples that had originated in America.

French Huguenots who settled in New Rochelle, New York, and along the northern shore of Long Island also brought with them a wide variety of fruits. Around 1730 Robert Prince established Prince Nurseries in Flushing, not far from the spot where the first commercially important American apple, the Newtown Pippin, originated. By 1845 the Prince catalog, which purported to offer only the best kinds of apples, was listing 350 varieties. Even though many farmers relied on seedling trees, the familiar and proven varieties offered by nurseries were popular among home orchardists, then as now. Farmers would "top-work" their trees, sometimes grafting many varieties onto a single trunk. The ultimate goal for homesteaders was "to furnish the home with fruit from the first of the season through the autumn, winter, and the spring, and even till early summer."[4]

Cider in America

By 1775 one out of every ten farms in New England owned and operated its own cider mill. There are numerous reasons why cider, like the apple itself, flourished in the American climate. For one thing, most early settlers preferred not to drink the local water, which could be unpalatable or even—close to settlements—polluted. This left milk and alcoholic beverages, but importing such a staple as ale from England was expensive and chancy, and early experiments in growing barley and hops in

New England had proved a dismal failure. For a time, desperate colonists sought creative, if dead-end, solutions to the problem, brewing beers out of pumpkins, corn (maize), molasses, maple sap, and even persimmons.

Apple trees, however, could be grown almost everywhere in America, and it didn't take long for the colonists to put down their persimmon beer and take up

The Harrison apple, renowned in early America for making superior-quality cider, was considered extinct until 1989. Modern cidermakers are now rediscovering this fine old variety. *Charlotte Shelton, Vintage Virginia Apples.*

cidermaking in earnest. Consumed by men, women, and children, by hired hands and Harvard students, cider quickly became America's national drink. In 1726 it was reported that a single village near Boston, consisting of about forty families, put up nearly 10,000 barrels of cider. One historian stated that in the year 1767 a per-capita average of 1.14 barrels of cider was being consumed in Massachusetts; that amounts to more than 35 gallons per person. President John Adams drank a large tankard of cider every morning until the end of his life, believing (probably correctly) that it promoted good health. One "Lazarus Redstreak" argued in 1801:

Experience shows that the use of [cider] consists with sound healthy and long life. Our inhabitants are settled in favour of it. The New Englanders are of all people the longest livers. Why then try an innovation so difficult, so doubtful, to say the least, in point of health and economy, as the substitution of beer in the place of cyder?[5]

Because it was so widely available and such a useful commodity in daily life, and because currency was relatively scarce, especially in rural areas, cider became a common unit of exchange, as it had been earlier in England. It was frequently used by farmers to pay the doctor, the schoolteacher, the minister, and other local professionals for their services. As it was plentiful, cider also tended to be quite inexpensive. The seventeenth-century historian John Josselyn wrote, "I have had at the tap houses of Boston an ale-quart of cyder spiced and sweetened with sugar, for a groat" (about fourpence), and in 1740 a barrel of cider cost about three shillings.[6] More than seventy years later, in 1817, the American pomologist William Coxe reported that cider in the Middle Atlantic states was selling for about five dollars per hogshead, and he advised cidermakers to convert part of their supply into vinegar, which would fetch three times the price of hard cider.

Chapter 1: The History of Cider

Although cidermaking was commonplace throughout America, the best quality of cider and the greatest commercial quantities were being made in New Jersey, especially in Newark. Local cider apples included the Harrison, which produced a cider described as having a "high colour, rich, and sweet, of great strength, commanding a high price in New York."[7] The Shaker community in Canterbury, New Hampshire, was making cider of such high quality that it sold in Boston for as much as ten dollars a barrel. In his 1817 book, *A View of the Cultivation of Fruit Trees,* William Coxe gives some indication of just how much cider (and cider brandy) was being made in its heyday:

In Essex county, N.J. in the year 1810, there were made 198,000 barrels of cider, and 307,310 gallons of cider spirits were distilled—one citizen of the same county in 1812, made 200 barrels of cider daily through a great part of the season, from six mills and twenty three presses. In the present season, 1816, 25,000 barrels of cider were made within the limits of a single religious society, as it is called, in Orange township, Essex county New-Jersey; comprising about three fourths of the township.[8]

An interesting footnote to this account is that 1816 came to be known as the Year without a Summer, due to a freakish global cooling event that occurred after the massive 1815 eruption of Mount Tambora in the Dutch East Indies. Killing frosts struck the northern United States and Canada in each of the three summer months, mowing down corn and other field crops and causing food shortages in North America and actual famines and bread riots in parts of Europe. On the bright side, though, the cold temperatures also decimated the insect population that year and produced one of the best apple crops ever.

American apples and cider were also being exported to the West Indies, and even to Europe. The first recorded shipment of apples from New England to the West Indies occurred in 1741. In 1758 a package of Newtown Pippins was sent across the Atlantic to Benjamin Franklin in London. And in 1773, when the English apple crop failed, merchants imported great quantities of American fruit.

Back at home, cider even played a part in American politics. When George Washington ran for the Virginia legislature in 1758, his agent doled out nearly three imperial gallons of beer, wine, cider, or rum to every voter. In the presidential campaign of 1840, Whig candidates William Henry Harrison and John Tyler, whose famous slogan was "Tippecanoe and Tyler too," played to anti-immigrant sentiments and used the symbols of the log cabin and cider barrel to represent self-reliance and traditional American values. Cider was freely served to all voters, and the Whigs won in an electoral landslide, 234 to 60.

Virginia fruit historian and orchard consultant Tom Burford, who rediscovered the famous Harrison cider apple. *Ben Watson*

Yet by this time cider's place in American culture was already starting to wane, and as the nineteenth century progressed, several independent and unrelated forces combined to weaken its standing still further. One major factor was urban migration. In 1790 the United States was an agrarian nation: Some 96 percent of Americans lived on farms and raised most or all of their own food; only 4 percent lived in towns or cities. By 1860, 84 percent still lived on the farm. But forty years later, this rural population had dropped sharply, to 44 percent, and by 1910 only 30 percent of Americans were still on the farm.[9]

Until around 1850, apple-growing and cidermaking remained closely linked to the small, self-reliant homestead farm, but the migration of workers to cities and to the fertile lands of the West after the Civil War meant that many old orchards were abandoned. Also, homemade farm cider, which was unfiltered and unpasteurized, didn't travel well to the new centers of population. Coupled with this growing urbanization and resettlement during the late nineteenth century, a steady stream of immigrants from Germany and northern Europe led to the establishment of more breweries in America and the increased consumption of beer, especially in cities.

At around the same time, in 1848, the first apple trees were being planted in central Washington State by a territorial legislator named Hiram F. "Okanogan" Smith. A century and a half later, the orchards of Washington now produce about half of the U.S. apple crop (or about 5 percent of the world harvest), but these apples are grown intensively for fresh shipping, not for cider. And although the planting of commercial apple orchards in western New York and other areas of the East also continued during the 1850s, growers were beginning to get discouraged by greater damage from insects like the codling moth and diseases like apple scab. This led to the widespread cutting of orchards during

The Newtown (or Albemarle) Pippin was one of the first American apples of commercial importance. It originated in the early 1700s in Newtown, New York, now part of the Borough of Queens. *Ben Watson*

the 1880s and a greater reliance on arsenical insecticides and fungicides.

Even more damaging to cider, though, was the rise of the Temperance movement, whose members considered the beverage once hailed as safe and wholesome even for children to be little better than demon rum. In fact, American cidermakers had for a long time been increasing the "octane," or alcoholic content, of natural cider (which normally ferments to around 6 percent alcohol, much lower than grape wines). At first this was done to improve the keeping qualities of cider, especially cider that was intended for long-distance shipping or export. Producers increased the final strength of the cider much as they do today, by adding a sweetener (honey, sugar, raisins, and so on) to the juice before or during fermentation. By the late eighteenth century, the alcohol content of the standard cider sold in taverns ran

Chapter 1: The History of Cider

around 7.5 percent—still not producing that much of a kick. Some producers, however, added rum to their rough cider, making it a less than "temperate" beverage. Also, the impurities found in traditional applejack (a strong, concentrated liquor that was made by freezing hard cider outside in the winter) gave drinkers awe-inspiring hangovers and, over time, led to the unfortunate condition known as apple palsy. Finally, just as had happened earlier in England, the good name of cider was besmirched by unscrupulous manufacturers, who made it out of just about anything, as is evident from this commentary from 1890:

The writer has found, by oft-repeated trials, that it [cider] is the most difficult of all articles to obtain in saloons, restaurants, and groceries. All keep an article they sell for cider; but in many cases it has but a small portion of fermented apple-juice, while in others there is no trace of the apple, the stuff sold being a villainous compound of vinegar, glucose, whisky, and pepper. Now it is perfectly patent that such a concoction could never be sold in this country for cider, any more than it could be sold in France for wine, if the knowledge of the true article prevailed here as does that of true wines in that country. But before such knowledge can prevail here, the cider makers must learn how to make cider correctly. There is where the fault lies, and the consumers will learn their part fast enough when a fairly good article is offered for their acceptance.[10]

Many farmers sympathetic to the temperance cause took axes to their apple trees and swore off alcoholic beverages of any kind. Others, not quite so fervent, started pasteurizing their pressed sweet cider and marketing it as inoffensive apple juice, or calling the fresh, unfermented juice from the press "sweet cider," a term that has been the cause of much confusion since then. Another blow came during the unusually frigid winter of 1917–18, when temperatures in the Northeast plummeted, wiping out whole orchards of cider apples, including an estimated one million Baldwin trees. (The winter of 1933–34 was equally hard, with -40°F weather sounding the final death knell for the Baldwin as the leading commercial apple; many farmers replanted their orchards with the hardier McIntosh variety.) By the time Prohibition was enacted in 1919, the production of hard cider in the United States had dipped to only 13 million gallons, down from 55 million gallons in 1899. Over the next several decades, the once proud American tradition of making hard cider was kept alive only by certain local farmers and enthusiasts.

Yet today, after a long hiatus, Americans are once again developing a taste for hard cider. In 2004 hard cider consumption in the United States exceeded 10.3 million gallons, up from 5.3 million gallons in 1996 and just 271,000 gallons in 1990. Demand for cider is also growing in traditional producing countries like England (which produces some 110 million gallons annually) new markets like China (the world's largest apple growing nation), and elsewhere around the world. Yet cider is still a relatively minor player in the overall alcohol industry, equivalent to only about 0.2 percent of the total U.S. beer market in 1999.

So what does the future hold? It really is anyone's guess, but there are encouraging signs. Increasingly these days, small orchardists and serious cidermakers in the United States are planting distinctive European cider apples and experimenting with both traditional and newer American varieties to see which are the best for making cider. Over the past few years it has become easier and easier for cider lovers to find high-quality beverages made by regional cider mills and wineries. And in the twenty-first century, blessed and encumbered as we are with our Information Age technologies, it's nice to know that something as old and traditional as the art of cidermaking is not only alive and well, but flourishing.

No fruit is more to our English taste than the Apple. Let the Frenchman have his Pear, the Italian his Fig, the Jamaican may retain his farinaceous Banana, and the Malay his Durian, but for us the Apple.

—Edward A. Bunyard, *The Anatomy of Dessert* (1929)

2. APPLE VARIETIES FOR CIDER

WHAT KINDS OF APPLES MAKE GOOD CIDER? On one level the answer is simple: the kinds you have available. Most amateur cidermakers, and even many professionals, use any varieties that are in season and readily available in sufficient quantities to press into juice. Almost any sound apple, from a mouth-puckering wild crab to the most refined dessert variety, is worth adding to your cider blend, at least in small amounts.

However, as with most simple things, there is an underlying art and subtlety involved in mixing and matching varieties to create the best ciders, both sweet and hard. Experienced cidermakers can tell by biting into an apple just what qualities it will contribute to the final product and about how much of that variety they should use in the mix. In this chapter I will describe some of the countless varieties of apples available and provide a few useful rules of thumb for evaluating and using them as potential cider fruits.

Sex and the Single Apple

First, though, it's useful to know something about the botanical nature of apples and to define what we mean by the term variety. The cultivated apple *(Malus pumila, often listed as M. domestica)* is a species that, like most important food plants, has been selected and refined over thousands of years for size, sweet taste, juiciness, and other useful or appealing qualities. Today there are thousands of named varieties in cultivation—more than 7,500 by some estimates. There are also untold numbers of unique "wild" varieties, apples that have escaped cultivation and that stand out only in spring, when the beauty and scent of their blossoms surprise us against the backdrop of woods or old stone walls, and then again in fall, when their untended fruits litter the ground beneath the tree or hang on the branches long after leaf fall, harvested only by the deer and the squirrels. In my home state of New Hampshire, 2007 will long be remembered as one of the most favorable years for wild apples that anyone can remember. Neglected roadside or pasture trees that rarely, if ever, bear fruit were absolutely loaded with red and yellow apples, some of them identifiable by taste and appearance as Baldwin or other old varieties, others

NONPOLLINATING APPLE VARIETIES

The apple varieties listed below are either pollen-sterile or triploids (having a third set of chromosomes), and are not reliable pollinators for other apples, though a few are somewhat self-fertile. To ensure that these apples produce a good crop of fruit, they require at least one other variety of apple growing nearby, one that blooms at around the same time.

Arkansas Black	Hibernal	Rhode Island Greening	Zabergau Reinette
Baldwin	Holstein	Ribston Pippin	**English Cider Varieties (triploids)**
Belle de Boskoop	Jonagold	Sir Prize	Bulmer's Norman
Blenheim Orange	July Red	Spigold	Court Royal
Bramley's Seedling	Jupiter	Spijon	Crimson King
Canada Reinette	Karmijn de Sonnaville	Stayman	Genet Moyle
Close	King's Acre Pippin	Summer Rambo	Morgan Sweet
Fallawater	Lady (Api)	Suntan	
Freiherr von Berlepsch	Mutsu (Crispin)	Tompkins County King	
Fukunishiki	Orin	Turley Winesap	
Gravenstein	Red Gravenstein	Winesap	

simply seedling varieties that were worth trying and, in some cases, preserving or grafting.

Apples rarely, if ever, reproduce themselves "true to type" from seed. This means that if you save a seed from an apple core (which, botanically speaking, is the true "fruit" of the apple), and plant it in the ground, the resulting tree will bear fruit that may differ slightly or even completely from its parent. And although bees can fertilize apple blossoms with pollen from other flowers on the same tree, most apples benefit from being cross-pollinated by another tree of a separate variety. In fact, some apples must have a different sort of tree blooming nearby at the same time in order to set fruit reliably. These are known as either pollen-sterile types or triploids (containing a third set of chromosomes); they include such familiar varieties as Gravenstein, Jonagold, and Mutsu (see "Nonpollinating Apple Varieties," on the previous page. Cultivated apples can also cross with other *Malus* species, including many kinds of crab apples, adding further to their promiscuous reputation.

This genetic variability of apple seedlings has proved to be good news for would-be cidermakers, especially in the United States, where farmers in the past created an almost infinite number of varieties simply by spreading the spent pomace (seeds and skins) from the cider press in broad bands in a sort of nursery planting, saving and transplanting any seedlings that appeared vigorous and healthy, then taking cuttings from any especially produc-tive varieties. Many fine old apples have been discovered growing as chance seedlings, including Red Delicious, which until recently was the world's most widely grown variety. Although today there are perhaps a hundred dif-ferent strains of Delicious, which at one time accounted for about one-fourth of the apples grown in the United States, they all trace their ancestry to a single tree that was discovered back in 1872 on Jesse Hiatt's farm in

Rich Stadnik

Peru, Iowa. (In fact, the variety was originally named Hawkeye after that state's nickname.) Hiatt tried three times to cut down the seedling tree, but each time it grew back. Finally, he gave up and allowed it to grow, and in 1893 its fruit won a prize at a show sponsored by Stark Brothers Nursery. The moral of the story is this: Never judge an apple tree until you taste its fruit. There is even an organization, the North American Fruit Explorers (or NAFEX; see "Resources" section), whose members are devoted, in part, to seeking out "wild" apples in hedgerows, abandoned pastures, and other obscure settings, with the goal of discovering neglected seedlings of unknown or forgotten varieties that someday may be worthy of widespread cultivation.

When we speak of a "variety," then, we are simply referring to a type of apple that possesses, in all environ-ments, at least one truly distinctive characteristic by which it can be told apart from all other apples. For instance, the old New England variety known as Blue Pearmain has a purplish red skin with a waxy bluish

Chapter 2: Apple Varieties for Cider

bloom; inside, its flesh is yellow and very aromatic. The recognition of these sorts of combined visible characteristics, rather than an apple's presumed parentage, has traditionally been the guiding rule in naming varieties.

In the past century or so, with the advent of scientific plant breeding, many apple varieties have been created not as "accidental" hybrids but by deliberately crossing two known parents and trying to express certain desirable qualities in the next generation, just as with other food and ornamental plants. For example, the variety Idared resulted from a cross between Jonathan and Wagener, and Mantet (one of my favorite summer apples) was named for its parents, McIntosh and Tetofsky. Such crosses are also known as seed hybrids.

Very, very rarely a new type of apple will result from a "graft hybrid." This sometimes occurs when one variety of apple is grafted onto another, yet the resulting fruit resembles neither of the parent stocks. More common, but still unusual, is what orchardists call a bud sport, when a characteristic like skin color changes spontaneously in the apples on a grafted fruiting branch. If this mutation persists, regardless of different growing conditions or environments, and passes on the new characteristic when the buds or scions are propagated in turn, then a new variety has been born.

For as long as there have been cultivated orchards, apple growers have recognized that, in order to increase the stock of a particular desirable variety, it is necessary to graft cuttings (shoots or buds) onto the limbs or rootstocks of other trees. Writing in 1572, the English horticultural expert Leonard Mascall observed, "When so euer ye doe replante or change your Pepin [pippin, or seedling apple] trees from place to place, in so remouing often the stocke the fruite there of shall also change; but the fruite which doth come of Graffing doth always keep the forme and nature of the tree whereof he is taken."[1]

Thus grafting, which is really just a low-tech form of cloning, offers the only sure way to transfer the precise genetic traits of a parent variety to new orchard trees. This ensures that a classic apple—Ribston Pippin, for example—will not only survive (so long as it is rejuvenated in newly grafted trees), but will also look and taste essentially the same today as it did three hundred years ago, when it was first grown in Yorkshire.

Basic Types of Apples

Fortunately, you don't have to be familiar with thousands of apple varieties in order to make terrific cider. All you really need to know are the broad, basic categories that describe the general tastes and uses of various apples. Then you can use that information in creating and blending a balanced, flavorful juice, either for drinking fresh or for fermenting into hard cider.

Foxwhelp is an old English cider apple classified as a bittersharp, with good tannins and acidity. *Ben Watson*

The first consideration, of course, is taste. Apples are generally classified as dessert (those eaten fresh out of hand), cooking, or cider varieties. Most people think of dessert apples as sweet, and they are, but the best kinds also have a good balance of acidity, so that they taste sprightly and not cloying to the palate. Also, the finest dessert varieties have a distinctive flavor (usually aromatic or spicy) that sets them apart from other apples. The heirloom American apple known as Mother, for instance, has a delicious balsamic taste and aroma. And once you taste them, it's obvious how varieties like Chenango Strawberry and Pitmaston Pineapple got their names.

Cooking, or culinary, apples taste brisker than dessert types either because they actually contain more malic acid or because they contain less sugar, which tends to mask the tartness that is present in the dessert fruit. The real "acid test" of a cooking apple, though, is whether it will cook down into a soft, pulpy puree (what French chefs call a *marmalade*). Some apples like Duchess and Yellow Transparent have what is known as "melting," or tender, white flesh, which cooks down into a wonderful applesauce. Other culinary varieties, such as the familiar Golden Delicious and Belle de Boskoop (a favorite for apple strudel), when sliced hold their shape in cooking. Even the most astringent, high-acid apples, like most crabs, are excellent for making jellies and tart applesauce. On the other hand, apples that are relatively low in acid and either very sweet (like Ribston Pippin) or very bitter (like Dabinett and other English cider apples) make lousy culinary apples, as their flesh tends to become only drier and tougher during cooking.

Cider apples are the most arbitrary category of the three, mainly because dessert and cooking apples are both commonly used in cider blends. A good fresh cider requires sweetness and body, sprightliness and aroma. Very few, if any, single apple varieties possess all of these

qualities. To achieve a good balance of these desirable characteristics, then, it is necessary to blend different kinds of apples. And while it is true that certain widely grown apples are used disproportionately as a base juice in commercial cider blends (Red Delicious and McIntosh, for example), small-scale orchardists and home cidermakers tend to strive for a more complex and interesting taste.

Because fresh cider in the United States is normally made from small, surplus, or "aesthetically challenged" fruit, the bulk of juice comes from dessert varieties that for whatever reason don't make the fancy grade. That's good news for cidermakers, as most American apples have a natural acid/sugar balance, which is important for both sweet and hard cider. Red Delicious is one notable exception; its juice is very sweet but also very low in acid. As a result, some cidermakers avoid it completely, while others make sure to blend it with plenty of more acidic apples. The table starting on the following page lists some popular and classic American apples that are especially good to use in cider.

True cider apples, though, are mainly bitter-tasting varieties that are used in making the classic hard ciders of northwest Europe and England. The bitterness and astringency of these apples come from tannins that are present in both the skin and the flesh of the fruit. Tannin is the same substance found on the skins of wine grapes; it acts as a stabilizer in both wine and cider, inhibiting the activity of certain bacteria and enzymes that can cause various disorders and off-flavors. It also contributes body and a dry finish, helps to clarify or "fine" the must (juice) during fermentation, and greatly improves the keeping qualities of finished hard cider.

I vividly recall the first time I bit into a true European cider apple, the aptly named Tremlett's Bitter. I was standing in an orchard, which was lucky, because I

Chapter 2: Apple Varieties for Cider

NORTH AMERICAN APPLES RECOMMENDED FOR CIDER

VARIETY NAME	SKIN COLOR/APPEARANCE	SEASON
1. Arkansas Black	Dark purple-red; glossy	Late
2. Ashmead's Kernel	Yellow russet; often scarlet cheek	Mid
3. Baldwin	Bright red; white dots; tough, thick skin	Mid to late
4. Belle de Boskoop	Green to yellow; rough russet; some red blush/stripes	Mid
5. Black Oxford	Dark purple; black bloom	Late
6. Black Twig	Green-yellow; dark red flush	Late
7. Blue Pearmain	Purple; bluish bloom	Mid
8. Bullock (American Golden Russet)	Yellow; some russet	Late
9. Calville Blanc d'Hiver	Pale green with red dots and pink blush; uneven ribbing	Mid
10. Campfield	Yellow with red blush and stripes	Late
11. Cortland	Dark red	Mid
12. Cox's Orange Pippin	Orange; red stripes	Mid
13. Egremont Russet	Yellow russet	Late
14. Empire	Dark red; waxy	Mid
15. Esopus Spitzenburg	Scarlet; russet dots	Mid
16. Fameuse (Snow)	Red over yellow cream	Early/early-mid
17. Freedom	Bright red	Mid
18. Geneva Crab	Red; dark red foliage	Early
19. Gilpin	Yellow; red stripes	Mid-late
20. Golden Delicious	Green/yellow; pink blush	Mid
21. Golden Harvey	Yellow russet; red cheek	Early-mid
22. Golden Pearmain	Green-gold with scarlet flush, red stripes	Early-mid
23. Golden Russet	Gray-green to golden bronze russet	Late
24. Golden Sweet	Pale yellow	Early-mid

NOTES

1. Hard, crisp yellowish flesh; distinctive aroma; long keeper; storage enhances flavor
2. Crisp yellow flesh; juicy, aromatic; sprightly, tart flavor when tree-ripe; acidity mellows in storage; as single-variety hard cider it benefits from extended bottle aging
3. Crisp, solid, juicy flesh; sweet, spicy flavor; good for sweet base or single-variety hard cider
4. Coarse, creamy white flesh is crisp, tender, and juicy; good acidity; requires pollinator
5. Firm, fine-grained, greenish-white flesh; insect- and disease-resistant; yields dense, dark, high-quality juice when pressed fully ripe; good single-variety or blended hard cider
6. Firm, fine-grained yellow flesh; good-keeping Southern apple
7. Coarse yellowish flesh is sweet, mild, and aromatic; skin shrivels in storage
8. Small, yellow-fleshed fruit with a rich, spicy flavor; tree hardy
9. High, sprightly flavor; good acidity; flavor develops with short-term storage or sweating; excellent for hard cider and vinegar
10. Sweet flesh; good keeper; very rare, but historic cider apple
11. Crisp, fine-grained, tender white flesh resists browning; tart, tangy juice for sweet base
12. Tender, juicy, yellow flesh; sweet, subacid flavor and wonderful aroma
13. Small to medium size fruit; greenish white flesh is sweet, nutty, and aromatic; good keeper; tree very hardy
14. Creamy white, crisp, juicy flesh; aromatic; keeps longer than McIntosh
15. Crisp, spicy yellow flesh; aromatic; sprightly and tart when tree-ripe, mellows in storage and reaches peak of flavor in December; juice holds up to pasteurization; for single-variety hard cider or blending; susceptible to fireblight
16. Bright white, juicy flesh tinged with red; spicy and aromatic
17. Crisp, juicy, fine-grained, greenish white flesh; strong subacid flavor; very disease-resistant
18. Red flesh is very acidic; good for blending; makes a highly colored early cider; tree is ornamental and hardy, but a poor pollinator
19. Firm, coarse yellowish flesh; sweet, rich flavor; old Virginia cider apple
20. Firm, crisp, tender flesh; sweet, mild flavor; bruises easily; use sparingly for sweet cider base, as milled pulp can be sloppy and difficult to press; self-fertile; excellent pollinator
21. Firm, crisp yellow flesh; sweet, spicy flavor; juice is very dense and good for hard cider
22. Firm, crisp, creamy yellow flesh; tender and juicy; old Southern apple variety or blended hard cider; disease-resistant
23. Crisp, fine-grained yellow flesh; adds body and depth to sweet cider; sugary juice ferments into good single-variety or blended hard cider
24. Very sweet, rich flavor; some disease resistance

VARIETY NAME	SKIN COLOR/APPEARANCE	SEASON
25. GoldRush	Golden yellow; brown dots; orange blush	Mid-late
26. Graniwinkle	Green/yellow; flushed dark red	Mid
27. Granny Smith	Light green; sometimes with reddish brown blush; peened surface	Mid-late
28. Gravenstein	Orange/yellow; red stripes	Early
29. Grimes Golden	Golden yellow	Mid
30. Haralson	Red-striped to deep red; yellow dots	Mid
31. Harrison	Yellow; black dots	Mid-late
32. Hewes (Virginia) Crab	Dull red with greenish-yellow streaks; white dots	Early-mid
33. Honey Cider	Light green; some russet	Early
34. Horse Apple	Golden yellow; ribbed	Early
35. Hudson's Golden Gem	Dull yellow russet; conical	Mid-late
36. Hyslop	Dark reddish purple; blue bloom	Early-mid
37. Idared	Bright red; waxy	Mid
38. Jonathan	Yellow with bright red stripes to all red	Mid
39. Jordan Russet	Yellow russet; red blush	Late
40. Keepsake	Red; yellow stars; some russet	Mid
41. King David	Dark red over pale green	Early
42. Kinnaird's Choice	Yellow, mottled or overspread with red	Early-mid
43. Lady (Api)	Light green; cherry red cheek; small, flat-round	Late
44. Liberty	Yellow overspread with red blush	Early-mid
45. McIntosh	Bright to dark red	Early-mid
46. Maiden Blush	Yellow; crimson blush; flat-round; waxy	Early-mid
47. Melrose	Yellow/green overspread with bright red	Mid
48. Mutsu (Crispin)	Yellow; occasional red blush	Mid-late
49. Newtown Pippin	Yellow/green; red blush	Mid

NOTES

25. Crisp, firm, juicy flesh with intense sweet-tart, spicy, winelike, flavor; very acidic when tree-ripe but mellows in storage; good keeper; high sugars for hard cider; very disease-resistant

26. Yellow flesh is very rich and sweet; juice is dense and syrupy; traditionally blended with Harrison

27. Hard, crisp, juicy white flesh; medium to high acid for blending

28. Crisp, juicy, fine-grained flesh; distinctive flavor; medium to high acid for blending; requires a pollinator

29. Crisp, juicy yellow flesh; rich, spicy, and aromatic; high sugar content is good for hard cider or brandy; self-fertile; excellent pollinator

30. Firm, white flesh; mild, aromatic, pleasantly tart

31. Yellow, coarse, rather dry flesh; rich, sprightly flavor; dark, dense juice makes a high-quality vintage hard cider with great body; rare variety, now being reintroduced

32. Yellow flesh is fibrous and astringent; high acid for blending and good tannins; makes a high-flavored dry hard cider.

33. Crisp, juicy, very sweet translucent flesh; use as sweetener with tarter apples

34. Coarse, tender yellow flesh; good acidity; very tart even when fully ripe; for early cider and vinegar

35. Light yellow flesh is crisp and juicy with high sugars and a pearlike, nutty flavor

36. Firm yellow flesh tinged red next to skin; press soon after harvest; subacid flavor with some astringency; good for blending

37. Crisp, juicy white flesh; good flavor and aroma when tree-ripe

38. Tender, juicy white flesh; brisk, subacid flavor; blend with mild juices; press right after picking; self-fertile

39. Juicy, hard fruit; excellent keeper; extremely hardy; rare

40. Crisp, fine-grained, juicy flesh; pleasant, complex, subacid flavor; extremely hardy

41. Rich, spicy, juicy yellow flesh; disease-resistant

42. Crisp, coarse-grained yellowish white flesh; aromatic, subacid flavor; old Southern apple

43. Tender, bright white flesh; mild and juicy taste; much of the flavor and aroma is in the skin; scab-susceptible

44. Sweet, juicy crisp, white flesh; contributes a bit of tannin; full flavor develops after a month in storage; scab-immune and very disease-resistant

45. Tart, spicy flavor; very aromatic; many strains available

46. Tender, creamy white flesh; sharp, acidic flavor; susceptible to scab and fireblight

47. Firm, coarse, creamy white flesh; juicy, aromatic, and subacid flavor

48. Dense, crunchy flesh; delicate spicy flavor; needs a pollinator

49. Rich, creamy yellow flesh; piney tartness; press soon after picking

VARIETY NAME	SKIN COLOR/APPEARANCE	SEASON
50. Northern Spy	Yellow; light red stripes	Late-mid
51. Ralls (Ralls Genet)	Green/yellow; marked with red; white stars	Mid
52. Red Delicious	Dark red; waxy	Mid
53. Red June	Deep red over yellow	Early
54. Redfield	Pink to red, waxy; reddish bronze leaves	Mid
55. Rhode Island Greening	Yellow/green; often orange-red blush	Mid
56. Ribston Pippin	Yellow/orange; russet	Mid
57. Rome Beauty	Solid red	Mid-late
58. Roxbury Russet	Green/yellow; russet	Late-mid
59. Sansa	Green overspread with scarlet red	Early
60. Smith's Cider	Clear pale yellow, striped red	Mid
61. Sops of Wine	Green/yellow; mottled red	Early-mid
62. St. Edmund's Pippin	Golden orange russet	Mid
63. Stayman	Dull red over green	Late
64. Tolman Sweet	Pale yellow	Late
65. Tompkins County King	Yellow flushed pale red with dark red	Mid
66. Vandevere (Grindstone)	Yellow; striped red	Late
67. Wagener	Pale red over light yellow	Late
68. Wickson	Yellow and red	Late
69. Winesap	Dark red	Mid-late
70. Winter Banana	Pale yellow with red blush; waxy skin with distinctive suture	Late
71. Yates	Bright red with dots	Late
72. York Imperial	Green/yellow; red flush	Late

NOTES

50. Fine-grained yellow flesh; tart, aromatic, subacid flavor; high sugars; long keeper
51. Green-tinged yellow flesh is crisp and dense; balanced sweet and tart flavor; susceptible to fireblight
52. Crisp, juicy white flesh; ery sweet and aromatic, but low-acid juice; use sparingly in blends
53. Brisk, subacid white flesh; add to balance sweeter juices
54. Rather dry, acidic red flesh makes a colorful, rose-like hard cider; press soon after harvest; tree is ornamental, hardy, and insect- and disease-resistant
55. Greasy skin;firm, greenish yellow flesh; tart, refreshing acid juice for blending; needs two pollinators
56. Hard, crisp, fine-grained flesh; rich, sweet, and aromatic; good acidity
57. Crisp, greenish white flesh; sweet juice; press soon after picking
58. Coarse, crunchy yellowish white flesh; lots of sugar and good acidity; very long keeper; makes high-quality varietal hard cider
59. Crisp, coarse-grained flesh; high sugars, low acidity; good for sweet blending
60. Crisp, fine-grained white flesh; subacid flavor; old traditional cider variety
61. Juicy, soft yellowish flesh; aromatic, mild, subacid flavor
62. Very juicy, crisp creamy white flesh; rich, sweet, aromatic; pearlike flavor; bruises easily
63. Tender, juicy yellowish white flesh; tart, subacid, rich, spicy, winelike flavor; needs a pollinator
64. Firm, white, rather dry flesh; high sugars, low acidity; bruises easily; susceptible to fireblight
65. Coarse, tender yellowish flesh; sweet, subacid flavor with good balance and aroma; susceptible to fireblight
66. Firm, tender, juicy yellow flesh; mildly subacid, lively flavor; old apple also listed as American Pippin
67. Tender white flesh; sweet, subacid, sprightly flavor; aromatic; good keeper
68. Small, sweet, highly flavored fruit; up to 25% sugar, balanced with high acidity
69. Crisp, very juicy yellow flesh; tart and sweet; spicy, winelike flavor; long keeper
70. Crisp, juicy yellowish white flesh; mild but distinctive flavor and aroma; bruised easily; good pollinator; susceptible to fireblight
71. Juicy, tender, yellowish white flesh, often stained red under the skin; sweet flavor; makes high-quality hard cider; Southern apple.
72. Juicy, coarse-grained yellow flesh; sweet to subacid and aromatic; good keeper; flavor develops in storage.

spent the next five minutes spitting the taste out of my puckered mouth as my companion, the orchardist, looked on in great amusement. If it is indeed true, as some people believe, that these apples have partly descended from the wild European crab apple *(Malus sylvestris)*, it's obvious why the Celts fermented them: A person would have to be very hungry indeed to actually eat more than a bite of these intensely bitter fruits—so beautiful in the hand, so galling on the tongue.

European cider apples fall into one of four basic types: 1) bittersweet (high tannin, low acid); 2) sweet (low tannin, low acid); 3) bittersharp (high tannin, high acid); 4) sharp (low tannin, high acid). Examples of varieties belonging to each of these types are listed in the table on page 42. As with American dessert varieties, the European cider apples are often blended together to make complex and well-balanced hard ciders. This blending can take place either at grinding time before pressing; immediately after pressing, when the fresh juices are mixed together; or after fermentation, once the various single-variety juices have each turned into nearly dry finished ciders.

Unlike most sweet ciders, there are numerous examples of single-variety (varietal) hard ciders. Varietal ciders are normally made from such "vintage" apples as Dabinett (a bittersweet) and Kingston Black (a bittersharp), which are common in the West Country of England, though cidermakers have experimented with many other nonblended hard ciders, including ones made from American varieties like Baldwin and Golden Russet. As a general rule, though, while single-variety ciders are fun to experiment with and often quite interesting and tasty, there are few if any that cannot be improved in terms of flavor, body, or bouquet by the addition of one or more other varieties of apples.

Keeping Things in Proportion

The basic components of any good cider are sweetness, acidity, bitterness, and aroma. How much of each quality the fresh-pressed juice exhibits depends very much on the personal tastes of the cidermaker and on the varieties of apples available for pressing at any one time. Beyond that, there are no hard-and-fast rules, although the percentages shown in the table on page 42 commonly invoked as an approximate rule of thumb in making a balanced juice, either for drinking fresh or for fermenting into a typical American-style still (dry) hard cider.

Obviously, not all orchardists follow these prescriptions when making their fresh or sweet ciders, particularly as regards the "bitter or astringent" category. It seems counterintuitive to think that bitter-tasting apples would contribute much, if anything, to a fresh juice,

Wickson is a modern American apple with high sugar and acid, making it useful for cider. Its only disadvantage is the extra time it takes to harvest the small fruits. *Ben Watson*

despite their importance in making traditional European hard ciders. But in fact, when used in moderation, astringent or bitter fruits can add a desirable "chewiness" or body to a nonalcoholic sweet cider; the juice does not pick up the bitterness of the fruit that's so evident when the apple is eaten out of hand. For most American cidermakers who don't have access to high-tannin English cider fruits, many "wild" apples or native crab apples provide a good alternative for adding astringency to cider. David Craxton, the former cidermaker at Lost Nation Orchard in northern New Hampshire, typically included as much as two bushels of wild apples in a single sixteen-bushel pressing, always tasting the "wild" fruit first to determine its characteristics and to gauge how much to add to the mix.

Apples vary widely in sugar content, anywhere from around 6 percent to nearly 25 percent in the case of Wickson, a small, high-sugar/high-acid variety that was created by intentionally crossing two classic American apples: Newtown Pippin and Esopus Spitzenburg. Environmental and growing conditions also affect the sugar content of the fruit, and even apples of the same variety may vary considerably in sweetness during different growing seasons. After a cool, rainy summer, apples will contain less sugar than they will following a hot, dry season. Some apples like Gravenstein or Newtown Pippin have a racy acidity when grown in Northeast, whereas in the milder Mediterranean climate of California the same varieties will often be dramatically sweeter and less acidic. Other apples ripen especially well in the warm days and chilly nights of a typical New England autumn. And apples are similarly variable in terms of acid content, ranging from less than 0.1 percent acid in some sweet varieties to more than 1.3 percent in the sharpest-tasting fruits.

Both sugar and acid, and ideally a balance of the two, are crucial for making good cider. Lots of sugary juice, as is found in yellow-fleshed apples like the various russets, gives a sweet cider depth and body, and makes for a naturally higher-alcohol and better-keeping hard cider. The malic acid found in apples is important to counteract the sweetness of fresh cider; to add a brisk, refreshing flavor to the juice; and to protect fermenting cider from unwelcome bacteria and discoloration.

Finding Your Cider Apples

Obviously, the ideal situation for any cidermaker would be to have his or her own orchard, filled with a variety of apple trees that have been selected specifically for the cider-worthiness of their fruit. This may sound like a pipe dream, but it is possible to have a diverse collection of apples even on a modest homestead—especially if you plant apple varieties grafted on semidwarfing or dwarfing rootstocks, which will begin bearing fruit much sooner than will standard-sized trees. If you plan to press lots of cider, though, keep in mind that a truly dwarf tree might yield only about a bushel of fruit; in contrast, you could reasonably expect to harvest four times that amount from a semidwarf tree, and ten times that (or more) from a standard tree.

Many of the classic older varieties of apples tend toward biennial production, meaning that you can expect a huge crop one year, and a relatively shy harvest the following year. There are some orchard strategies to encourage annual bearing, but most apple growers either go with the flow or select apples that crop well every year. One time I helped my friend Roger Swain harvest an old seedling tree on his property whose high-acid fruit we add to our cider blend; that year we picked twenty-eight bushels of fruit from the "Castle Rock" tree, whereas most seasons we might harvest half that

Chapter 2: Apple Varieties for Cider

APPLE TYPES AND PROPORTIONS FOR BLENDING

Type of Apple	Percentage of Total Juice
Sweet or dessert varieties (examples: *Baldwin, Cortland, Golden Delicious,* *Golden Russet, Mutsu, Rome Beauty, York Imperial*)	30%–60%
Subacid or tart varieties (examples: *Ashmead's Kernel, Bramley's Seedling,* *Calville Blanc d'Hiver, Granny Smith,* *Gravenstein, Jonathan, Newtown Pippin,* *Rhode Island Greening, Wealthy*)	10%–40%
Slightly astringent to bitter varieties (examples: *Cortland, Liberty, Northern Spy,* *many russets and crab apples (Hewes, Hyslop, etc.);* *European bittersweet and bittersharp varieties*)	5%–20%
Aromatic varieties (examples: *Black Twig, Cox's Orange Pippin,* *Fameuse, Grimes Golden, McIntosh, Ribston Pippin,* *Red Delicious, Roxbury Russet*)	10%–20%

amount. Either way, once you plant or adopt a standard-size apple tree, it becomes abundantly clear why cider-making is such a good idea. What else does one do with twenty-eight bushels of apples from a single tree?

On an October weekend several years ago, I pressed cider with Farish and Eleanor Jenkins on their farm in Eaton, New Hampshire, and I saw firsthand what a little planning and patience can produce in terms of a home cider orchard. The Jenkinses were not full-time farmers; in fact Farish at the time was a paleontologist and the Agassiz Professor of Zoology at Harvard University. Yet over the course of several years the couple lovingly plant-ed, pruned, and tended a number of apple trees that grow around the stone walls of their well-kept farm, with its prospect of Mount Chocorua across the fields in the distance. During this annual cider-making weekend, the barn was filled with bushel boxes of different apples that had been ripening and "sweating" for several days or even weeks. They included Macouns and Spartans, Cortlands and Roxbury Russets, King Davids and Ribston Pippins. There were also Mother, Lady, Horse, Sheepnose, Idared, Fameuse, Westfield Seek-No-Further, Red Rome, Golden and Red Delicious, Northern Spy, the enormous Wolf River, and Cox's Orange Pippin. There was even a foundling variety that they had chris-tened Bubbaliciosa. The possibilities made my head spin, and by the end of the day I had a stomach to match, just from sampling all those apples.

If you aren't an apple grower yourself, and don't aspire to be, there are still plenty of options available to you. One is grinding and pressing your own cider using a homestead screw-type press (see chapter 3). For relatively small amounts of cider, or with the help of friends, this strategy allows you maximum control, as you can purchase utility or cider-grade apples and then mix them yourself in very precise quantities before pressing.

Some small local cider mills and orchards will agree to do custom pressing for you, though there is typically a minimum quantity of apples that they will press at any one time. Talk to the proprietor, find out what kinds of apples he or she typically uses at various times of the year, then get together some cider-making friends to share the costs as well as the abundance of fresh cider. It used to be much simpler to find cider mills that would allow you to bring in your own apples for them to cus-

tom-press. Unfortunately, given the current regulatory climate and liability issues, fewer and fewer orchards are willing to assume the risk of pressing apples that they have not picked and controlled from the tree to the press.

The easiest course for beginners who are interested in making hard cider is to purchase unpasteurized sweet cider. This may sound simple, but real, high-quality fresh cider has become increasingly hard to find of late (see chapter 3). Still, if you have retail orchards in your area that press cider, they will probably make their own natural, unpasteurized product, or be willing to sell you a quantity of fresh-pressed juice, perhaps at a bulk price. Even if you buy in gallon quantities from the orchard store, talk with the orchard manager or cidermaker to find out which varieties of apples were used in the batch you're buying. Some cidermakers are inexplicably tight-lipped about the specific quantities and varieties they use, as if their formulas were proprietary. If you like their cider, though, don't sweat the details; if you don't like the taste, look elsewhere, or consider the homestead or custom-pressing options.

Whichever strategy you use, be prepared to put your teeth into as many different varieties of apples as possible. You may understand in theory what properties make a good cider, but your own taste buds are still the final arbiter of sweetness, tartness, and aroma. Look for apple tastings in the fall at local orchards or at historical and farm museums. Antique apples like Esopus Spitzenburg and Roxbury Russet have become popular in recent years, and many small retail orchards now sell them. Try to buy a few bushels of any nonfancy or "orchard run" fruit to bring home and press yourself. Even if you are only making your own sweet cider and never ferment a drop, the results will be well worth it.

Cider apples harvested at Poverty Lane Orchards, Lebanon, N.H. *Ben Watson*

Chapter 2: Apple Varieties for Cider

ENGLISH AND EUROPEAN CIDER APPLES

Note: Varieties marked with a "V" are generally considered to be "vintage" cider apples—those whose juice is sometimes left unblended to make single-variety hard ciders.

Type/Variety Name	Notes (Taste, Season)
BITTERSWEETS (high tannin, low acid)	
Ashton Bitter	Full bitter; aromatic juice; early
Ashton Brown Jersey (V)	Medium bitter; hard tannin; full body; late; scab-resistant
Bramtot (France)	Full bitter, biennial bearer; hard tannin; high sugar; mid
Brown Snout	Mild to medium bitter, soft tannin, late
Brown Thorn (Argile Grise)	Mild bitter; old Norman apple; late; susceptible to fireblight
Bulmer's Norman	Medium bitter; hard tannin; juice ferments quickly; biennial bearer; triploid; mid
Burrow Hill Early	Full bitter; fruity, full-bodied juice; early
Chisel Jersey	Full bitter; full-bodied juice; late
Coloradona (Spain)	Mild bitter; low acid; early-mid
Dabinett (V)	Full bitter; soft tannin; late; self-fertile; reliable crops
Ellis Bitter	Medium bitter; soft tannin; early-mid
Harry Masters Jersey (V)	Medium to full bitter; soft tannin; mid-late
Major (V)	Full bitter; soft tannin; early-mid
Medaille d'Or (France)	Full bitter; soft tannin; late; scab-resistant
Michelin (France)	Medium bitter; soft tannin; for blending; mid; reliable crops
Nehou (France)	Full bitter; biennial bearer; early-mid
Reine des Hatives (France)	Mild bitter; biennial bearer; early-mid
Reine des Pommes (France/V)	Medium bitter; makes dark, rich cider; mid
Somerset Redstreak	Mild bitter; biennial bearer; early-mid
Stembridge Jersey	Full bitter; biennial bearer; mid-late
Tardive Forestière (France)	Full bitter; biennial bearer; late
Tremlett's Bitter (V)	Full bitter; hard tannin; early-mid
Vilberie (France)	Full bitter; full-bodied juice; late
White Jersey (V)	Mild to medium bitter; early-mid
Yarlington Mill (V)	Medium bitter; biennial bearer; mid-late

SWEETS (low tannin, low acid)

Court Royal (V)	Biennial bearer; triploid; juice ferments quickly; late prone to scab
De Jaune (France)	Rich, sweet; also for dessert, cooking; late
Dunkerton's Late	Makes light, fruity cider; late Duron Arroes (Spain); good balance of acid and tannin
Morgan Sweet	Pure sweet juice ferments rapidly; triploid; early
Northwood (V)	Soft, fruity low-tannin juice; late
Reine des Reinettes	Balanced acid; also for cooking; mid (King of the Pippins)
Slack-Ma-Girdle	Rich, full bodied, aromatic juice; late
Sweet Coppin (V)	Soft, white flesh; biennial bearer; mid-late
Taylor's Sweet	Sweet to mild bitter; for blending; mid

BITTERSHARPS (high tannin, high acid)

Breakwell's Seedling	Medium bitter, mildly sharp; biennial bearer; early-mid
Cap of Liberty (V)	Full bitter; high acid; fruity; mid
Dymock Red (V)	Medium bitter; well balanced; early-mid
Foxwhelp (V)	Musky flavor; good blender; mid; bruises easily
Genet Moyle	Light juice; triploid; also for cooking; early-mid
Kingston Black (V)	Mild bitter; good balance; juice ferments slowly; mid-late
Meana (Spain)	High acid and tannin; late
Porter's Perfection	Very sharp, medium bitter; late
Stoke Red (V)	Medium sharp, aromatic juice; high tannin; late; scab-resistant

SHARPS (low tannin, high acid)

Bramley's Seedling	High acid; triploid; also for cooking; mid
Brown's Apple (V)	Fruity, fragrant juice; biennial bearer; mid; scab-resistant
Crimson King (V)	Medium sharp; light, fruity juice; triploid; late
Frederick (V)	Fruity, aromatic juice; mid-late
Gin (V)	Fruity, full-bodied juice; early
Raxao (Spain)	Very sharp, little astringency; late
Stembridge Cluster	Biennial; fruit in clusters; mid-late; prone to scab
Tom Putt	Soft, mildly sharp flesh; also for cooking; early

What is more melancholy than the old apple-trees that linger about the spot where once stood a homestead, but where there is now only a ruined chimney rising out of a grassy and weed-grown cellar? They offer their fruit to every wayfarer—apples that are bittersweet with the moral of time's vicissitude.

—Nathaniel Hawthorne, *Mosses from an Old Manse* (1846)

3. SWEET CIDER: FROM TREE TO JUICE

ONLY IN NORTH AMERICA does the word *cider* refer primarily to the freshly pressed, nonalcoholic juice of the apple. Throughout Europe and in the rest of the world, *cider* always indicates a fermented beverage. Even when the French mention *cidre doux* ("sweet cider") they are talking about a low-alcohol drink (about 2 to 4 percent) in which fermentation has been stopped or greatly slowed down before bottling, leaving behind the residual sweetness of the fruit.

America's cider schizophrenia dates back to the late nineteenth century and the years before Prohibition, when the making of alcoholic cider was declared illegal and apple orchards in the East were abandoned, grubbed out, or chopped up into firewood. Although fermented cider was considered the devil's brew, fresh apple juice was being recognized and marketed as a healthful drink, and the term *sweet cider* was coined to suggest the simpler, more wholesome aspects of life on the farm.

The designation stuck, and today most Americans who hear the word *cider* still picture the sweet, cloudy juice that is made seasonally at local orchards and cider mills (or, increasingly, that insipid, denatured drink that can be found year-round at the supermarket). The New Hampshire Department of Agriculture defines cider as simply "the unfermented juice of apples with an alcohol content of less than one percent by volume at 60 degrees F." Yet this definition is much too broad for our purposes. So, at the risk of confusing matters even further, I suggest we use a new term, *real cider,* to mean the natural pressed juice of apples, unfiltered, unpasteurized, and without additives or artificial preservatives.

From a purist's perspective, there is no clearer explanation of what real cider is and is not than the one offered some forty years ago by Professor Robert LaBelle of the New York State Agricultural Experiment Station: "The term fresh, sweet, or farm cider should be reserved to the simple, old-fashioned product, normally oxidized in color and flavor and still containing all the suspended solids that render it almost opaque. . . . However, all processing, such as heating [pasteurization] or the addition of ascorbic acid [vitamin C] that largely prevents oxidation, produces 'apple juice,' not cider."[1]

LaBelle might also have mentioned the addition of potassium sorbate or sodium benzoate, two preservatives that are commonly used to extend the brief refrigerated shelf life of fresh cider and allow large producers to sell it to distant markets. The bottom line is this: For most anyone who has ever tasted the genuine article, juice containing preservatives is simply not the same as real cider.

In Defense of Real Cider

In our present economic climate, when it is considered un-American to oppose anything done in the name of free trade or the global economy, this uncompromising view of cider and other traditional foods is often regarded as eccentric and elitist at best, subversive and neo-Luddite at worst. Yet why should this be so? If apples can be grown in virtually all temperate growing regions, in the United States and around the world, why can't tens of thousands of small, regional cidermakers turn out a good product primarily for local consumption? Left to its own devices, a natural cider has an extremely short shelf life; even under refrigeration it will begin to ferment and turn fizzy in ten to fourteen days after pressing. But most fall and early-winter apples (the kind best suited to making cider) will store well for months, and some classic varieties, such as Esopus Spitzenburg and Ashmead's Kernel, develop their fullest, richest flavor only after several weeks of storage. With the right varieties on hand, cider can be pressed fresh in small batches all winter long. And even if larger batches of cider are made during the fall, cider freezes well and can be kept in this way for six months or more without losing any of its flavor, zest, or nutritional qualities.

The reason that natural, real cider has become so hard to find these days has much more to do with our industrial, centralized system of agriculture and food distribution than with any technical difficulties in making or keeping sweet cider fresh. High-quality cider requires a balance of characteristics that are found in different varieties of apples: sweetness, tartness, aroma, and astringency. Making such complex and excellent cider requires an artisan's touch and experience, as well as a diverse selection of fruit. This is possible for small farmers and orchardists, and not surprisingly these are the people who still make the best sweet cider. But large-volume cider and juice producers generally do not operate their own orchards, instead buying cider-grade fruit in bulk. This virtually ensures that the majority of juice will be pressed from the most widely grown varieties of dessert

Chapter 3: Sweet Cider from Tree to Juice

apples. As of 2004, just eight varieties comprised nearly 80 percent of the U.S. commercial apple crop: Red Delicious, Golden Delicious, Gala, Fuji, Granny Smith, McIntosh, and Rome Beauty.[2] The majority of these apples will *contribute* to making a good cider; but without a good percentage of other apples that add depth, body, and a balanced acidity (such as the various russets), it is no wonder that mass-produced juice from large-scale cider operations so often ends up tasting banal and uninspiring.

A good natural cider is deep, dark, and mysterious, like a good pint of stout or a bowl of homemade gumbo. Drinking it refreshes the soul and leaves you wanting more. It has an effervescence, an aliveness that is a precursor to the fizzier fermentation to come. A heat-pasteurized juice, by contrast, tastes dead and flat. At best it is good, unrefined apple juice—which is nothing to sneeze at—but a true connoisseur knows that it is not the same thing as real cider. You sip it instead of quaffing, and one glass at a time is plenty. We know that real, honest-to-goodness cider won't remain at its fresh flavor peak for very long, and so we drink it down in generous gulps that celebrate the fleeting joys of the season and nature itself—like Indian-summer days and cold, clear, moonlit nights.

Even more unfortunate from the standpoint of taste is the use of preservatives, which are added to extend the refrigerated shelf life of cider and are found in almost all ciders made by larger producers and sold by national and regional supermarket chains. Erick Leadbeater, who owns the hundred-acre Gould Hill Orchards in Contoocook, New Hampshire (which has been growing apples since 1764), is a master cidermaker with an inquiring and open mind about such things as preservatives. Leadbeater says he has experimented with potassium sorbate, adding it to his fresh farm cider in small increments, but that he could never find a level at which the chemical would effectively preserve the cider and yet not be noticeable—and objectionable—to his taste buds. Almost anyone who has ever tasted real, natural cider would agree with him.

How Safe Is Real Cider?

The news that something as wholesome as fresh, sweet cider could actually be hazardous to your health came as a shock in 1996 when one child died and other people became sick from a new strain of bacteria that, it was reported, had contaminated unpasteurized apple juice. This new microorganism, which was classified as *E. coli* 0157:H7, was recognized as a serious public health threat, with the potential to contaminate not only apple and other unpasteurized fruit juices, but other foods as well. Government food safety agencies and consumer groups soon began insisting that the only cider safe to drink was pasteurized cider. As a result of the hysteria, products containing unpasteurized juice must now carry advisory labels, which resemble the warning labels found on alcohol and cigarettes.

Partly as a result of these health concerns, unpasteurized cider (which, aside from its superior taste, is indispensable for making natural hard cider) has become increasingly hard to find. For some small orchardists, this new level of consumer concern and the promise of increased government regulation proved to be the last straw; fearful of lawsuits, they have thrown in the towel on their own cider operations, shipping their lower-grade apples instead to large manufacturers that can afford the expensive pasteurization equipment, and buying pasteurized juice for resale at their own farm stands or orchard stores.

Yet, to paraphrase Mark Twain, rumors of the death of real cider have been greatly exaggerated. Nevertheless, some people still consider drinking unpasteurized cider to be reckless behavior, and see those of us who prefer it to pasteurized juice as eccentric thrill-seekers, furtively looking for our next illicit fix. One orchardist, who has had to shut down his cider business largely as a result of the *E. coli* flap, showed me a cartoon of a shady character opening up his trenchcoat and saying, "Psst . . . Hey buddy. Want to buy some cider?" Before we compromise away this honorable American tradition—the making of natural sweet cider—it's worth examining exactly what *E. coli* is, how much of a threat it poses to cider, and what we can do to guard against it.

The bacterium *Escherichia coli* was first described back in 1883 by Dr. Theodore Escherich. It is one of the many organisms that live in the intestinal tracts of warm-blooded animals, especially livestock and poultry. Fortunately, most types of *E. coli* are harmless or even beneficial to humans, and some strains help in binding solid wastes or in producing antibiotics and vitamins like B_{12} and K in our intestines. However, four kinds of *E. coli* are harmful and can cause food poisoning and sickness, including the familiar malady known to world travelers as Montezuma's revenge.

The new virulent strain called *E. coli* 0157:H7 was first identified in 1982, and since then it has caused several outbreaks of food-borne illnesses, most of them linked to contaminated, undercooked ground beef. The news that the new bacteria could contaminate apple cider came as something of a surprise; at first it was thought that the acidity of cider (around 3.6 to 4.5 pH) would inhibit the bacteria's growth. However, researchers have since found that *E. coli* can survive at a pH as low as 2.0. Refrigerating or freezing the cider doesn't help, either, as the bacteria can survive even deep freezing and were found to produce toxins at temperatures between 40°F and 120°F.

Cow manure is the main source of *E. coli* contamination in food, and it can also be transmitted through contact with infected people. In every reported case of food-borne illness caused by cider, the juice in question had been pressed from unwashed orchard "drops"—apples that had lain on the ground for some time and had become infected from contact with animal feces or cow manure used as a fertilizer. The most obvious solution to this problem is prevention: keep animals from grazing in orchards, particularly for a certain period before harvest time; refrain from using old or unwashed drops, and bruised or cut fruit, for making cider (something that is not done by reputable cider mills in any case); follow good sanitation practices inside the mill; and keep good records, as would any other food service business. Almost every commercial cider operation is state-inspected and already has to follow these basic sanitation and safety procedures. Orchardists are also extremely conscientious about regulating themselves. After all, who would risk a few cents' profit to make an inferior product

A GLASS A DAY KEEPS THE DOCTOR AWAY

Besides the issue of taste, there are good nutritional reasons to bemoan the lack of real, unpasteurized cider in retail markets today. Natural apple cider is full of vitamins, and is more flavorful but less sweet than pasteurized juice. As a health drink, the temperance boosters were right: Natural cider contains lots of pectins and other suspended solids and is excellent for the body, especially for people who are on a cleansing or reducing diet. It benefits the liver and the gallbladder, and it tends to speed up bowel function. By contrast, heat-processed apple juice is much sweeter than real cider and has a significantly lower level of vitamins, particularly vitamins A, B_9, C, and E.[3]

Chapter 3: Sweet Cider from Tree to Juice

that might make somebody sick? That's a sure way to go out of business, particularly when your business is mainly retail and relies on repeat customers. And because of the heightened concerns over *E. coli*, cidermakers have become even more conscious of sanitation in their orchards and mills. As a result, according to author, home cidermaker, and food service consultant Paul Correnty, "The quality of the cider is the highest I've seen in the fifteen or sixteen years that I've been making hard cider, and the sanitation is the best. There is no safer time to buy sweet cider."

Fortunately, after an initial wave of consumer uneasiness, the pendulum seems to be swinging back in favor of real, unpasteurized cider. Retail sales of sweet cider in general have remained stable or are rising, despite the bad publicity, perhaps because there is a growing awareness of cider among consumers, and because these same people are demanding a better-tasting beverage, one made with good cider apples, not just any variety available. In the fall of 1998, Ian Merwin, of Cornell University, told me that although their research farm's sales of pasteurized and unpasteurized cider had been about equal the year before, sales of unpasteurized cider had rebounded sharply, to around 90 percent. However, less than a decade later, New York consumers were denied the right to choose which kind of cider they wanted to buy. The New York Apple Association lobbied that state's legislature and pushed through a bill banning the sale of *all* unpasteurized cider, even when it was made and sold on-premises at the farm, as is permitted in many other states and by the U.S. Food and Drug Administration (FDA). Until a few years ago, the only way to be absolutely sure of killing any *E. coli* bacteria in cider was with a heat treatment known as flash pasteurization, which exposes the fresh-pressed cider to a relatively high temperature—usually in the range of 160°F to 165°F—for a short time, from as little as ten to twenty seconds to as long as three minutes. The main problem for cidermakers—aside from pasteurization's adverse effect both on the taste of cider and on the yeasts and other microflora necessary for natural fermentation—is the cost of the equipment, which can range from $20,000 to $200,000, depending on the size of the operation. The fear among many small, seasonal orchardists is that if they have to pasteurize, they may be forced out of business, leaving only a few large producers to dominate the market.

Ultraviolet light pasteurization is the latest technological innovation in cidermaking, and it appears to offer smaller producers a more affordable way to protect their cider against *E. coli*. In this new process, a thin film of cider is pumped past a UV light at a rate of two or three gallons per minute. Tests have shown that UV treatment can reduce *E. coli* contamination from one hundred thousand microorganisms to one per milliliter, thus achieving the FDA's goal of a "five-log [10^5] reduction" in the total bacterial load. Ultraviolet units eventually may cost as little as $6,000, making them more affordable than heat pasteurization equipment.

I've sampled many UV-pasteurized ciders over the past decade, and I must admit that some of them tasted pretty good. In December 2006, I even had the opportunity to taste the top three sweet ciders in the state of Michigan, as awarded by a panel of judges at the Great Lakes Fruit, Vegetable and Farm Markets Expo in Grand Rapids. The top two winners were UV-pasteurized; third place went to a heat-pasteurized cider. All were virtually indistinguishable from good fresh raw cider. None of them contained preservatives, which was crucially important in terms of taste. And all were made with care and pride by apple growers who clearly knew how make great cider. The problem comes in when inferior fruit is deemed "safe" by a large industrial-scale cider producer because it has been cooked or irradiated, then dosed with preservatives and shipped all over the region, passed off as the real article.

Don't get me wrong: I still prefer raw cider; every year I make it myself and also buy from local farmers I know and trust. However, UV treatment in the right hands may help to calm some of cider's critics, especially in this age of media-fueled fearmongering, obsessive germophobia, and government nannyism. Keep the caution labels on real cider, by all means; very young children, very old people, and anyone with an impaired immune system probably *should* steer clear of the unpasteurized juice, no matter how safely made. Yet increasingly, real-food advocacy groups, like Slow Food and the Weston A. Price Foundation, are arguing that, in many cases, our human immune system problem is a chicken-and-egg situation. Our centralized, industrialized, corporate food system has simply grown too big, and our government regulatory agencies have neither the staff nor the money to guarantee food safety. Most consumers can't make informed food choices because we are buying indirectly from distant producers whose operations we don't know. So the typical top-down response from government and industry is to sterilize and irradiate everything, in an attempt to make even the dirtiest food "safe," from a legal as much as a health standpoint. Their first response is to impose technological fixes to correct what is in fact a societal problem: each of us should make it a point to know who is growing our food, and how, and then decide for ourselves whether it's safe for our family. Otherwise, the immune systems of even healthy people will continue to be compromised, as we consume food that is essentially dead and that lacks much nutritive value, unless it is "fortified," or added back in after processing.

Getting back to UV-treated sweet cider, I was initially concerned that it would be difficult if not impossible to make good hard cider from irradiated juice. Fortunately this appears not to be the case. Again, I (as well as most other amateur and commercial cidermakers) prefer to start fermentation with raw sweet cider, not UV-treated juice. But it seems that UV radiation, while it kills bacteria, has little or no effect on the natural yeasts in cider (something that can't be said of heat pasteurization). Charles McGonegal of AeppelTreow Winery in Burlington, Wisconsin, has reported that using UV juice delays the start of natural fermentation in cider by only a day or so.

Speaking of hard cider, the good news is that both peer-reviewed scientific research and experience have shown conclusively that *E. coli* 0157:H7 is eliminated from the alcoholic product through the natural fermentation process. There has never been a documented case of *E. coli* sickness attributed to drinking hard cider. So even in jurisdictions where real sweet cider can't be sold for fresh consumption, there is generally some allowance for selling it to amateur cidermakers for fermentation purposes.

Making Your Own Sweet Cider

Of course, the ultimate way to ensure the quality and purity of your fresh cider is to press the apples yourself at home, using either a small hydraulic cider press or a screw-type cider/wine press. Growing a few different cider apple trees at home or buying a selection of utility- or cider-grade apples from a local orchard will provide you with the range of varieties needed to produce a rich, good-tasting cider for immediate consumption, freezing, or fermenting into hard cider.

The basic technology and methods of turning apples into fresh sweet cider have changed surprisingly little over the past few centuries. For instance, a modern cidermaker would have no trouble understanding the following instructions from medieval times for making "verjuice" (a fermented cider made from crab apples):

Gather crabbs as soon as the kernels [seeds] turn blacke, and lay they in a heap to sweat and take them into troughs and crush with beetles [heavy wooden mallets]. Make a bagge of coarse hair-cloth and fill it with the crabbes, and presse and run the liquor into Hogsheads.[4]

Beating the fruit to a pulp in a trough or hollowed-out tree trunk is one of the most primitive cidermaking techniques, almost certainly dating back to prehistoric times; yet it was still being practiced in parts of England as recently as the seventeenth century. In fact, the wooden trough, which the French called *l'auge*, lent its name to the most celebrated cider-making region in Normandy, the Pays d'Auge (*pays DOE-guh*).

The next real development came with the adaptation of another old technology used by the Greeks and Romans for crushing olives. A heavy millstone set on edge was drawn around and around a circular trough, usually by a draft animal like a horse or an ox attached to a wooden axle (also known as the sweep), which passed through the center of the wheel. This milling technology was adopted widely throughout the Arab world and was reintroduced to medieval Europe by way of North Africa and Moorish Spain. The advantage of this system was that a fairly large amount of apples could be squashed quite effectively into a pulpy mass ready for pressing, all with very little human labor. The major disadvantage was that the millstone was so heavy that it crushed not only the apples but also the apple seeds, which contain moderate amounts of amygdalin, a chemical that breaks down into cyanide and can impart an unpleasantly bitter taste to cider, even after fermentation.

An elegant solution to this problem came in the seventeenth century with Englishman John Worlidge's invention of a new kind of apple mill, which he called the Ingenio. This hand-powered mill was adapted from the design of similar mills that were used in the Caribbean to crush sugar cane. It was small, portable, and efficient, and used wooden rollers (two closely spaced counter-rotating shafts) that ground the apples without crushing their seeds. The pulp was then pressed in a screw-type cider press (see illustrations on pages 20 and 21). The whole process is virtually the same as that used by today's homestead cidermakers, although grinders today are often powered by an electric motor and typically have a wooden drum fitted with stainless-steel teeth to assist in breaking up the fruit.

The basic steps in making fresh cider, examined separately and in detail below, are these: 1) harvesting the fruit; 2) "sweating" the apples; 3) milling (crushing or grinding) the fruit; 4) pressing the juice.

Reducing the cider-making process to its essential ele-

The traditional millstone and circular stone trough used for centuries in Europe for milling apples. The millstone was attached to a draft animal by the wooden axle, or "sweep." *Wikimedia Commons*

ments in this way reminds me of T. S. Eliot's famous take on life in *Sweeney Agonistes:* "Birth, and copulation, and death. / That's all the facts when you come to brass tacks." Making cider seems simple and straightforward, and it is; yet to make the best-quality cider, it helps to know a little more about the hows and whys of the process.

Harvesting the Fruit

Apples intended for cider should be harvested only when they are fully tree-ripe. There are several indications as to when an apple is ready to pick. First, fruits may begin to drop of their own accord from the tree, even when there isn't a wind. Second, when you pick an apple—cradling it in your palm, then lifting and twisting in a clockwise motion—the stem should release easily, without your having to tug. If the stem does separate easily from the branch, the apple is ripe. Finally, cut the fruit in half horizontally. The seeds of a ripe apple will appear dark brown; those of an unripe apple look greenish tan.

Skin color is not a reliable indicator of ripeness, as climate and exposure to sunlight greatly influence the final appearance of the fruit. A Granny Smith apple grown in Washington State will be uniformly grass green when it is ready to pick. On the other hand, a Granny grown in New England may be 50 percent red. All apples start off green, with most developing a yellow "ground color" as they ripen. The additional reddish "surface color" that many varieties achieve can range from splotches or streaks to a complete paint job, overspreading and finally obscuring the ground color of the fruit.

Another simple method for determining ripeness, one that is often used by commercial apple growers, is the starch iodine test. Basically, you put a few drops of a tincture of iodine onto half of an apple that you've sliced horizontally, Wherever the color turns a bluish black or gray, it indicates starches that haven't yet converted into sugars. Where the color remains yellowish brown, the iodine is not reacting with starch. Of course, the ideal ripeness of an apple will depend on whether you are planning to press the fruit soon after picking, or "sweat it" or store it for a longer period for later cidermaking. Also, different apple varieties reach their optimum maturity at different points in the starch conversion process.[5]

The ultimate test of ripeness is taste: Although the full flavor and aroma of many varieties of apples will develop only after storage, at harvest time you should be able to tell, with a bit of experience, how close to ripeness the apple is by how sweet or sweet/acid it tastes, which indicates how far the conversion of starch to sugars has progressed. The starch content of a green, unripe apple is between 5 and 8 percent. When the apple is fully mature, the starch content is only 0.5 to 1.0 percent; the rest has turned into sugar. Refractometers and other scientific gadgets for measuring precise levels of sugars and acid are no substitute at this stage for your own taste buds, which will unerringly tell you which varieties of apples should be mixed and pressed together to produce a balanced, sweet, and sprightly juice. (See chapter 10, though, for more discussion on measuring instruments.)

Don't consider using any apple in your cider blend that you wouldn't eat yourself, in terms either of flavor or of quality. (The exception to this general rule would be the addition of small amounts of "wild" or crab apples, or even some truly bitter European cider apples. These fruits will set your teeth on edge, but added in moderation they can be great in a cider blend.) Smaller apples are perfect for cider, though, as are those that are cosmetically challenged. In other words, don't reject an apple simply because it doesn't meet the supermarket's superficial standards of beauty. A winding sawfly scar or a bit of fly speck or sooty blotch (summer fungal diseases that rub off with a little spit and elbow grease and don't affect the quality of the fruit) isn't reason enough to reject a cider apple—or an eating one, for that matter. Cut or seriously bruised fruit should never be used, however, and the same goes for "drops"—apples that have been lying on the ground for any length of time.

Drops are often considered the same as windfalls, and some people insist that any fruit that has fallen to the ground—no matter for how short a time—should not be used for making cider. Given the recent concern about *E. coli* in cider, you definitely need to be cautious, but windfalls have been used to make cider for thousands of years, and the fact that trees naturally drop some of their apples as they ripen makes the gathering of windfalls (think of the positive connotations of that word) not only economical but inevitable as well. Use your own judgment, however. Any minor bruising that may result from apples falling on soft orchard grass usually doesn't warrant composting them or feeding them to the sheep, *so long as they are picked up soon after they fall*. Drops, on the other hand, are fruits that have sat around on the ground for a longer period of time—typically a day or more.

This last point cannot be emphasized enough. Many orchards hire workers in the fall to patrol around the trees, picking up any sound apples that may have fallen during the night. In fact, one of my first jobs as a junior high school student was picking up bushels of McIntosh and Cortland windfalls that were destined for a local orchard's cider press. I forget what we earned per bushel; suffice it to say that it was not enough to retire on. But it was a good excuse to go switching through the dewy grass on a frosty October morning.

Avoid using damaged or badly bruised windfalls for cidermaking, and certainly don't use any that have brown rotted spots. Apples that have been lying on the ground for any length of time can pick up acetobacter, various organisms that will turn cider into vinegar, or

they can become infected with the potentially dangerous *E. coli* 0157:H7 strain of bacteria. Even if you don't graze livestock in your orchard or use manure as a fertilizer around your trees, it's difficult to prevent deer from hanging around, and they too, as well as other wildlife, may be a vector for *E. coli*. Having said that, though, timing is everything, in orchard management as in

SUPPORT YOUR LOCAL CIDERMAKER

The best way to ensure that you are getting fresh cider that is both safe and good-tasting is to get to know your local cidermakers, as well as their products and their operations. Ask them to take you on a tour of their facilities; ask questions about their orcharding and cider-making practices, and about the sanitary and safety measures they take. Establish personal relationships with them. Just as with the growing movement known as Community Supported Agriculture (CSA), where the point is to know and support local farmers, buying locally produced cider can give you an added sense of security, certainly more than what you would get from a mountain of government-mandated regulations and inspections. After all, ground beef is inspected, too, and there are still a lot more reported cases of *E. coli* contamination in meat than in cider. Buying cider from a local orchardist you know and trust, who presses only his or her own fruit, may cost you a few pennies more than buying a flat-tasting, inferior cider at the supermarket. But it provides you with something far more valuable. As the Japanese say, it's "food with the farmer's face on it."

standup comedy. Jim Koan, a respected apple grower in eastern Michigan, has recently attracted a lot of press attention for running Berkshire hogs through his orchard to clean up after the annual "June drop" of immature fruit. The pigs efficiently gobble up any of the young plum curculio beetles that are inside the apples. But Koan keeps his hogs and apples far apart from this point on in advance of the harvest.

Yet another reason to eschew drops that have been lying around for more than a few hours is the earthy, musty, disagreeable flavor of cider made from them. This is caused by the patulin toxin, which results in the off-flavor that the French call *gout de terroir*. Regardless of how much of a flower child you are, in this case "earthiness" is definitely not a good thing, and the unpleasant taste of the cider doesn't go away, even after fermentation.

If you are picking your own apples, handle them gently and transfer them from picking bags to wooden or plastic containers that have been thoroughly sanitized, rinsed, and air-dried. Large, heavy-duty woven plastic bags that have some ventilation, like those used to hold vegetables, also work well. Extra-careful pickers don't let their storage boxes or bags sit directly on the orchard grass or ground during harvest, to avoid any risk of *E. coli* infection. If you're buying cider fruit from an orchard, be very selective and try to pick into bushel boxes or bags from their bins—those large wooden containers most commercial orchards use, which hold about fifteen bushels of fruit when full. Wood is great, but some orchards are now switching over to plastic containers because they hold up well with repeated use and are easier to sanitize than wooden bins.

Finally, consider the season and check to see when the best apples for making cider will be available in your area. In general, the richest-tasting cider fruits are those that mature fairly late in the season, from October onward. It's not that cider made from early apples can't be good; but without the depth and body of russets and other sweet, dense, yellow-fleshed fruits, early cider tends to be somewhat thin and vinous ("winey"-tasting) rather than full and complex, as it becomes later in the season.

In fact, French cidermakers traditionally distinguish among the qualities of their hard ciders based on the ripening season of the apples from which they are made. September fruit produces "precocious" or "petite" cider; October fruit yields "ordinary" or common cider; and the late apples that ripen in November make "grand" (great) cider. The precocious cider is weaker, has less color, and doesn't keep as long as the later ciders. The November cider, however, when made with the right kinds of fruit, can be cellared and drunk for four to five years after fermentation and bottling.

Even though these distinctions relate to hard cider, they hold true for sweet cider as well. Most orchardists and cider connoisseurs agree that the best cider (hard or sweet) is produced from late-season apples. For this same reason, most cidermakers also maintain that apples that ripen at different times should not be blended to make a single cider. Whether there is any basis to this beyond tradition and practicality is unclear. In most cases, though, it isn't an issue: Early apples like Gravenstein and Red Astrachan typically don't store well for more than a few weeks at best. In other words, by the time you get around to pressing or buying cider in the mid- to late fall, these late-summer apples will be only a pleasant memory (unless you press them and freeze the juice for later blending), and the varieties that are available later on will be similar in age and maturity.

Sweating the Apples

"Sweating" refers to the practice of storing apples for several days to several weeks after they have been harvested and before they are pressed into cider. After they are picked, apples continue to ripen and respire, losing excess water content, giving off ethylene gas (the reason that tomatoes will ripen faster when placed in a paper bag with an apple or a banana), and converting starches in the flesh into sugars. In times past, apple growers would often leave the fruit outdoors, piled up on the grass, for a week or two before pressing, to trap some of the ethylene gas and promote faster ripening. Orchardists today bring the harvested apples under cover—to a barn, porch, or other space with good air circulation—and store them, typically for two to four weeks before pressing, in bushel boxes or bins.

Sweating apples at room temperature, even when the "room" or barn is relatively cold, as it is in the fall and early winter, violates just about every rule in the book for the long-term storage of fruit. The softening rate and respiration of apples are both about twice as fast at 40°F as they are at 32°F, and about three times faster at 60°F than at 40°F. Furthermore, if the weather is warm, every one day's delay in cold-storing apples after picking reduces the potential storage life of the fruit by eight to ten days. However, the whole point of sweating is that you *want* to accelerate the ripening of the apples, so that they can be pressed into cider as soon as possible, when they have reached their peak of flavor and sweetness, rather than slowing down their metabolism by putting them into a cold, controlled-atmosphere storage room.

Up to 10 percent of an apple's excess moisture content can be lost during the period of sweating, and the relative gain in fruit sweetness can be as much as 6 to 8 percent. So, that water loss from sweating can make a significant difference in the sweetness of the pressed fresh cider. This can be especially important for making hard cider, because a juice that contains more sugar, if fermented completely to dryness, will have a higher alco-

A typical bench-mounted grinder box. *Terence Bradshaw*

holic content than will a less sweet juice—which is desirable for a host of reasons (explained further in chapter 4).

Not all apples benefit from sweating. Certain North American dessert varieties, like Jonathan, Newtown Pippin, and Rome Beauty, can and should be pressed soon after harvest. And some orchardists who make perfectly fine cider don't even bother sweating their apples, preferring instead to let the fruit's flavor ripen and develop slowly in long-term cold storage. If you have a lot of apples and plan to press them in small batches throughout the winter, this "no-sweat" strategy makes sense. But if you plan on having only one or two cider-making sessions each year, consider collecting your fruit at least a week or two in advance and letting it mellow before pressing.

You can tell whether your apples have sweated long enough and are ready for grinding and pressing by squeezing a few of them gently in your hand. If they have softened but are still sound, and if your thumb and fingers leave an impression on the surface of the apples, they are ready to be made into cider.

Milling the Fruit

Once the fruit is ripe and ready for pressing, the next step is to grind the apples into a pulpy mass, known as pomace. Before you do this, it is advisable to wash the apples to remove any soil, litter, spray residue, or foreign substances that might be clinging to them. Strictly speaking, this washing step may not be absolutely necessary with fruit that you have hand-picked off the tree yourself, then sorted and stored with care in a clean place under cover. But it's still good sanitary practice. Use a large tub filled with clean, cold water that you change or refresh after each batch of fruit. (Having a garden hose nearby makes this simple.) Swirl the apples gently in small batches and drain off any excess water before pressing. A wicker or plastic laundry basket is ideal for draining the fruit.

Sound, healthy apples will float on the surface of the water; any fruits that don't should be picked out and dis-

This pedal-powered apple grinder is an ingenious use of appropriate technology, as well as good exercise and lots of fun (especially with friends). *Emily M. Herman*

carded. Scrubbing the fruit or adding chlorine to the wash water—both routinely done by commercial cider operations—probably amounts to overkill on the home scale. If your main concern is *E. coli* contamination, take the steps outlined in the harvesting section earlier to guard against it; neither scrubbing nor washing in chlorinated water has proved 100 percent effective in eliminating these bacteria.

Some new cidermakers, especially those who want to try making natural hard cider using wild yeasts, are afraid that washing the fruit will rinse away the "bloom" of yeast that clings to the surface of the apples. It won't. What's more, there are plenty of natural yeasts inside the fruit, not to mention on the press cloths and other equipment if you've been making cider for some time.

Home-scale apple grinders are either separate, stand-alone units or, more often, attachments mounted on homestead cider/wine presses. Well-made grinders are heavy-duty, made from cast iron with a flywheel attached to a grinding shaft (for hand-powered models) or to a small electric motor. Inside the grinding box, any knives or other attachments that pulverize the fruit should be made of stainless steel, never iron. That's because iron (as well as copper, lead, and other metals) will react with the acidic apple juice and can ruin an otherwise good batch of cider. An optional feature often mounted on top of the grinder box is a wooden hopper, which holds a batch of apples and makes feeding the grinder a quicker and easier proposition.

A perennial topic on the Cider Digest and other Internet forums is the efficacy of using a commercial garbage disposal unit as a grinder for milling apples. In theory, this sounds terrific, since that's what garbage disposals do. But in practice some people have had problems either with the motors overheating after only short periods of grinding, which is frustrating when you

58

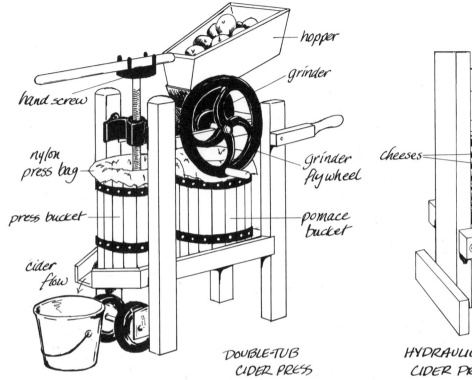

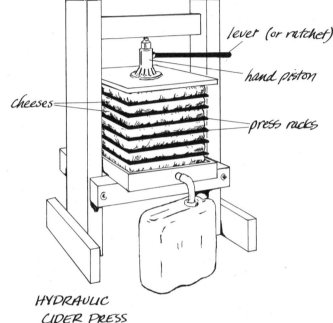

hopper

grinder

hand screw

nylon
press bag

press bucket

cider
flow

grinder
flywheel

pomace
bucket

DOUBLE-TUB
CIDER PRESS

lever (or ratchet)

hand piston

cheeses

press racks

HYDRAULIC
CIDER PRESS

A double-tub home cider press

are trying to keep up a continuous pressing process, or with the consistency of the pomace, which is ground too fine. The goal in grinding apples is to achieve a uniform pulp that will press well and yield the maximum amount of juice possible. If necessary, use a large wooden pestle (an ordinary two-by-four works well for this) to encourage the apples through the grinder teeth; obviously, this is a job for adults, not children. If the apples still aren't grinding well, add a little water to the grinder box. Try not to grind the apples too fine; aim for pea-sized pieces to make pressing easier. If you are lucky

A hydraulic rack-and-cloth cider press

enough to have some true European cider apples, these press very well, as their flesh is dry and fibrous. Some North American dessert apples, such as Golden Delicious, yield a slimy, applesaucy pomace, which can clog up the press cloth and reduce the amount of juice you can extract from the fruit. Commercial cider-makers compensate for this by adding rice hulls or wood pulp before pressing such fruit, but the best strategy is avoid the problem altogether by mixing good cider varieties together with dessert apples before grinding and pressing.

Cider, Hard and Sweet

In fact, combining different kinds of apples is probably the most creative part of cidermaking, with infinite variations possible, depending on the supply of fruit you have available. In making sweet cider, the different types of apples are almost always mixed together during grinding; keep baskets of a number of varieties close at hand and feed them into the hopper or grinder as you go. If you are bottling in gallon jugs right off the press, you might want to pay closer attention to the relative proportions of each apple you're feeding into the grinder than if you're mixing the cider from several pressings in large carboys or other storage or fermentation tanks.

People who make hard cider are more apt to press one variety of fruit at a time and blend the juices later; this gives them more control over the proportions used. They are also more likely to experiment with fermenting single-variety ciders from apples like Golden Russet and Baldwin. Although varietal sweet ciders are less common, it might be worth trying to press one type of apple at a time before blending if you really want to see exactly what each variety tastes like and what qualities it will bring to other juices in a blend. I've tried varietal sweet cider made from various apples such as Mutsu (Crispin) and Golden Russet, and found them to be good and sweet, though a bit one-dimensional for my taste. (For more on the qualities of different cider apple varieties, see the table on pages 34–39.)

In a typical homestead grinder/cider press, the pomace falls into a cylindrical, slatted wooden tub that is lined with a heavy nylon press bag. The double-tub models of cider presses make it possible for two or three people to run a continuous grinding-and-pressing operation. While one person is grinding the fruit and filling the rear bucket with pulp, the other worker can press the previous batch of pomace in the forward bucket into juice.

At this point, right after grinding the apples into

Using a sturdy homemade hydraulic cider press.
Terence Bradshaw

pulp, most cidermakers immediately proceed to pressing the pulp into juice. However, there is some advantage to letting the pomace stand in the press tub for fifteen minutes or more after grinding, to let a little oxidation take place (indicated by the darkening color) and to begin the process of cell breakdown, which helps the juice flow a bit more freely during pressing.

Chapter 3: Sweet Cider from Tree to Juice

Pressing the Juice

The final stage in making fresh, sweet cider involves pressing the juice out of the ground apple pulp. Home cidermakers generally use a screw-type cider/wine press. The screw is tightened by turning it with a two-by-four or a length of pipe, exerting increasing force on a wooden press disk that sits on top of the slatted hardwood tub containing the pomace. The press disk, along with a pressure foot on the bottom of the screw, distributes the force evenly over the surface of the tub. If you are interested in buying one of these presses, or in assembling one from a kit, go for the more expensive, heavy-duty models made of forged cast iron (for recommended manufacturers see "Resources"). A cider press must be sturdy to stand up to the pressure you will be exerting, not only on the apples but also on the frame. A new, top-of-the-line double-tub press, mostly or completely assembled, currently costs a little over $700, plus shipping. Single-tub presses are slightly less expensive, as are kits. For the slight difference in price, I recommend buying one of the double-tub models (unless you make more wine than cider), which allow for simultaneous grinding and pressing.

DEUTSCHE POMOLOGIE. I.59.

Cider, Hard and Sweet

Another option is the homemade or small-scale hydraulic model, which resembles a traditional rack-and-cloth cider press. There are several sources of plans for making such presses; a little searching on the Internet or in the other cider books listed under "Resources" at the back of this book will turn up several leads. Operating this type of press involves building up several layers of pomace (collectively known as the "cheese") within a wooden form or frame, which looks like a dresser drawer without a bottom. First, you put the form on top of a wooden rack with holes or channels cut into it for drainage. Next you lay a heavy nylon press cloth inside the form and distribute about three to five inches of pulp on top of it. (In the old days, the pomace was enclosed not in nylon but in twisted straw and reeds—as in Devon—or in horsehair cloth, as in Herefordshire.) Then fold the corners of the cloth over the pulp, remove the form, place another wooden rack on top of the pomace-filled press cloth (called a pillow), and place the form on top to start another layer. Novice cidermakers should try pressing only two or three layers at a time until they get the hang of it. With these hydraulic presses, the force is delivered not by a screw but with a hydraulic jack that pushes down onto a press plate.

Whichever kind of press you use at home, you won't be getting as much juice out of your apples as commercial cidermakers do with their large hydraulic presses. That's because you are exerting far less pressure. A homestead press might squeeze only a gallon or so of juice out of a bushel of fruit. Larger presses, on the other hand, might press three gallons or more from the same amount of apples.

If you have the time, and don't have to press bushels and bushels of apples in a single day, it is possible to squeeze a little more juice out of your apples. After you have pressed all you can from a single tub, or "cheese," take a fifteen-minute break, then turn the screw or work the jack once more; this should yield a bit more juice. In northern Spain, where traditional cider presses are monstrous affairs made of oak or chestnut, a single large batch of pomace might take five to seven days to press.

Collect the fresh-pressed juice in plastic or stainless-steel containers, then strain the juice through cheesecloth into clean plastic gallon cider jugs and cap them. The word *juice* is the operative term here: Straight out of the press, the light-colored liquid essence of your apples is not yet true cider, though it is quite refreshing to drink as you work up a sweat, grinding and pressing away. Store the juice for about twenty-four hours at room temperature, during which time the cider will oxidize quickly, becoming darker and cloudier and leaving a gray deposit (lees) on the bottom of the jugs. Carefully pour off the cider into new plastic jugs, leaving the lees behind, then store in the refrigerator for immediate consumption, or leave about three inches of empty space at the top of the jug and freeze the cider for later use. Freezing preserves sweet cider with no loss of flavor for at least six months. This is useful not only for extending the fresh cider-drinking season, but also because frozen cider can be thawed out and used during the winter for "topping off" jugs or carboys of fermenting hard cider as you rack them off into different containers.

Even the spent pomace left over after pressing is useful for much more than compost material (though it is good for that, too). In the old days, water would be added to refresh the spent pomace, and it would be pressed again to produce a weak cider that was known variously as water cider, ciderkin, purr, or purrkin. In England this ciderkin was used to make a low-alcohol drink for servants and laborers, analogous to the "small beer" made from a second working of spent barley. In America, ciderkin was mainly a drink for children. Spent pomace can also be used as a livestock feed (dole it out sparingly, though, since cows and pigs will eat all the pomace like Halloween candy and can get sick) and as a natural weed killer when spread on fields. I even knew a fellow in Berlin, Vermont, who used to spread out pressed pomace and dry it, then added it to his apple-

MACERATION

Many traditional cidermakers in Europe let the freshly ground apple pomace sit for anywhere from 8 to 48 hours before pressing. This practice, known as maceration, or *cuvage* in French, involves putting the pulp into shallow vats to allow for maximum exposure to air. Advocates of this practice claim that maceration results in better color in the finished cider, a greater yield of juice and a more intense aroma of fruit. Critics counter that it promotes acetification, greatly reduces the amount of tannin in the juice (by 80 to 96 percent), creates a disagreeable aroma, and leads to too much color (or complete decoloration) in the finished cider.

Unless you are an experienced cidermaker or are trying to make an authentic French style of cider, it's best to avoid long maceration. (See the discussion on keeving in chapter 10.) If you do decide to experiment with this method, though, try to use varieties of apples that oxidize (turn brown) slowly after they are cut, such as Cortland, and macerate the fruit for only a few hours before pressing. You may find that you get more juice, with a higher sugar content, which can be useful when making hard cider. For sweet cider, though, there's no clear advantage to maceration: Either press right away or let the pulp sit for a few minutes, just to get the juices flowing.[6]

wood chips, which he sold for smoking meat and fish. If that doesn't exemplify those twin Yankee traits of ingenuity and frugality, I don't know what does.

Apple Juice

My preference for real, unpasteurized cider notwithstanding, there is definitely a place in this world for good apple juice. Many apple growers, especially the bigger ones, would have a difficult time selling their lower-grade fruit if it weren't for juice processors, who every year buy large quantities of surplus North American fruit at a low, but predictable, wholesale price. According to the U.S. Department of Agriculture, only a small portion of American apples are grown strictly for juice; most juice apples are culled from fresh packing lines because of their size or appearance. Some 64 percent of apples go into the fresh market; the remaining 36 percent (some 3.5 billion pounds in 2005/06) are sold for processing, though not all into juice. Even so, this isn't enough to satisfy the growing domestic market; in 2005/06 the U.S. imported around $270 million worth of apple juice from other nations, about half of that coming from China. Any way you slice it, that's a lot of apple juice.

Economic arguments are one thing; taste is something else altogether. Most of the apple juice sold in this country is extremely sweet, bland, and uninteresting. The solution to this problem is to put up some of your own juice, made from your own sweet cider. Not only will you be making a better product than almost anything you can find on the market, but pasteurized juice is also another good way to preserve some of the flavor of the harvest.

TRADITIONAL CIDERMAKING PHOTO SERIES *All photos by Hannah Proctor*

Sanitizing wooden press racks with bleach solution and water.

Apples sweating in the grinder room.

Feeding apples into the grinder box.

Cider, Hard and Sweet

The basis for both tasty apple juice and high-quality hard cider is a good sweet cider. The old expression "You can't make a silk purse out of a sow's ear" definitely applies in this case. However, whereas a high proportion of sugar is definitely a plus in sweet cider that is going to be fermented into hard cider, when making apple juice it's crucial to have a good balance of sweetness and acidity. Commercial juicemakers measure this balance precisely, using the Brix/acid ratio, which indicates the percentage of sugar divided by the percentage of acid; this ratio is more important than the absolute amount of either sugar or acid in the juice. Home juicemakers don't have to worry about such niceties. The main thing is to add enough tart apples or crab apples to your dessert fruit to make a sprightly or even somewhat sharp-tasting cider. This is the kind of cider that makes the most interesting and flavorful apple juice. Gingerbrook Farm in South Washington, Vermont, makes its own apple juice using a mix of wild and other unsprayed apples, and the resulting product can be quite racy and mouth-puckering. It's not to everyone's taste, but to me it seems much more healthful and stimulating than the flat, "cooked" taste of supermarket juices.

To make a cloudy apple juice, strain the fresh-pressed cider from the press as described above, then add about 0.5 gram of ascorbic acid (vitamin C) per quart of juice. Use pure powdered ascorbic acid, which is available from winemaking and canning supply stores. Adding the ascorbic acid allows some oxidation to take place in the juice, which helps develop its flavor, but it prevents the browning of the tannins in the juice and sedimentation.

Apples fall down onto a turning metal scratter drum and are finely milled.

The ground pomace drops down through a chute from the grinder box onto the press, where it is spread out in heavy-duty press cloths, which are stacked and separated by slatted wooden racks.

Placing a wooden rack onto the top of the stack (or "cheese") before pressing.

The next step is to pasteurize the apple juice, either in beer bottles that will accept a crown cap, or in pint or quart canning jars. In any case, you'll need to sterilize the bottles or jars beforehand, along with their lids and caps, in a boiling-water bath.

Fill the sterilized bottles or jars with apple juice, leaving a one-inch headspace. Then arrange them in a large kettle on top of the stove, immersing them in water as far up their necks as possible. Gently heat the water until it reaches a temperature of 170°F, then hold it at that temperature for thirty minutes. When the temperature inside the middle bottle or jar measures at least 165°F, the yeasts and other unwanted organisms should be destroyed.

If you're using bottles, remove them from the kettle, cap them immediately, and lay them on their sides to cool slowly so that the hot juice will sterilize the inside of the cap. Be sure not to place the hot bottles or jars directly on a cold countertop or other surface! If you've used canning jars, screw on the tops loosely and process for a few minutes in a boiling-water bath, just long enough to ensure a good vacuum seal. Let the jars or bottles cool slowly and completely for a day or so, then store them at room temperature. Apple juice keeps well for quite a while, but it tastes best if chilled before opening.

To make a clear apple juice, you'll want to skip the ascorbic acid and instead add a pectic enzyme (also available from wine or beer supply stores) to the juice after pressing. Keep the juice cool overnight to discourage yeast growth. The next morning the juice should appear clear and golden, having precipitated its pectins and left a sediment on the bottom of the container. Carefully siphon or strain the juice off this sediment into sterilized bottles or jars, and pasteurize as described above.

This old 1908 rack-and-cloth cider press has a movable bed that rotates a full 180 degrees, positioning the cheese under the press mechanism.

The juice is expressed as pressure is applied from above.

Cider, Hard and Sweet

It's also worth experimenting with single-variety apple juices when you have fruit that has a good sugar/acid balance. Pure Gravenstein juice is produced every year out in Sonoma County, California, and other apple varieties that I'd like to try as fresh varietal apple juices include Esopus Spitzenberg, Newtown Pippin, and Wickson.

Another alternative way to use fresh raw cider (aside from pasteurizing it and making juice) is to culture it with a bit of sea salt and either whey or kefir grains to make a naturally lacto-fermented drink. I haven't made this myself, but have had some deliciously sweet and smooth-tasting lacto-fermented cider courtesy of my friends Noah and Dove Elbers at Orchard Hill Breadworks in East Alstead, New Hampshire. The process is very simple and straightforward, and can be found in Sally Fallon's excellent book, *Nourishing Traditions.*[7]

Good, natural apple juice—the kind that is full of flavor, minimally processed, and contains no preservatives—is a wonderful drink, perfect in kids' lunchboxes or as a snappy, refreshing start to the day. Over the past few decades, the Florida and California citrus industries have managed to persuade us that orange juice is the all-American breakfast drink. However since apples—unlike oranges—grow all over North America, shouldn't apple juice enjoy the home-field advantage? Perhaps some day it will.

Real sweet cider is a uniquely American tradition, one that is well worth seeking out. Fortunately, there are still people out in the suburbs and the countryside who are making and selling great-tasting cider. Like other artisans who care about putting out a good-quality product, they deserve our admiration, our respect, and—most importantly—our patronage.

Removing the press cloths filled with spent pomace, which is composted or used as a feed supplement for grateful cows and pigs.

Sampling the juice straight out of the wooden press box, below, as the shaft and gear assembly keeps squeezing.

Filtering and transferring fresh-pressed cider into carboys from a bulk holding tank.

O bid the cider flow
In ploughing and in sowing,
The healthiest drink I know
In reaping and in mowing.
O the jovial days when the apple
trees do bear,
We'll drink and be merry all the
gladsome year.

—Anonymous verse from Devon, England

4. HARD CIDER: FROM JUICE TO BOTTLE

HARD CIDER HAS ALWAYS SUFFERED FROM an identity crisis of sorts, stuck in the alcoholic no-man's-land between beer and wine. Even today, when interest in cider is high and sales of major commercial brands are soaring, many people don't quite know what to make of hard cider—what it should taste like, when to serve or drink it. Americans, especially, are still in the process of reinventing a "cider culture," gradually rediscovering the refreshing and distinctive drink that has played such a prominent role in our historical and folk traditions. And although cider will probably never regain the stature it had in colonial days, when the average person quaffed thirty-five gallons in a year's time, the current proliferation of choices and products in the marketplace bodes well for cider's future.

The continued popularity of homebrewing, and the explosion in the number of microbrewed beers since the 1980s, is evidence of a strong demand for high-quality, craft-brewed beverages with a regional or connoisseur appeal. And cider is a natural extension of this trend: For one thing, hard cider is much easier to make than beer, and is ready for drinking much sooner than homemade wine, which typically needs to mature anywhere from six months to a year in the bottle. It's also cheap to produce: In a recent fall season, the wholesale price of fresh local cider stood at $6.25 for a five-gallon carboy, filled right at the orchard. Even if you have to pay the full retail price ($5 a gallon or more), sweet cider is still very affordable, particularly when you are turning it into a "value added" hard cider for your own consumption. As cider author and consultant Paul Correnty likes to say, "It's the cheapest buzz you can get in a bottle."

If everyone knew how simple and inexpensive it was to make wonderful hard cider at home, millions of people would be doing it. You don't need a degree in chemistry or microbiology; you don't need to buy specialized brewing equipment like a wort chiller or a lauter tun; you don't even need to sacrifice half of your garage to the operation. The main ingredients that go into creating a traditional, all-natural hard cider are nothing but good unpasteurized juice and a bit of patience. Books that explain cidermaking may intimidate first-timers, because of the sheer number of variables and details that *can* be involved in the process. Fear not. Whenever I get confused or frustrated, I always think back to the ancient Celts. After all, they were making cider more than two thousand years ago—are we really any less intelligent or capable than they were?

This chapter offers a basic introduction to home cidermaking, providing all the information you need to make a successful first batch of still (uncarbonated) or sparkling hard cider in the traditional English or "farmhouse" style. First, I'll outline the general steps involved in the cidermaking process, then go on to discuss in much more depth the equipment, ingredients, and other relevant topics. Once you have produced your first batch of cider and gained some experience, you may be inspired to try your hand at making different styles of cider or apple wine (see chapter 5), or to consult other sources and read up on more advanced techniques (see chapter 10). For now, though, it's enough to understand in general terms what is going on throughout the entire process, from the unfermented juice stage to that moment of truth when the bottle is opened and you decant the golden fluid—impressing your family, your friends, and maybe even yourself.

Cidermaking 101

About ten days after pressing, sweet cider starts to "turn" and gets increasingly fizzy, as yeasts and other microflora in the juice begin to convert sugars into ethyl alcohol and carbon dioxide. The cidermaker's job is simply to encourage the kind of microbial activity that will ensure a successful fermentation and produce a good-tasting, stable hard cider, and at the same time to discourage or impede unwelcome organisms, which can spoil fermentation, create off-flavors or aromas, and take the cider beyond the alcohol stage, resulting in acetification—the conversion of alcohol to acetic acid, or vinegar.

Or think of it another way—in terms of gardening or farming. Your role as the "yeast farmer" is to create the conditions in which good cider-making yeasts and other useful organisms will thrive, while at the same time suppressing or eliminating "weed" species, like acetic acid bacteria, that can cause problems. A real, natural hard cider, like a garden plot, plays host to millions of tiny living organisms, many of which continue to work even after the cider is in the bottle and safely ensconced in your cellar—just as the garden ecosystem doesn't completely shut down after the crops have been harvested, the geese have flown south, and the snows are blanketing the land.

Various factors can influence the taste and quality of the final hard cider. One is the nature of the fresh, unfermented apple juice you are starting with: how much sugar it contains, as well as the relative amounts of acids, tannins, and other substances that contribute to the finished body, character, and taste of the cider. Another is the kind of yeast you use (wild yeasts or a variety of commercial yeasts) and the temperature at which fermentation takes place: Cooler temperatures generally result in a slower fermentation; higher temperatures, a faster one. I will go into more detail later in this chapter. In the meantime, the following list presents a brief overview of the basic steps involved in turning sweet cider into a natural hard cider:

1. Fill a fermentation vessel (jug or carboy) nine-tenths full of sweet cider. That would mean leaving out half a gallon of juice in a five-gallon carboy, or a little less than a pint from a gallon jug. Cover the container loosely with plastic wrap and place it in a cool location out of direct sunlight.

2. In a few days, the cider should begin to froth up vigorously and "boil over." Remove the plastic wrap and let the cider continue to cleanse itself. Wipe off the sides of the container every day to remove any scummy residue.

3. Once this vigorous fermentation subsides (which might take a week or more, depending on the temperature), clean off the sides and neck of the container as much as possible. Fill up the vessel with fresh
cider, leaving about a two-inch headspace at the top. Fit the jug or carboy with a fermentation lock filled with boiled or sanitized water to exclude air.

4. Let the cider continue to ferment slowly for a month or two, until the steady glub-glub of escaping carbon dioxide slows down considerably and the cider begins to clear. There will be a lot of sediment on the bottom of the container.

5. Insert a siphon hose and rack the cider off into another clean container, leaving the lees, or sediment, behind. Place a fermentation lock filled with a new water solution on top. Let the cider continue to age and mellow for another month or two.

6. Approximately four to five months after you've started, the cider should be completely fermented to dryness, or nearly so, and ready for bottling. The cider's flavor will improve if it is aged in the bottle for another month or two before drinking.

And that, in its simplest terms, covers the basic, no-frills cidermaking process, one that will produce a dry, still (uncarbonated), traditional farm-style cider. Because fermentation temperatures and other conditions will vary from house to house, it's good to use the directions above as a guideline for what you can expect and approximately how long the whole process should take.

However, the process outlined above assumes that you are making cider in the traditional way: that is, without any added sugar or other ingredients; relying on wild rather than cultured yeast strains; and without the use of sulfites, yeast nutrients, or other fermentation aids. All of these ingredients are optional, but in many cases they are used by home cidermakers to achieve more predictable and consistent results. I'll describe all of these options in the course of this chapter; whether you decide to employ any or all of them is entirely up to you.

On your first attempt at cider, though, I would suggest trying a half-gallon control batch, using no added sugar, cultured yeast, or sulfites, just to see how the all-natural method works for you. You may be supremely underwhelmed by the results when you compare this test batch against other ciders. On the other hand, you might just find that the nothing-added cider has a better taste and aroma than anything else you've produced.

Basic Equipment

The following categories describe the main items you will need to purchase or scrounge before you start making hard cider at home. None of this equipment is prohibitively expensive or hard to find, and some of it (especially bottles and fermentation vessels) can be obtained for free as recycled materials.

Only utensils and containers that have been thoroughly cleansed and sanitized should come in contact with your cider, and then only ones that are made of plastic, glass, wood (mainly barrels or casks for fermenting), or stainless steel. Other metals, including copper, iron, and lead, will react with the acids in cider, and can irreparably spoil an otherwise good batch.

Fermentation Vessels

These can either be glass or plastic carboys (available from homebrewing and winemaking supply stores, usually ranging in size from 3 to 6.5 gallons) or recycled one-gallon glass wine jugs. In terms of carboys, glass is preferable to plastic because it is transparent and allows you to keep a closer eye on fermentation and clarity.

Another option is to purchase a food-grade plastic fermentation pail, along with a lid that fits tightly and has a hole drilled into the top with a rubber grommet that will accept a fermentation airlock. These are useful for the first vigorous stage of fermentation, after which you can transfer the cider to a carboy or jug to continue the process.

For your first attempt at cidermaking, I recommend using the one-gallon (four-liter) glass wine jugs. They cost nothing, as they're usually easy to find in the recycling bins at your town's transfer station or bottle redemption center. They are also available from many restaurant kitchens, or you can save your own if you buy cheap jug wine for cooking, for sangria-making, or even (God forbid) for drinking.

The one-gallon size is useful if you have limited space or if you decide to press and ferment single varieties of apples separately, either to blend the juices later or to bottle them individually after fermentation. For a first-timer, the gallon jug also means that if a particular batch of cider goes bad for some reason, you're out only the cost of a single gallon of sweet cider.

Another useful size of container to have around the house is the half-gallon "growler," which is commonly used by brewpubs and microbreweries for take-out retail sales. These growlers come in handy for making small control or experimental batches of cider, or for bottling off a larger "party-sized" amount of finished hard cider.

Finally, a stainless steel or plastic funnel is essential for pouring and straining cider or other liquids into carboys and jugs.

Other Fermentation Equipment

Probably the most crucial piece of equipment for cidermaking is the fermentation lock (also called a water lock or airlock). These locks are small plastic gadgets that come in a variety of shapes—some cylindrical or globelike, others multichambered—and they are designed to be filled with sanitized water, which keeps both air and aerobic

Fermentation lock

organisms away from the fermenting cider but allows carbon dioxide gas from the feeding yeasts to escape.

Some fermentation locks are designed be screwed onto the top of a gallon or half-gallon container by means of a threaded circular adapter at their base. Others can be inserted into a bored rubber cork or stopper that fits snugly into the mouth of the fermentation vessel. Bring an empty gallon fermentation jug to the brewing supply store and check stopper sizes before you buy them. Depending on the mouth size of your jug or carboy, you will generally need a size $5^1/2$ to $6^1/2$ stopper; use the one that seems to fit best. Both the stoppers and the fermentation locks are inexpensive (usually less than a dollar apiece), but it's frustrating to get home only to find that you should have purchased a larger or smaller cork, or that your airlock doesn't fit easily yet snugly into the stopper's bored hole.

Measuring Tools

The two most important measuring tools for the beginning cidermaker are a hydrometer and a thermometer.

The *hydrometer* is a blown-glass tube, weighted at the bottom with lead shot, that contains a piece of paper inside with various scales printed on it. This tool is used to check the fresh juice and, later, the fermenting or finished cider to determine its specific gravity, sugar content, and potential alcohol (see page 73). You can buy a decent triple-scale hydrometer for less than ten dollars from a beer or winemaking supply store or catalog, and for a few bucks more a glass or plastic tube that is used to hold the cider sample. The hydrometer is inserted into the cider and bobs up in the sample tube, allowing you to take a reading.

The thermometer is handy for monitoring the temperature of your fermentation room. One with a long sensor that can be inserted into a jug or bottle is useful for checking cider temperatures, or if you are making pasteurized apple juice (see chapter 3). Beer or winemaking supply stores also carry floating thermometers, which are quite handy as well. Another useful item is a long plastic wine thief, which enables you to draw a sample from the carboy or other fermenter for testing.

Along with these tools, a set or two of stainless-steel measuring spoons, a nested set of measuring cups, and a two-cup Pyrex measuring cup are essential. Odds are you will already have these items in your kitchen cupboard.

Hydrometer

Racking and Bottling Equipment

Racking, or drawing off cider from one fermentation vessel into another, is easily accomplished with a length of clear plastic vinyl tubing, available from most hardware stores. Get a couple of sizes and try siphoning with them to see how fast they draw off the liquid and how easily you can manage the flow. Experiment with tubing that has an inside diameter measuring $1/4$, $5/16$, or $3/8$ inch to see which size works best for you. Usually a four-foot length of tubing is sufficient, and it will cost between one and two dollars. An optional but useful item is a bottle filler, a rigid plastic wand that fits onto the end of the siphon tube, filling when the tip touches the bottom of the jug or bottle and stopping the flow when it's lifted.

There's no reason in the world to go out and buy bottles when they probably go begging at your town's recycling center every weekend. It makes very little sense to pay maybe a quarter for the cider and other ingredients that you put in the bottle and then spend a dollar for the bottle itself. Save your own bottles throughout the year and scrounge around at the dump or a restaurant or bar for the others.

Still ciders (those that are noncarbonated and either fully fermented to dryness or stabilized to prevent further yeast activity) can go into just about any kind of wine or other bottle. Sparkling ciders (those with added pressure from natural or forced carbonation) require stronger beer or champagne bottles to avoid accidental and violent bursting. American champagne bottles generally have a smaller mouth (26 mm) and will accept a crimped (or crown) bottle cap as well as a cork; French champagne bottles have a slightly larger mouth (29 mm), and usually won't take a regular crown cap (though you can find caps with the "long skirt" to fit the European bottles). Confirm this fact before you start to bottle, though; I once spent an hour or so cleaning and sanitizing about a dozen American champagne bottles and laboriously scrubbing off labels, only to find that I then couldn't fit them with the regular crown caps I had on hand.

Other bottling equipment includes crown caps (not the twist-off kind), corks, and plastic champagne stoppers; wire cages for the champagne stoppers; and a hand corker or capper. A good two-handled lever corker currently costs less than forty dollars, and a two-handled bottle capper runs maybe half that much. Both are fine if you're just getting started or not doing lots of bottling. However, if you continue making cider, wine, or beer, consider investing in a somewhat more expensive "one-handed" model of capper or corker, which sits on a base and will last a long time, plus make bottling much easier. Some models of cappers will require a larger "bell" fitting to work with the European-style champagne bottles.

Cleaning and Sanitizing Equipment

It's extremely important to keep fermentation vessels and all cider-making equipment clean and sanitary, to protect cider from coming into contact with unwanted bacteria and other microorganisms that can spoil it. Regular household chlorine bleach is inexpensive and fine to use on glass and stainless steel. You don't need much; add a quarter to a half-cup of bleach to a glass fermentation vessel and fill it with water. Set aside for an hour or so, then scrub with a nylon bottle brush or carboy scrubber to get rid of any residues. Rinse out thoroughly with hot water, then cold, to get rid of any traces of bleach before adding fresh cider. Make up a bleach solution in a large bucket to soak the rest of your cider-making equipment (measuring spoons, fermentation locks, hydrometer, plastic tubing, and so on) after every use.

Other sanitizing products include a chemical cleanser, sodium percarbonate, which is sold under the brand name B-Brite, as well as similar substances, available from all homebrewing supply stores. B-Brite costs more than chlorine bleach, but it has an advantage in that it sanitizes on contact (no waiting or soaking the equipment), and can then be rinsed off immediately.

Campden tablets (sodium or potassium metabisulfite) are often used in home-scale cider- and winemaking to release sulfur dioxide gas into the juice, where it kills or suppresses harmful bacteria and wild yeasts before fermentation (see page 77); they are also sometimes added to cider at racking and bottling time to prevent oxidation and microbial activity. Regardless of whether you use them to sanitize juice, though, Campden tablets make a good sanitizing solution for filling plastic fermentation locks. Crush one Campden tablet and dissolve it in a pint of water, then pour the solution into the airlocks. Changing the solution in the airlocks every few weeks during fermentation isn't a bad idea, either.

Miscellaneous Items

A large standing freezer or a deep chest-type freezer is a handy appliance for home cidermakers to have—not because it's needed for fermentation, but because you can store a few gallons of fresh sweet cider in it for later use in topping up fermentation containers. Many smaller orchards operate only seasonally, closing around Christmas or even earlier, so it's wise to purchase extra sweet cider in the late fall when it is widely available and of a high quality and freeze it for winter and spring use. (Better yet, press some of your own sweet cider and freeze a supply of that.) When cider freezes, it forms "slip ice," which expands but doesn't shatter containers like water and other liquids. So, when you are freezing a jug of cider, be sure to leave about three inches of head space to allow the frozen juice to expand without blowing its lid and seeping out.

Other items for the well-stocked cider operation include packaged aids for fermentation, such as cultured yeast strains, yeast nutrient, tannin powder, and malic acid. Whether you use any of these substances, or other

additives, depends on both the style of cider you are making and the composition and balance of your unfermented juice. I'll describe them on a case-by-case basis later. All of them are available, though, from a well-stocked homebrewing supply store.

The Juice Before Fermentation

Good hard cider starts with the fresh-pressed, unfermented juice of the apple (also known as the must), which comes straight from the plastic jug or cider press. And while it is possible to ferment an antiseptic kind of hard cider using pasteurized juice or juice concentrate, this is not the way to produce a natural, traditional cider at home. For one thing, pectic enzymes in the juice are destroyed by heat pasteurization, so the resulting cider will remain cloudy instead of clearing during fermentation. And while the "cooked" taste of a heat-pasteurized juice will eventually disappear, much of the fresh, fruity flavor and delightful bouquet of a natural hard cider will be absent. In other words, it's best to use only natural, unpasteurized, preservative-free sweet cider for making hard cider. Concerns about *E. coli* seem irrelevant in this case; to date there have been no reported cases of illness that have resulted from drinking fermented hard cider.

One exception to this rule is UV-treated cider. Although I still prefer using raw, natural cider as the basis for making the best hard cider, it is possible to find well-made UV-treated juice (it is often referred to as "UV-pasteurized," but it involves irradiation with ultraviolet light, not heat pasteurization. When done effectively, this process kills bacteria, including *E. coli* 0157:H7, while leaving the natural yeasts in the juice unaffected. Anecdotal evidence suggests that the UV treatment can slow down the start of natural fermentation, but not by very much. As mentioned earlier, though, avoid buying any juice for hard cidermaking that has been treated with a preservative to extend its shelf life, typically sodium benzoate or potassium sorbate.

Sugars, Specific Gravity, and Potential Alcohol

Before you pour the sweet cider into your fermentation vessels, it's important to test the specific gravity of the juice, using the hydrometer described above. The specific gravity (S.G.) measures the sugars and other soluble solids in the juice, on a scale where 1.000 is the equivalent of distilled water. For an accurate reading, measure the juice at the temperature to which your hydrometer is calibrated; typically this temperature is 60°F (15.6°C) or 20°C (68°F); check your instructions or the printed scale inside the instrument. Insert the hydrometer into a sample jar filled about half full with cider. Then direct your eye to the bottom of the curve in the liquid (called the meniscus) take your reading on the printed scale inside the instrument. Again, refer to the instructions that come with your hydrometer: if your juice isn't at the nominal temperature, you can often find a conversion chart that allows you to adjust the observed reading (or see the temperature conversion chart in the Appendix).

Most American fresh ciders are pressed from a blend of dessert apples and will typically have a specific gravity between 1.040 and 1.050. If you allow a sweet cider with a 1.050 S.G. to ferment fully to dryness, it will result in a hard cider with around a 6.9 percent potential alcohol content. This is easy to see if you look at the corresponding columns on the hydrometer's printed scales. Another measurement of sugar content in the juice is the Brix or Balling scale, which is also printed on most hydrometers. This measures the number of grams of sugar per 100 grams of solution; in the example above, a juice with an S.G. of 1.050 and a 6.9 percent potential alcohol content would measure roughly 13 degrees Brix.

The reason it's important to measure the potential alcohol of a juice before fermentation is that low-alcohol ciders tend to be less stable than higher-alcohol ciders in storage, and they may permit unwanted microorganisms to continue working in the bottle, ones that would be inactive at a higher level of alcohol. If your juice has a specific gravity of less than 1.045 (less than about 6 percent potential alcohol), it is wise to add sugar to the juice to bring it up to at least that minimum S.G. reading. Also, if you are making a higher-alcohol product like New England–style cider, apple wine, or cyser (see chapter 5), you will want to add some form of sugar or other sweetener at this point. (For a table showing the equivalent values for degrees Brix, specific gravity, and potential alcohol, see the Appendix.)

Just how much sugar you add will depend on the natural sweetness of the juice and how much you intend to raise its specific gravity. The basic rule states that 2.25 ounces of sugar (or 3 ounces of honey) will raise the specific gravity of 1 gallon of juice by five points—for example, from 1.045 to 1.050 S.G. To raise the S.G. by twenty points, from 1.045 to 1.065, you would add 2.25 ounces times 4, or about 9 ounces total (roughly equivalent to a rounded cupful of sugar per gallon). Sugar can either be added as is to the carboy or other fermentation vessel, or gently heated and dissolved in an equal amount of water, then cooled and poured into the juice.

What type of sugar you add depends on your personal preference and the recipe for the style of cider you are making. *Cyser* is the term for a cider that has been sweetened with honey, and all kinds of other sugars—from granulated cane sugar to light and even dark brown sugar—may be added. The cheapest option, and the one that you should start with when making basic cider, is plain old granulated sugar (sucrose). Sweet cider naturally contains some sucrose (around 15 percent of its sugar content, along with 74 percent fructose and 11 percent glucose), and the cane sugar becomes indistinguishable from the fruit sugars produced in nature once it comes in contact with the organic acids in the solution of apple juice. In other words, once it is in the juice, the sucrose can never be removed and reconstituted as cane sugar.

Acids

The two other major flavor components of fresh apple juice are acids and tannins, and, as with sugar, it's good to know before fermentation whether you need to adjust the levels of either one. This is especially important if you are buying fresh sweet juice from an orchard or cider mill: You may not be able to find out exactly which varieties of apples were pressed, and in exactly what proportions. When you are pressing your own cider, you have much more control over the process and can make sure to blend in varieties of apples that will provide sufficient acids and tannins to the juice (see chapter 2 for a description of apple types and varieties).

Malic acid, the primary acid in apple cider, contributes a sharp taste to the fresh juice and a refreshing character to the fermented hard cider. Low-acid ciders taste flat and insipid; those with a high total acidity (above 0.7 or 0.8 percent) can be excessively sharp and harsh-tasting. An ideal level of total acidity in a juice is 0.3 to 0.5 percent. Acidity also helps guard against discoloration and discourages certain unwanted bacteria, thus helping to establish a dominant fermentation of the beneficial yeast strains and protecting the cider in storage.

Most American dessert apples contain a good, balanced amount of acidity, with Red Delicious being one notable exception (it makes a very fragrant but low-acid juice). Home acid-testers are available from most brew-

DEUTSCHE POMOLOGIE

MUSCAT REINETTE

ing supply stores and may be useful to experienced cidermakers, but they're rather expensive and not really necessary when you're just starting out. The best way to test for acidity is to taste the unfermented juice: Try to ignore the sweetness and the astringent tannins, and focus instead on the amount of "tang" that you can sense in the cider. If it tastes flat or insipid, you might want to blend in some juice from tart apples or crab apples, or add a measured amount of malic acid, which you can buy in powdered form at a homebrewing supply store. Add about 20 grams (2 rounded tablespoons) to a 5-gallon batch and taste it again, or follow the directions on the acid-tester you're using. This amount of malic acid will raise the total acidity of the juice by about 0.1 percent. If, on the other hand, the juice that you're starting with is extremely acidic, you can try neutralizing it by adding a small amount of calcium carbonate (precipitated chalk), at the rate of about 1 teaspoon to a 5-gallon batch, until you reach the desired level of acidity. But this should be your last resort, and it's rarely necessary. If you use a mix of dessert and culinary apples (see chapter 2), you should be able to press a cider with a good sugar/acid balance, and of course any cider you buy from a cider mill or orchard will, if anything, be lacking in sharpness. Unless you're pressing cider dominated with wild or crab apples, or a highly acidic variety like Bramley's Seedling, your fresh cider should be fine for fermentation purposes.

Another measure of acidity is the familiar pH scale. A good acidity reading for juice is somewhere between 3.0 and 3.8 pH. At a higher pH, the juice won't be acidic enough to discourage microbial infection, which can cause problems with spoilage and flavor. European bittersweet apples generally contain little acid and are typically blended with more acidic varieties (sharps or bittersharps), either before or after pressing. Most winemaking supply outlets sell narrow-range pH strips, which give a pretty good estimate within a range of 0.5 to 1.0 pH. For more accurate testing, you'll need to use a pH meter (see chapter 10).

A cider that is highly acidic and very sharp following the primary fermentation of sugar to alcohol will often mellow as it ages into a quite acceptable, even delicious beverage. This is because half or more of the malic acid may be converted into lactic acid in the process known as malolactic (or secondary) fermentation. The resulting cider becomes much smoother and nuttier-tasting because of the efforts of the lactic acid bacteria, which occasionally start working at the same time as primary fermentation, but usually wait until after the cider has completed its initial yeast fermentation and has been racked into a new container to mature and mellow.

Some commercial cidermakers (and winemakers) encourage ML fermentation; others try to prevent it at any cost, which is fairly easy if you add sulfites to the juice after primary fermentation. If you do want to reduce the sharpness of your cider and don't want to

leave things to chance, you can purchase an ML culture from winemaking supply sources, or direct from companies that sell liquid yeast strains (see the "Resources" section). ML bacteria don't work in temperatures cooler than 60°F, which is why this secondary fermentation tends to occur in the spring or early summer.

However, if a cider becomes more acidic during the fermentation process, it usually means that acetobacter (aerobic organisms that produce acetic acid) have been at work. A certain amount of acetic acid is always present in cider, but when the vinegary taste becomes too pronounced, the cider can become unpleasantly harsh or even undrinkable. At this point, it's best to save it for salad dressings.

Tannins

Tannins are the chemical flavor compounds that make red wines different from white wines. As with wines, tannins give a hard cider body and a dry finish, as well as having an antiseptic effect on various bacteria that can cause problems in fermentation or storage. In addition, tannins in the juice help to clarify, or fine, the cider, making it less hazy and more brilliant.

Apple tannin is colorless in the fruit cells, but that quickly changes, as anyone knows who has cut open an apple and let it sit around for a while. The tannins soon oxidize in the presence of air, and the apple slices become progressively darker in color. Cider experts classify the taste of tannins in an apple or cider as either "hard" (very bitter-tasting) or "soft" (more astringent or drying in the mouth than bitter).

It is unlikely that your juice will contain too much tannin unless you are using an especially high percentage of crab apples or European cider apple varieties. If you are using mainly North American dessert apples in your blend, you can add tannin to the juice before fermentation in a couple of different ways. The easiest method is to purchase powdered grape tannin at a brewing supply store. Add about 1 teaspoon to a 5-gallon carboy of juice, or a scant ¼ teaspoon to a 1-gallon jug. Another way to increase the tannins in a cider is to make a specialty cider by blending in some juice from another high-tannin fruit like elderberries, cranberries, or blueberries (see chapter 5). Raisins, used in making traditional New England-style cider, will also contribute some tannin.

Yeast Nutrients and Pectic Enzymes

Some cidermakers add other substances to the juice before fermentation, either to give the yeast a boost or to ensure that the finished cider will be brilliantly clear.

Yeasts require a food source, of course, and this consists of the natural sugars in the sweet cider, as well as any extra sugar that you may add to the juice before fermentation begins. However, yeast cells also need some soluble nitrogen in the juice to produce the proteins and amino acids that are necessary for their growth. A cider with a low nitrogen content (such as one pressed from apples that come from wild or unfertilized trees) will ferment more slowly than will one with a higher nitrogen content. The most common cause of a "stuck" (stalled or incomplete) fermentation is either a lack of free amino nitrogen, which inhibits yeast growth, or a lack of thiamine (vitamin B_1) and in the worst cases can result in the cider having a "rotten egg" smell from hydrogen sulfide (H_2S). For that reason, some cidermakers add either some form of ammonium sulfate or thiamine to their juice before and during fermentation (especially if they also are adding sugar), to ensure a quick and complete conversion of sugar to alcohol. Old-time cidermakers used to hang a piece of beef or mutton in the fermenta-

tion vat to accomplish the same thing. Both thiamine and ammonium sulfate are known as yeast nutrients, and are available from homebrewing supply stores.

For small-batch cidermaking, only tiny amounts of either kind of yeast nutrient are necessary to get things going. (Think of it as sprinkling pixie dust.) I have rarely found it necessary to use yeast nutrients, but you might want to consider using them if you are adding a lot of sugar to your fresh cider, or if your fermentation seems to "get stuck" or stop in mid-process. General recommendations are to add half of the recommended dosage of DAP (diammonium phosphate) before fermentation starts, and the other half once it starts up. Fermax is another commonly available brand of yeast nutrient. The recommended dosage is about 1 teaspoon per gallon, and the recommendation here is to add a third of the total needed pre-fermentation, the second third once fermentation starts, and the final third when it is well underway, when the must measures around 8 to 12 degrees Brix.

Pectic enzymes help break down the pectins in the juice. Pectins are a kind of natural adhesive that binds together the cells in an apple. In the finished cider, the pectins contribute a viscous quality, or oiliness, which sounds terrible but actually means that the cider is softer and more pleasant to drink. Although pectins are soluble in water, they are often precipitated by alcohol, which can lead to a persistent "pectin haze" after fermentation—something very common with homemade or traditional farmhouse ciders. This haziness doesn't affect the quality of the cider, just the appearance, but many people prefer a cider that has brilliant clarity. To achieve this, they add a pectic enzyme at some point in the process, either sprinkling it onto the milled apple pulp before pressing, or adding it to the pressed juice before or after primary fermentation.

For your first few batches of homemade cider, I would avoid complicating things and leave out the pectic enzyme. See how clear a cider you can produce without it. Then, if you like, experiment with it later to make an aesthetically pleasing cider that will sparkle in the glass and delight the judges at any cider tasting. Dosage rates are normally indicated by the manufacturer, or you can inquire when you buy the enzyme at a brewing supply store.

The other reason for adding a pectic enzyme would be if you are trying to create a cider that naturally stops fermenting before it reaches complete dryness. This is an advanced procedure that's traditionally used in making sweeter French-style ciders, and in English it's called "keeving" (for more on this, see chapter 10). It involves the intentional stripping of nutrients out of the fresh juice—but since that is diametrically opposed to what we just discussed under yeast nutrients, let's ignore it for the time being.

Sulfur Dioxide

Since ancient times, sulfur dioxide (SO_2) has been used in winemaking to sterilize fermentation vessels, usually by burning sulfur candles or strips inside a wooden cask or barrel. Sulfites are still used to make both wine and cider, either to sterilize the juice before adding a cultured yeast strain or to suppress microbial activity, prevent oxidation or infection, and protect a cider during racking or bottling.

Today, instead of sulfur candles, most amateur cidermakers use Campden tablets (sodium or potassium metabisulfite), which are available from all homebrewing supply outlets. Adding sulfites before fermentation either kills off or suppresses all of the wild yeasts and bacteria in the sweet cider. How much you'll want to use depends chiefly on the acidity of the juice, as measured by pH (see the table below for a simple overview). Campden

ADDITION OF SULFUR DIOXIDE (SO_2)

Juice pH	SO_2 Needed in Parts per Million (ppm)	Campden tablets (50 ppm) needed per gallon
Above 3.8 (insipid)	Lower pH to 3.8 with addition of malic acid	
3.8–3.5	150	3
3.5–3.3 (balanced)	100	2
3.3–3.0	50	1
Below 3.0 (sharp)	None	None

Notes: If a pH meter or narrow-range pH strips are not available, use the taste of the juice as your guide. Campden tablets are typically formulated to give the equivalent of 50 ppm SO_2 when dissolved in one gallon of liquid. Check the specific rating/yield that's listed on tablets you buy commercially and adjust quantities if needed. *Adapted from Andrew Lea's Wittenham Hill Cider Portal (www.cider.org.uk). Used with permission.*

COMMON CIDER DISORDERS

A number of possible problems can make a good cider turn bad. Usually these are the result of unwanted microorganisms working away in the cider and producing undesirable tastes or smells. Fortunately, most of these conditions are 100 percent preventable, and are relatively rare if you follow good sanitary practices and limit the cider's exposure to air during fermentation and storage.

Acetification is caused by various organisms (collectively known as acetobacter), which are aerobic (operating in the presence of oxygen). They oxidize the cider, thus forming acetic acid—in other words, vinegar. Acetobacter are present in all cider, and they can even survive sulfiting and the high-alcohol conditions of a fully fermented cider. Eventually they will form a wispy gray film on the surface of the cider, which turns into the gelatinous culture known as mother of vinegar. A little acetic acid in a finished farmhouse cider may not completely ruin its taste, but once acetification is under way in earnest, you might as well make vinegar instead of cider (see chapter 8). The best strategy, though, is to keep the acetobacter from reproducing in the first place, by not exposing the cider to air: Top up all fermentation jugs and bottles with fresh cider, water, or sugar solution so as not leave a large airspace.

Film yeasts also operate in aerobic conditions and produce something known as "flower," a greasy or powdery film on the surface of the cider. A cider affected with flower will smell like solvent (from the acetates these yeasts produce) and will taste moldy or musty. If you notice it in time, the cider can be treated with 100 parts per million of sulfur dioxide (typically equivalent to two crushed Campden tablets per gallon). Take special care in sterilizing containers where film yeasts have been working before you use them again for cider.

Cider sickness is most common in ciders that are low in acid and naturally sweet, like traditional French cider. North American apples generally have enough acidity to avoid this condition, which is caused by *Zymomonas* bacteria. These bacteria ferment sugars and produce acetaldehydes, which give the affected cider the odor of rotten lemons or banana skins. (To the French nose, this fruity aroma smells like raspberries, so they also call this disorder *framboise.*) It is often accompanied by the smell of rotten eggs (hydrogen sulfide), and the cider sometimes has a dense, milky white turbidity or haze. If you catch it early on, you can add malic acid or blend in juice from acidic apples to lower the pH to below 3.7.

Ropiness or **oiliness** sometimes occurs in low-acid ciders after bottling or in bulk storage. It is caused by certain lactic acid bacteria that produce a gel-like substance. When the cider is poured, it will have the slimy texture of light oil or a raw egg white. The flavor is not affected. This condition does not occur in ciders that have been treated with sulfur dioxide before fermentation. To treat it later on, pour the cider into another container and stir it vigorously to break up the clumps. Then add 100 ppm of SO_2 (two crushed Campden tablets) per gallon, and rack into new bottles or jugs.

Mousiness is also caused by certain lactic acid bacteria as well as certain strains of yeast. It creates an unpleasant "mouse droppings" aroma and a taste that lingers at the back of the throat and that has been compared to fresh-baked bread, beer, or popcorn. Some people are more sensitive to the off-flavor than others. It occurs slowly over time in stored ciders, and nothing really can be done to prevent it, although it seems to be less common in ciders that have been treated with sulfur dioxide.

Black or green breakage is a discoloration caused by the reaction of cider with metals. Often the color doesn't develop until you open the bottle and the cider comes in contact with air. Contact with iron can cause a black or greenish black color; copper gives cider a greenish hue. The flavor will be harsh, metallic, and unpleasant. There is nothing you can do after the fact to remedy this condition. Keep your cider away from iron, copper, and other metals in equipment and utensils, except for stainless steel.

Oxidation is caused by cider coming in contact with air during storage, or containing high levels of dissolved oxygen. The cider may be dark and discolored, appearing orange, coppery, or dark golden brown; the taste is variously described as stale, leathery, or sherry-like. The solution is, first, to keep stored cider from contacting the air (especially important with wooden casks or barrels, which "breathe"), and, second, using sulfites when racking or bottling as needed.

tablets used to be standardized to provide the equivalent of 50 parts per million (ppm) of free SO_2 when dissolved in one gallon of liquid. In recent years, I've purchased Campden tablets that say on the label that they provide anywhere from 30 to a whopping 120 ppm of SO_2. Clearly, if you use them, you will need to check the label carefully and adjust your dosage accordingly.

The other option (and the one some amateur and nearly all commercial cidermakers employ) is to buy metabisulfite powder and make up their own 5 percent stock solution of sulfur dioxide. To do this, dissolve 10 grams (about 0.35 ounce or 2 teaspoons) sodium or potassium metabisulfite in 100 milliliters (about $3/8$ cup or 3 fluid ounces) water. Adding 1 teaspoon of this solution to a 5-gallon carboy of cider will correspond to around 50 ppm SO_2.

As we can see from the table on page 77, adding 100 parts per million of sulfur dioxide is more than enough to knock out all undesirable microbes in the juice in a typically sugar/acid-balanced American sweet cider. Some cidermakers prefer to use less than this, around 50 to 75 ppm per gallon. Very acidic juice (lower than 3.0 pH) doesn't really need sulfites, as the acids provide protection against spoilage organisms, including acetobacter. On the other hand, very low-acid ciders (which are unusual, unless you are fermenting a single-variety English bittersweet variety or a low-acid juice from mostly Red Delicious apples) may require more sulfur dioxide. I once sampled a barrel of a still-fermenting Foxwhelp cider: The flavor and body were indeed musky and interesting, but the high level of sulfites that the cidermaker had to use to protect this low-acid, single-variety juice lent the immature cider all the aftertaste and insouciant charm of a wet matchbook.

After adding the sulfur dioxide, you will need to let the cider sit for a full day before adding, or pitching, the

Chapter 4: Hard Cider from Juice to Bottle

commercial yeast culture into the juice. Most beer and wine yeasts are somewhat sulfur-tolerant, and they should begin to work within a few days of pitching them. Adding the sulfite to the juice eliminates the competition for the commercial yeast strain and lets it take over as the dominant fermentation agent in the cider.

Of course, if you want to make use of wild yeasts and other microorganisms, you won't want to add any sulfur dioxide before fermentation. My advice for the beginning cidermaker is to add sulfur before fermentation if you plan on using a cultured yeast strain. If nothing else, it will ensure that the qualities you detect in the finished cider are due to the commercial yeast you're using and not a result of some unknown interloper. However, you can also pitch a commercial yeast culture into a natural, unsulfited cider, and in most cases this is enough to ensure that the culture you want to encourage will eventually dominate the fermentation process. It doesn't guarantee against possible infections or other problems, but I've made good cider both with and without sulfur.

Finally, some people (asthmatics and others) are highly sensitive to sulfites in wines and ciders. This usually isn't a problem if you use sulfur dioxide at the beginning of the process; it will bind to other chemicals during fermentation. However, sulfur dioxide is more noticeable if it is added later on, before bottling, so use it with discretion and only when you are making a low-alcohol cider that is meant to be sweet or semidry, or after sweetening a dry cider before bottling. Again, one or two crushed Campden tablets per gallon (50 to 100 ppm) is the generally recommended dosage, but the overall sulfur dioxide content of a cider (prefermentation through bottling total) should never exceed 200 ppm.

Fermentation

The process of fermentation, in which yeasts and other microorganisms convert sugar into alcohol, can be likened to gardening or farming, with your role as the cidermaker to provide the appropriate growing conditions that will favor a good "crop" of yeast and discourage unwanted yeasts and bacteria from taking hold. I am indebted to my farmer/writer friend Gene Logsdon for introducing this simple, but not necessarily obvious, conceit to me in his excellent book *Good Spirits:*

Growing yeasts and harnessing their energy is the fundamental agriculture. Until Pasteur looked into the matter, the role of yeasts was not understood (although good drinking alcohol and sourdough bread were made for centuries before him—a point not to forget). Most scientists thought the change from sugar to alcohol was a chemical one, and that was true in the sense that everything is chemical in the final analysis. But the role yeasts play in the conversion of sugar into alcohol is fundamentally a biological process. To make alcohol by feeding sugar to yeasts is at least metaphorically like feeding cows hay to produce milk. . . . Managing yeasts is really a kind of farm and garden work, not a test tube maneuver.[1]

My simplified overview of the cidermaking process as described so far relies on the activity of wild yeasts and bacteria—which are naturally present in the fresh cider—to ferment the sugars into alcohol. This is the traditional way to make hard cider, and it still works well today. However, there are many other cultured strains of yeast that can be used to ferment cider, and lots of homebrewers depend on these commercial yeasts to ensure more consistent and reproducible results, or to create certain flavors or styles of cider.

Yeasts, Wild and Domesticated

The most important yeasts involved in the fermentation of alcohol are those belonging to the genus *Saccharomyces*. However, most of the yeasts that are found growing wild on the skins and even in the flesh of ripe apples (fewer than 500 cells per gram by some accounts, up to 45,000 cells by others) are weaker-fermenting types like *Kloeckera* and *Candida*, which will get fermentation going but then die off once the cider reaches 1 or 2 percent alcohol. *Saccharomyces* and other alcohol-tolerant yeasts will then take over and help ferment the cider to completeness; these yeasts can build up over time on the press cloths, equipment, and walls and floor of the cider house itself, and thus get into the fresh-pressed juice. And just as real sourdough bread will taste slightly different depending on whether it was made in San Francisco or in Savannah, so traditional farmhouse ciders made with wild yeasts have unique and distinctive tastes that vary with each individual producer.

Wild yeasts are anathema to commercial cidermakers, who want a product that will taste the same, or nearly so, batch after batch. Home- and farm-scale cidermakers, though, can frequently produce delicious, aromatic, and complex ciders by using wild yeasts. However, be prepared to throw consistency to the winds. In order to ensure success and avoid disappointment the first time out, make only a half-gallon or gallon batch of cider using wild yeasts. For the bulk of your run, try making cider with one of the many cultured yeast strains that are available from homebrewing supply stores.

The complex bouquet of a hard cider is partly due to the aromatic varieties of apples used in the blend, but partly due as well to the fragrant compounds produced as a result of yeast fermentation. Louis Pasteur first noted that fruit juices fermented with wine yeasts acquire

DEUTSCHE POMOLOGIE

WINTER-GOLDPARMÄNE

a vinous (winey) aroma, and the same holds true for beer. This means that the type of cultured yeast you use in cidermaking will have a profound effect on the character of your finished cider. Although many large cideries have developed their own strains of yeast specifically for cider, there are currently only one or two specific cider yeasts that are commercially available for home cidermakers. This means that you'll be faced with a choice as to which yeast you'd like to use.

Once you've made your first successful batch of cider, it's definitely worth experimenting with some of the thousands of strains of commercially available yeast to see which one produces a cider with the aroma and taste you like best. For starters, though, try and keep things simple and base your choices on the temperature of the room or space where you will be fermenting your hard cider.

Slow fermentation at cooler temperatures (40° to 55°F) is recommended by most cider experts, as this creates the best conditions for making a fine-tasting hard cider that retains as many of the complex or fruity esters as possible. Because the best cider is generally made from

Chapter 4: Hard Cider from Juice to Bottle

late-harvested apple varieties, the ambient air temperatures found in your garage, barn, or cellar at this time of year (late fall and early winter) might be perfect for cool fermentation. I use a walk-in closet located on an outside wall of my house, where throughout the year the temperature rarely climbs above 60°F or dips below 45°F. Terry Bradshaw, a serious amateur cidermaker in Calais, Vermont, has partitioned off a portion of his basement, with much the same effect. A small window helps to regulate the temperature of his fermentation room, keeping it in the range of ideal temperatures for a long, slow ferment, or warming up a bit in spring and summer, when the cider is done fermenting and might perhaps benefit from a bit of secondary, or malolactic, fermentation, which requires a higher temperature to get started.

In this kind of environment, you might want to use

An active fermentation in progress. Note the use of the "blow-by" tubes that extend into the vessel full of water, allowing for the escape of carbon dioxide and other purged solids while protecting the fermenting cider from outside air, microbes, and other interlopers. *Terence Bradshaw*

a champagne, white wine, or lager yeast, all readily available from most homebrewing supply outlets. Each one leaves its own distinctive fingerprint on the finished cider. For a beginner, I recommend using Pasteur champagne yeast for making at least one batch: It produces a dry, clear, golden cider and is pretty foolproof, although it does take a little longer than other yeasts to begin working. Another good choice is Côte des Blancs (Epernay 2) wine yeast, which will ferment at a lower temperature and produce more aromatic estery by-products than will a typical champagne yeast.

If you are fermenting your cider at a temperature higher than 55°F, try using a variety of ale yeast (*Saccharomyces cerevesiae*) instead of a wine or lager yeast. Ales are meant to be fermented at a cool room temperature of 55° to 65°F, so this kind of yeast will be most successful in making a fruity, refreshing cider with a nice "draft ale" quality to it. At these warmer temperatures, the fermentation will proceed quickly and should be quite vigorous. (See sidebar on pages 83–84.)

Starting a Yeast Culture

Yeast comes in two basic forms, either dried and sold in small foil packets like baker's yeast, or as a liquid culture packaged in foil "smack packs" by laboratories. Both types are usually available at homebrewing supply stores. Dried yeasts are convenient: One 5-gram packet contains enough granules to pitch into a 5-gallon carboy. However, there is often a large percentage of dead yeast cells in a dried yeast. Lab yeasts offer more variety, but they are more expensive (six dollars or more, versus less than a buck for most dried yeast packets). The foil smack packs are convenient, though; you place the foil envelope on a flat surface and whack it firmly to release the yeast culture into the nutritive medium. In short order, the yeast starts working and the packet puffs up like a blow-

Some Commercial Yeast Strains Used for Cidermaking

The following is certainly not a comprehensive listing of all the yeast strains that are available, nor does it provide a full description of each yeast's characteristics. A good place to find an updated list of available yeasts is on The Winemaking Home Page (http://winemaking.jackkeller.net/strains.asp). Other good sources of information are the websites of the commercial yeast manufacturers themselves; many of them sell to home winemakers directly and you can place an order on the Web. Homebrewing and winemaking supply stores do carry yeasts, both dry packet and liquid cultures, from the manufacturers, but they might not have the specific strains you're looking for.

When choosing a yeast to try, look for information on what kind of flavor notes it is said to bring out. It's fun over time to experiment with different yeast strains, keeping notes of how they perform in your ciders and your fermentation conditions. However, many cidermakers come back to the basic few types, mainly champagne yeasts (*Saccharomyces bayanus*), which can do their business even in cool conditions (under 50°F), and rarely stop or stick until they fully ferment the cider to dryness. Also, these yeasts are rather neutral in terms of taste profile, and tend to express the qualities of the fruit rather than masking or overshadowing them.

Producer	Yeast Strain	Type	Characteristics
Red Star	Pasteur Champagne	dry	good for sparkling cider, cold ferments
Red Star	Premier Cuvee (Prise de Mousse)	dry	low-foaming; good for barrel fermentation
Red Star	Cote des Blancs (Epernay 2)	dry	slow, cold ferments; floral and fruity
Lalvin	DV10 (Epernay)	dry	tolerates high SO_2, low pH, ferments clean in wide temperature range
Lalvin	ICV DV47 (Cotes du Rhone)	dry	quick-fermenting, low-foaming; forms compact lees; good mouthfeel
Lalvin	EC-1118 (Prise de Mousse)	dry	low-foaming; good for barrel fermentation; compact lees; good for bottle conditioning and restarting stuck fermentations
White Labs	Champagne (WLP 715)	liquid	clean and quick ferment; neutral flavor profile; high alcohol tolerance

Producer	Yeast Strain	Type	Characteristics
White Labs	Sweet Mead/Wine (WLP 720)	liquid	slightly fruity character, leaves some residual sweetness
White Labs	English Cider (WLP 775)	liquid	ferments dry, but retains flavor from apples; sulfur produced in fermentation dissipates with two weeks aging
Wyeast	Activator™	liquid	live yeast cells in a "smack pack" with liquid nutrient pouch; for cider and mead

fish. At this point, you can simply sanitize the outside of the packet and cut it open, pitching it into your must. Still in all, for beginners, the easiest and cheapest option is probably dry yeast.

When using dried yeast, it's not a bad idea to grow a starter culture for a day or two, so as to multiply the number of yeast cells before pitching them into the carboy or fermentation jug. To do this, sterilize a pint-sized beer bottle or canning jar by placing it in a boiling-water bath for ten minutes or so. Pour the packet of yeast into a bowl containing $1/4$ cup of warm water (95° to 105°F). Then funnel about $3/4$ cup *pasteurized* cider or apple juice at room temperature into the sterilized and cooled beer bottle. If you can't find pasteurized cider or juice without preservatives, simply heat some raw, unpasteurized cider to 170°F on the stovetop for a few minutes, then let it cool to room temperature.

Funnel the liquefied yeast slurry into the beer bottle, give it a swirl to aerate the yeast, and cover loosely with a piece of plastic wrap secured around the neck with a rubber band, to prevent contamination. Set the bottle aside at room temperature for a day or so, then pitch it into your carboy or jug filled with cider. Gently swirl the jug around a bit to incorporate the yeast, then cover the fermenter loosely with plastic wrap and wait for the yeast to start working vigorously. The most efficient strategy is to start your yeast culture at the same time you add the crushed Campden tablets to the fermentation vessel—you will have to wait for at least a day in any case before you can pitch the yeast into the sulfited cider.

Primary Fermentation

The yeast that you have cultured has now been pitched into the carboy or fermentation jug, and within a few days the vigorous primary fermentation will have started. At this point, the carbon dioxide gas that is being expelled should protect the cider, even though the top of the fermentation vessel has been left open. However, when using wild, champagne, or other slow-starting yeasts, or when fermenting in especially cool conditions, I often feel more comfortable using an alternative to the open-mouth method—one that makes it even more unlikely that any acetobacter, fruit flies, or other unwanted visitors will drop into my cider.

Fit the top of the carboy or jug with a bored rubber stopper. Then push the end of a length of plastic tubing through the hole in the cork, leaving it above the level of the cider, in the empty space that winemakers call the *ullage*. Place the other end of the tubing in a pail or jar half filled with water and set next to, and a little lower than, the fermentation vessel (see photo on page 82). This arrangement is known as a blow-by fermentation lock, and it is routinely used by folks who make cider in wooden barrels. In the inimitable words of my cidermaking friend Farish Jenkins: "This will allow the enthusiastic fermentate, which is the product of the yeasts all arising from a Brunnhilde-like slumber kissed by the warm sucrosed lips of the cider and at once plunging into the sexual frenzy of reproduction, to blow off. The fermentate is not pretty, and I would not attempt to explain it to your friends."

Once this messy (and rather naughty) phase of fermentation is over, you can remove the stopper and the tube, clean up the top of the jug or carboy as best as possible, and fill it up with fresh sweet cider, leaving about a two-inch headspace at the top. Then fit it with a regular plastic fermentation lock filled with sulfur dioxide solution. I try to replace the sanitized water in the airlock every month or so.

How can you tell when fermentation is complete? Eventually, usually after one or two months, the cider will look clear or slightly hazy, and you will no longer see or hear carbon dioxide bubbles glubbing up in the fermentation lock. There will be a thick sediment of yeast on the bottom of the container, and you will probably still notice bubbles rising gently to the top of the cider.

At this point, it's a good idea to sample the cider and check its specific gravity again with the hydrometer. The cider has fermented to dryness, or close to it, when it registers an S.G. of 1.005 or less. The basic rule of thumb is that when fermentation is going well, the cider's specific gravity drops about one point a day. If the cider stops fermenting at an S.G. much higher than 1.005, you may have a "stuck" fermentation on your hands. If this happens, add a yeast nutrient and stir the cider vigorously for about twenty minutes to aerate the yeast and get it working again.

Once the cider has reached this stage, you can either rack it off into a new sanitized container using a plastic siphon hose or let it stay in the same vessel and sit on its lees for a while. When racking off, try to pick a fair day when the barometric pressure is high: These weather conditions help keep suspended yeasts to a minimum, while retaining the dissolved carbon dioxide in the cider.

Incidentally, my friend Claude Jolicoeur, who is a skillful and passionate cidermaker in Quebec, doesn't just throw out his old lees after racking. Instead he uses them to create rich, thick sauces or as a braising liquid for meat. Sandor Katz, author of the fascinating book *Wild Fermentation* (Chelsea Green, 2003), likewise uses his wine and cider lees, which are rich in B vitamins, in soups and salad dressings. Waste not, want not, I say.

At this point, taste the cider. It won't be anywhere near ready to drink at this point, but you should be able to gauge the level of malic acid. Ciders that taste excessively sharp and acidic should be left standing on their lees for a while; this seems to encourage a secondary, or malolactic fermentation, which converts some of the malic acid into smoother lactic acid. Ciders that are low in acid, however, should be racked off into a clean container at this point and not left standing on their lees. And in no case is it good to leave a fully fermented cider standing on its sediment for more than a month or so: The dead yeast can "autolyze" and create off-flavors.

Maturation and Bottling

Unlike wines, most ciders do not require long-term aging before they are ready to drink. A month or two after you have racked the cider off its lees into a clean container and fitted it with a new airlock, it should be ready for bottling. Work quickly but carefully as you siphon cider into cleaned and sanitized bottles. Try to avoid excessive splashing and oxidation of the cider, and leave about a half-inch of headspace. It helps to have someone assisting with this operation; you can siphon and fill the bottles while a friend adds priming sugar and caps them, or tips and holds the carboy steady while you extract all the clear cider you can from above the bottom sediment.

Traditional farmhouse or English cider, which I have been describing in this chapter, is dry and still. If you want to have a bit of natural carbonation in your cider, add 1/2 teaspoon of sugar per pint to the bottles before filling and capping. It's possible to simply use granulated cane sugar in this way, but I prefer using dextrose or "corn sugar," which is familiar to anyone who has ever used it for priming (naturally carbonating and bottle-conditioning) home-brewed beer or ale. It gives the remaining yeast cells in the bottle a little something to nosh on, and the carbon dioxide gas that they release creates a lightly sparkling beverage. Once the sugar is all used up, the spent yeasts precipitate and form a light sediment on the bottom of the bottle, which doesn't affect the quality of the cider and is neither very noticeable or objectionable. The advantage of using dextrose, which is made from hydrolyzed cornstarch, is that it creates finer bubbles in the finished cider than regular granulated sugar.

Please don't assume that if a little priming sugar is good, then a lot must be better. Adding too much sugar at bottling can have explosive consequences if you don't watch out. A sturdy beer bottle will typically withstand about three atmospheres (3 atm) of pressure from carbon dioxide building up in the bottle, and a heavy champagne bottle can handle roughly twice that, or 6 atm. But you never want to overcarbonate your cider, whether you're doing it through secondary bottle fermentation or by force-carbonating with a CO_2 tank and counter-pressure bottle filler (see chapter 10). Even if you aren't awakened by the sound of shattering bottles in the cellar, no one wants to have a gusher when they pry open a bottle. For safety's sake, never bottle an unstabilized cider in a beer bottle if it has a specific gravity of 1.005 or higher; if you're using champagne bottles, you can go a little higher, up to 1.010 S.G. The nicest sort of cider, in my opinion, is what the French call *petillant,* where the tiny bubbles lazily curl upward in the glass, giving the drink a light effervescence, but certainly not a foaming head of bubbles.

Alternatively, you can sweeten a whole batch of cider with a simple syrup or sugar solution. In a nonreactive saucepan boil 1/2 to 3/4 cup granulated cane sugar in a pint of water with a bit of lemon juice for about five minutes and let it cool, covered, before mixing it into the cider thoroughly (to disperse the solution and introduce a bit of oxygen, which the yeast will need to get restarted. This will prime a 5-gallon batch of cider. By boiling the cane sugar (sucrose), you are transforming it into an invert sugar, which the yeast can more readily to work on, without having to produce invertase, an enzyme that can produce a sour taste. After mixing, you're then ready to bottle.

Store the capped or corked bottles at room temperature for a month or two before drinking; this allows the yeast to carbonate the cider and lets the flavors continue to develop and mature. Then chill a bottle and open it up. Pour the cider carefully into the glass, so as not to stir up the yeast sediment at the bottom of the bottle. Hold your glass up to the light, sniff the bouquet, then take that first, long-awaited sip of your own homemade cider. For pure satisfaction, it doesn't get much better than this.

What makes the cider blow its cork
with such a merry din?
What makes those little bubbles rise
and dance like harlequin?
It is the fatal apple, boys,
the fruit of human sin.

—Christopher Morley, "A Glee upon Cider"

5. CIDER STYLES AND TRADITIONS

THERE ARE AS MANY DIFFERENT STYLES OF CIDER as there are cidermakers. The taste and quality of traditional cider varies not only with the knowledge and skill of the producer, but also according to the specific blend of apple varieties he or she uses. What's more, unseen factors such as wild yeasts and other microorganisms, which are always present, even in the most spotlessly clean operation, combine to make each producer's cider unique.

Traditional cider is at heart a local product, one that has until recent years been made primarily in small regional cideries or sold directly at the farmhouse gate. In some regions, such as the West Country of England and in northern France, it still is made and sold this way. Real cider has never traveled well because of its relatively low alcohol content and its sensitivity to heat, among other factors. Ciders specifically designed for export—especially from England, Spain, and the United States—tended to be less delicate products that were fortified by adding sugar or other sweeteners to the juice. Especially important in an age before electric power and refrigeration, this strengthening would increase the cider's final alcoholic content after fermentation and help preserve its stability, keeping qualities, and shelf life.

The Influence of Soils and Climate

Another important contributor to the character of any cider is something the French call *terroir*. In the broadest sense, this term refers to the place where the fruit is grown—from the composition of the soil and subsoil, to the local or regional climate (sunshine, rainfall, seasonal temperatures, prevailing winds), to the microclimate or aspect of a particular orchard. Usually applied to discussions of wine and vineyards, terroir can be just as important when considering which areas make the best cider. Georges Warcollier observed that excellent hard ciders were produced from apples grown on soils that derived from schists and quartzites, and as early as 1588 Julien Le Paulmier considered soil conditions to be even more important for cider than for wines. In America, too, the importance of certain soils in growing good, flavorful apples has long been recognized. As Vrest Orton wrote in his classic *American Cider* Book: "We were informed by a leading orchardist years ago that the primary reason for [the superior quality of New England's apples] is that the soil of New England is made up of glacial deposits left here many centuries ago, rich in minerals and trace elements, which make the fruit so healthful and flavorful. The soil on the West Coast, however, consists largely of volcanic ash and seems to lack something that New England soil has."[1]

Whether this is, in fact, the case or merely an excuse for claiming regional bragging rights is an open question. Certainly apple growers in other regions of North America, from Michigan to New Jersey, from Arkansas to Washington State, would vigorously dispute this conclusion.

Less debatable is the influence of climate over which apple varieties can be grown where, and how successfully. S. A. Beach observed back in 1905 that the Esopus Spitzenburg apple seemed to grow best in the Schoharie Valley of New York, that Newtown Pippins reached their greatest perfection on the north shore of Long Island, and that the Fameuse, or Snow, apple thrived in the Saint Lawrence Valley and along the shores of Lake Champlain. In *The Apples of New York*, Beach noted that "the adaptability of a variety to a particular region is not altogether a matter of latitude, or length of season, nor prevailing temperature during the growing season. The general character of the soil, the prevailing climate condition during the blooming season, and other conditions peculiar to the local environment also enter into the question."[2]

Many varieties of apples produce their best fruits only with a sufficient period of heat in the spring and summer and a certain minimum number of "chilling" hours over the winter, when the trees are dormant and temperatures dip below 45°F. Although England is famous for its own apples, many North American apple varieties when grown in England do not thrive or devel-

DEUTSCHE POMOLOGIE

LANDSBERGER REINETTE

Cider, Hard and Sweet

op as fine a flavor or color as they do on these shores, because the English summer climate is not as extreme. And the reverse can also be true. For instance, the climate in Britain is generally better suited to growing the beautiful dessert and cider apple known as Ribston Pippin, a variety that one writer said "stands as high in Great Britain as the Bank of England . . .[and] to say that an apple has a Ribstone [sic] flavour is there the highest praise that can be bestowed."[3] The American orchardist William Coxe recognized the importance of climate back in 1817 when he wrote: "Cold and heat are equally necessary to the production of a fine apple; neither must predominate in too great a degree. It is remarked by Knight in his treatise on the fruits of Hereford, that the flavour of the liquor for which particular orchards in that country are celebrated, is ascribed to their warm and favourable exposure in every instance which had come to his knowledge."[4]

Regional Ciders

Different apple-growing regions of the world have always produced distinctive styles of cider. The ciders of Germany and Switzerland, for instance, are made almost exclusively from surplus dessert varieties of apples and are called *Apfelwein*. And in fact they do more closely resemble a thin white wine than a full-bodied English or French bittersweet cider. Germany makes around 8 percent of the world's cider, yet its products remain relatively unknown in the United States. (Another major cider-producing nation is South Africa, which is second only to the UK in terms of cider, with 14 percent of the world market in 2004. However, virtually all of South Africa's production is industrial or draft-style cider sold in multipacks.)

Perhaps this lack of recognition is because Germany has a colder, continental climate (like Finland and Scandinavia, which together make up another 6 percent of the world's cider production), whereas the greatest, oldest, and most highly regarded cidermaking areas of Europe—England's West Country, Normandy and Brittany in France, and Asturias and the Basque region of Spain—all have longer growing seasons and mild climates tempered by the Gulf Stream. They also have rich soils where apple trees flourish, traditionally planted on wide spacings in fields of sod, where animals graze beneath the trees.

Spain

In northern Spain, where the ancient Celts may well have cultivated the first domestic apples in Europe, possibly hybridizing them with the wild European apple *(Malus sylvestris),* small farmers still grow apples whose ancestry dates back to these original varieties. These orchardists spray their trees very little, because cosmetic appearance is not a major concern with cider apples, as it is with table fruit. More than a hundred small, regional cidermakers still operate in the traditional way, buying lots of varieties of apples from local farmers and selling their cider in corked wine bottles to local cider bars, or *sidrerias*. There are no labels on these bottles; the only way to identify the cidermaker is to look for the stamp on the cork. The largest producer is El Gaitero, a company that is almost as important to the Spanish cider industry as the venerable firm of H. P. Bulmer is in England. Like Bulmer's cider, Gaitero is sweet and carbonated, and a lot of it is exported to Latin America, particularly to Brazil and Argentina.

Jose Maria Osoro, director of the Asturian Cidermakers Association reported in 2005 that the total annual cider production was 100 million liters, with about 40 percent of this being the industrial style of sweet, sparkling cider just mentioned and the other 60 percent comprised of all brands of traditional Spanish cider, or *sidra natural*. The region of Asturias alone accounts for 82 percent of Spanish cider production, about equally split between industrial and traditional cider.

Some 11 to 14 million liters of cider are produced in the Euskadi, or Basque country, which includes territory in both Spain and France. The Euskera (Basque language) name for their traditional cider is *sagardoa* or *sagarnoa*, and it is virtually impossible to find it anywhere but in the Basque regions, where it is ready to be consumed beginning around the end of January in the many rural ciderhouses *(sagardotegias)* just inland from San Sebastian (Donostia). Here, typically in a simple, rustic hall, visitors pay for a multicourse meal punctuated by generous tastes of true "draft" cider that shoots out in a golden stream from large chestnut cider barrels tapped for the occasion. This draft cider party atmosphere lasts until April, after which the remaining cider is bottled and sold from the farm ciderhouse.

Traditional Spanish cider is very dry and tart, even acetic, and has a good tannic structure and an alcohol content around 6 percent. Only slightly effervescent and never pasteurized or filtered, it frequently appears somewhat turbid. It's a most convivial drink that is served, in addition to the ciderhouses, at the cider bars of northern Spain, along with the Basque-style tapas known as *pintxos*. To serve it, the bartender ceremoniously uncorks a bottle and flourishes it high over his head, letting the cider flow in an arc into a widemouthed, paper-thin glass that he holds tilted upward at his waist. This pouring ritual helps to aerate the cider and open up its flavor, in much the same way that an experienced taster "chews" a cider in the mouth to release its full bouquet (see chapter 6). The customer then drinks off the glassful of cider, except for the lees, which are thrown on the floor; some *sidrerias* even have troughs to catch this runoff. This is cider drinking at its best: lusty and passionate, full of joy and life. It is to polite cider-sipping what bullfighting is to walking your pet schnauzer.

France

In England and France these days you are more apt to see intensively planted apple trees, which have largely replaced the widely spaced standard apple farms of yore. France has the most tightly regulated cider industry in the world, and arguably produces the consistently highest quality of cider. Most high-end artisanal cidermakers make a completely natural product, using no extra sugar, sulfites, or added yeasts. They do, however, filter the cider before bottling to strain out most of the yeast. In the Pays d'Auge, the most famous cider region of Normandy, the cider is made exclusively from locally grown apples and so has a very distinctive character, with a fine head of little bubbles (known as the *mousse*), an amber color, and a complex, intense, sweet taste. Normandy cider in general tends to be sweeter than the sharper, drier cider of Brittany and usually contains 4 percent alcohol or less. Breton cider is brilliantly clear and a little stronger than its Norman counterpart. Traditionally, the French countryfolk drank their cider from ceramic mugs that looked like oversized teacups. Given the fact that French cider is almost always sparkling from natural bottle carbonation—*cidre bouche*—it seems a shame to pour such a magical drink into anything but a glass, so you can fully admire it.

The things that makes French cidre so appealing to the sweet-toothed American public—low alcohol, residual sweetness, and natural fruity character—mean that it doesn't always travel well, or cellar for very long. More than occasionally I've encountered scale or "breakage" (floating things) in the bottle. Although this isn't always fatal to the taste, it isn't acceptable from a visual stand-point, and such cider needs to be decanted through a filter before serving (an unbleached coffee filter does the trick).

Cider purchased directly at the farm gate in France is much less sweet than the typical Normandy export cider for sale in the U.S. The French generally classify their products by relative sweetness, as Cidre Doux (up to 3 percent alcohol by volume), Demi-Sec (3 to 5 percent abv.); and Cidre Brut (over 5 percent abv.). Cidre Bouche indicates a highly carbonated sweet cider that has had a secondary in-bottle fermentation.

In 2004 France made about 9 percent of the cider produced worldwide. Alongside cider, of course, the French also produce quite a lot of Calvados and other distilled cider brandy, as well as pommeau (a blend of cider brandy and unfermented apple juice). For more on both of these wonderful products, see chapter 8.

United Kingdom

The UK is far and away the leader in cider production, making about 48 percent of the world's total in 2004.[5] English cider operations vary widely, from small farm-scale cider mills to the huge H. P. Bulmer Ltd., an old and renowned company that dominates the British cider industry. Bulmer contracts with local orchardists for their apples, going so far as to provide trees, technical assistance, and a contract guaranteeing growers that the company will buy their apples for five to six years. Dabinett, Michelin, and Ellis Bitter are among the favored bittersweet varieties that Bulmer's contract growers raise.

In addition to its domestic sales, Bulmer also exports some of its brands overseas. North Americans are most likely to have encountered their sweet Woodpecker brand or the semidry Strongbow cider. In the 1990s Bulmer

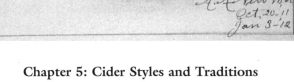

Chapter 5: Cider Styles and Traditions

even gained a brief foothold in the U.S. with its purchase of two cidermakers based in Vermont that make the popular Woodchuck and Cider Jack brands of industrial draft ciders. However, a few years ago Bulmer fell on rather evil times and the old family company was sold to Scottish & Newcastle, the huge beer company, which divested itself of Bulmer's North American holdings. The company's future, in this age of acquisition and consolidation, is at present anyone's guess.

Most of the English factory cidermakers resemble their large American counterparts in making a consistent product that is a bit higher in alcohol than French cider and fermented to dryness, then resweetened and artificially carbonated. They also frequently supplement fresh-pressed cider with concentrated apple juice. Instead of being sold like wine in champagne bottles, as in France, most mainstream English cider is sold on draft at pubs, where it competes for the beer drinker's pound or euro.

However, there is also a strong "real cider" movement afoot in Britain, spurred on by tradition and by organizations like the Campaign for Real Ale, or CAMRA (see "Resources"). A tour around the West Country of England and other cider-making counties proves that there is still a lot of regional variation among traditionally made ciders. Devonshire produces a sweet cider from apples with names like Tom Putt and Slack-My-Girdle. Devon cidermakers also use the process known as keeving (or *défécation* in French) to produce a slow-fermenting cider with residual sweetness (see chapter 10). Somerset cider is full-bodied and made from bittersweet apples like the various Jerseys, and the classic mild bittersharp known as Kingston Black, which produces one of the best and most distinctive single-variety ciders. Herefordshire and Worcestershire ciders use dual-purpose culinary/cider varieties like Cherry Norman and Genet Moyle, as well as bittersweets. Gloucestershire

produces a brisk-tasting cider with plenty of acidity, from apples like Foxwhelp and Redstreak.

In 2004 Ireland produced about 6 percent of the world's cider, not bad for a small island nation, and testament to the fact that the Irish like apples and cider, though not as much as Guinness. The major Irish brand is Magners, produced by the Irish company Bulmer (no relation to the English cidermaker). Several years ago Magners made a big push to enter the American market, and almost anyone who has had cider on draft at a big city bar has had this brand. The company's success has spurred sales of all kinds of cider in the UK as well, and a renewed demand for traditional ciders from smaller West Country producers.

In North America, amateur and small commercial cidermakers have only in recent years begun to explore the possibilities of using native apple varieties in their hard cider. To some extent, Americans have been looking to Europe for inspiration, with more and more orchardists planting classic English and French bittersweets and bittersharps. Yet many classic American apples also can be blended to produce distinctive and wonderful hard ciders, from the various russets to once famous commercial varieties like Baldwin and Newtown Pippin. Someday the U.S., too, may have its own distinctive and world-renowned cider regions, styles, and traditions. In fact, to some extent this is already happening, spurred on by the increasing awareness among consumers for local and regional foods. In time we may see regional cider styles emerging (or re-emerging) out of the Blue Ridge Mountains of Virginia and North Carolina, from the Great Lakes and Midwest, and in the Northeast and Northwest corners of the country. Until then, we owe it to ourselves to remain excited and open-minded, making and sampling any and all types of cider with an eye toward the best blends and varieties.

Basic Cider Styles

Despite the great variety of ciders out there, it is possible to identify and define a few basic categories into which most ciders fall. One of the best attempts at listing different styles of cider was made several years ago by Cézanne and Morgan Miller from Portland, Oregon, who created the Cider Space Web site, from which the following categories are drawn.[6]

In 2004 the Beer Judge Certification Program (BJCP) adopted its own style categories and specific guidelines for use in evaluating ciders, and these have been recently updated as of 2008. These guidelines were developed to assist both entrants and judges in sanctioned cider competitions like the annual Great Lakes Old World Syder Competion (GLOWS), held in Michigan. They are meant to provide a common vocabulary when discussing cider styles and production methods, and are definitely worth checking out online (www.bjcp.org).

Draft Cider

This is the most widely available style of cider in America, sold in six-packs like beer or sometimes in quart bottles or draft kegs. Draft cider is made from the juice of surplus dessert apples and fermented to dryness, to a much higher alcohol level than natural, unsweetened cider (up to 14 percent). Then it is filtered, cut with carbonated water and/or apple juice to around 5 or 6 percent alcohol, and sulfited before bottling. It is sweet or semisweet and should be drunk very cold, like lager beer.

Farmhouse or Farm Cider

This is the kind of cider discussed in chapter 4; it is also known as traditional or "real" cider or English dry cider. It is usually still and dry, fully fermented to 5 percent alcohol or higher, depending on the sweetness of the fresh juice and whether any sweeteners have been added.

French Cider

Also known as *cidre doux,* this style is popular in France and parts of England and Canada. The traditional method of making this type of cider relies on a process known as keeving or *défécation,* in which pectins and nitrogenous yeast nutrients are precipitated out of the fresh cider; then the clarified juice is siphoned into another container to begin a long, slow period of fermentation. French cider has some residual sweetness and is lower in alcohol than other styles, coming in at only 2 to 4 percent. It can be either still or effervescent.

Sparkling Cider

This term simply refers to a cider that has been carbonated in some way. This can be the result of natural carbonation, which is accomplished by secondary bottle fermentation of a small amount (a *dosage*) of sugar, or by the French "closed *cuvée*" method of making champagne, in which a few hundred gallons of hard cider are refermented in a closed vat, which is treated like an enormous champagne bottle. Alternatively, sparkling cider may be made by means of forced or artificial carbonation, in which carbon dioxide is injected into the cider during kegging or bottling.

The main difference between "sparkling" and "effervescent" ciders is the clarity and brilliance of the former, which is achieved through the removal of spent yeasts and other residues at the bottom of the bottle. This is done through the procedure known as *dégorgement,* in which the stoppered bottles are placed upside down in a rack placed in a freezer or ice/salt mixture (see chapter 10). In this way the lees in the bottle collect on the bottom of the cork and freeze there. Then the bottles are removed and wiped off, and the corks are expelled, taking the lees with them. Finally this sparkling "champagne cider" is fitted with new stoppers and wire cages. In contrast, "effervescent" ciders—though they also are carbonated by adding sugar and subjected to secondary, or bottle, fermentation— usually have a small residual yeast deposit at the bottom of the bottle.

Cyser

Cyser is a cider to which honey has been added as the only adjunct or sweetening agent. Cysers typically are slow to begin and to complete fermentation, and must be aged for anywhere from several months up to a year after bottling to mellow and improve in flavor, much like an apple wine.

The BJCP guidelines treat cyser as a subcategory of mead, or honey wine; they base this distinction on the

amount of honey added, and whether the honey or the cider provides the dominant flavor notes. They consider a product with honey added, but not dominant, as a type of specialty cider.

Apple Wine

To produce an apple wine (sometimes called "cider wine") sugar is added to cider to raise its specific gravity high enough to ensure that the final alcohol level will be between 10 and 12 percent. Some people prefer to add sugar to the fresh cider before fermentation; others advocate fermenting a hard cider to dryness, then adding sugar and sometimes raisins to start a second fermentation. Fresh cider is normally treated with sulfites before fermentation to suppress wild yeasts and bacteria, and then pitched with a white wine or champagne yeast; often, yeast nutrient and pectic enzyme are added as well (see chapter 4). For a fuller discussion of apple wine, see he following page.

New England–Style Cider

This is a still or effervescent cider fortified with either white or brown sugar, molasses, concentrated cider, or other sweeteners to achieve a final alcohol level of 8 to 14 percent. Sun-dried, preservative-free raisins are usually added following the first vigorous fermentation phase to contribute a bit more sugar, tannin, and natural yeasts. Carbonation must be natural, and only wild or wine yeasts may be used.

Specialty Ciders

These include ciders that contain either juice from other fruits or herbs, spices, or other flavoring. Some draft cider companies make cranberry- and raspberry-flavored ciders that are flavored with stabilized juice or concentrate after fermentation; however, a better way to make these specialty ciders at home is to blend the fruit juice or whole fruit in with the fresh cider and let everything ferment together. Generally speaking, the volume of non-apple juice should be 25 percent or less, with the possible exception of pear/apple cider, which works well as a half-and-half blend (sweet or fermented) and which the British sometimes call "pider." For information on real perry, fermented pear juice, see chapter 7.

Specific recipes for making all the above cider styles and variations can be found in many of the how-to books that deal with homebrewing or winemaking. The best recipes I've used come from Paul Correnty's excellent book *The Art of Cidermaking* (Brewers Publications, 1995), which is currently out of print, but available used. It is particularly strong on cysers and specialty ciders. For good information on making French cider or sparkling champagne cider, consult the classic book *Cider: Making, Using & Enjoying Sweet & Hard Cider,* by Annie Proulx and Lew Nichols (Storey, 2003), now in its third edition.

Recipes are great to consult when you're first starting out, but once you've made a few batches of cider you will probably discover, as I have, that cidermaking is mainly about understanding the basic process and then finding and using the best-quality fruit that you can get your hands on.

Apple Wine

Except for apple wine's greater alcoholic strength, there is really little or no difference between it and hard cider. Both can be made in the same way, and in fact a cider that has been sweetened with sugar, raisins, or other adjuncts like honey, and fermented to dryness using a wine or champagne yeast (like some New England–style ciders), is more or less indistinguishable from apple wine, and may be even stronger.

Just as an aside, the technical term for adding sugar to raise the specific gravity of a wine or cider must (juice) is *chaptalization.* Almost no one except winemakers use the word, but it's a common practice in northern Europe and other grape-growing regions where the climate in general, or the specific growing season, may not be warm enough to produce grapes with a consistently high Brix (fruit sugar) level. Although he didn't invent the idea, the term is named for Jean-Antoine Chaptal, who was not only a chemist, but also Napoleon's minister of the interior at the beginning of the nineteenth century. Commercial winemakers often add cane sugar (in much the same way as was described in chapter 4 for bringing up a low specific gravity in cider), but they also make use of other types of sugar, including beet sugar and concentrated grape must. In a similar way, some cidermakers amend the sugar levels in their fresh juice with apple juice concentrate.

Because apple wine is usually aged longer than hard cider before drinking, some cidermakers take this opportunity to mature it in oak barrels, or suspend a mesh bag of oak chips in the wine, to give it more of a winelike complexity and structure (see chapter 10 for more on oak chips and barrel fermentation). Most authorities agree that the best-tasting apple wines are a bit lighter and more delicate than grape wines, with an alcoholic content of only 10 to 11 percent. Because most apples don't contain nearly as much natural sugar as wine grapes, it is necessary to sweeten the fresh-pressed juice, to bring the sugars up to about 20 or 21 degrees Brix (see the discussion of specific gravity in chapter 4 and the specific gravity/Brix/potential alcohol table in the appendix).

There is great potential for making wonderful single-variety apple wines from North American dessert fruits. Greg Failing, who developed several award-winning varietal apple wines for the former Joseph Cerniglia Winery in Cavendish, Vermont, knows a lot about wine—and about draft cider, too. When I met him back in the late 1990s, he was the winemaster at Green Mountain Cidery in Springfield, Vermont—one of the largest cider producers in North America and the maker of Woodchuck ciders, a brand that also originated with the Cerniglia Winery and that in its history has been owned by such major industry players as Stroh's Brewing and England's H. P. Bulmer.

Failing says that every apple has its own distinctive characteristics when it is made into wine, which can be described in terms of classic white wine styles to someone who already knows about different grape wines. Take, for instance, Golden Delicious. The Golden Delicious wine that Greg made for Cerniglia contained about 3.5 to 4 percent residual sugar and had all the sweetness of a classic Sauternes, but with the distinctive flavor and bouquet of a Golden Delicious apple.

Other familiar apple varieties that Failing experimented with include McIntosh and Macoun, which share many of the same characteristics; Empire, which he made like a Chardonnay, aging it over oak chips; Granny Smith—one and a half times sweeter than McIntosh, with twice the acidity—which produces a wine that resembles Chablis, but a little tarter; and Northern Spy, whose spicy bouquet is reminiscent of a classic Gewürztraminer. All of these varietal wines have a fresh, fruity character when they are drunk young. However, after a year or two they develop into an even closer approximation of fine grape wines, perfect for sipping or as an accompaniment to any foods with which you would serve white wine.

Failing told me that the wines he developed for Cerniglia had at first to overcome the prejudice against non-grape wines. Most people still think of apple wines as something like Boone's Farm or Thunderbird, served al fresco on a park bench or railroad siding, usually inside a paper bag. But when Cerniglia entered its wines in a Dallas competition, in the "mixed varietal" category, the judges weren't informed that they were made from apples, and awarded them silver and gold medals the first time around. Wine critic Robert Parker tasted Cerniglia's wines and also gave them high marks, in the 1980s and 1990s. And although the U.S. government doesn't allow non-grape wines to call themselves a "vintage," Cerniglia's apple wines were among the first to have the harvest date of the apples printed on their labels. A far cry from Thunderbird.

In the years since this book first appeared, I've had the chance to sample a number of apple wines from various regions of the country. Most small wineries produce an apple wine, though few of them in my opinion are very distinguished, mainly because they are too sweet, too alcoholic, or use indifferent dessert apples. However, one producer who is making superior and interesting wines is Charles McGonegal of AEppelTreow Winery (pronounced "apple true") in Burlington, Wisconsin.

Clearly, there is as much to learn about making fine apple wines as there is about hard cider. But the fact that people like Greg Failing and Charles McGonegal have tried and succeeded in making distinctive, high-quality wines from all kinds of American apples should encourage and inspire amateur and commercial winemakers alike. Good wine grapes are choosy about where they grow; very few of them are hardy enough to grow in New England or other regions of North America that experience cold, harsh winters. Rather than waiting for global warming to occur, it makes a lot more sense to produce great wines from the fruit that *does* grow well for almost everyone—the apple.

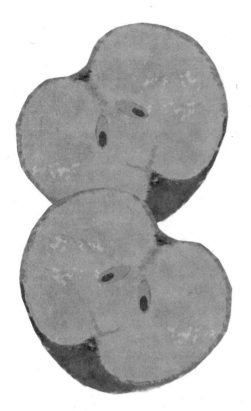

Heaven's sweetest blessing, hail!
Be thou the copious matter of my
song, and thy choice nectar; on
which always waits Laughter and
sport, and care-beguiling wit,
and friendship, chief delight of
human life. What should we wish
for more? or why, in quest
Of foreign vintage, insincere, and
mixt, Traverse th'extremest world?

—John Philips (1676–1709) from *Cider, Book I*

6. TASTING AND EVALUATING CIDER

NO MATTER HOW SATISFYING THE PROCESS OF CIDERMAKING MIGHT BE, the real payoff comes when you uncap or uncork a bottle—preferably your own homemade stock—and pour it out for friends and family to enjoy. A well-made cider is a sociable drink, one that is almost guaranteed to create a sense of generosity and goodwill. Not as strong as wine, nor as filling as beer, hard cider warms the heart and frees the spirit in a unique and wonderful way that must be experienced to be truly understood.

I can still recall my first taste of real hard cider, brought up from the cellar in a quart bottle by a farmer friend I was visiting in Springfield, Vermont. It was late February, the season of lambing and blustery pre-spring snow squalls. Everything on the kitchen table that Sunday afternoon had been grown or made within a stone's throw of where we were sitting. From the rich golden butter on home-baked bread to the carrots and roast chicken, the freshness and flavor of simple food that tasted like it is was meant to make this meal one of the best and most memorable of my life. And the cider itself—still and cold, fragrant and fruity—provided the perfect foil for both dinner and conversation. We lingered long over the table, and made more than one return trip to the cellar. That cider was nothing short of a revelation to me and my poor unwitting taste buds; the full flavor of golden apples fairly burst in my mouth. Suddenly I understood what people meant by "the good life," and I wouldn't have traded that dinner, or that company of friends, for King Solomon's riches.

On a social drinking level, cider has certain advantages over its close cousins, beer and wine. For instance, two people can easily split a large bottle (750 ml) of hard cider over lunch and still manage to function for the rest of the day—especially if they choose one of the naturally sparkling ciders made in the French style, which typically contain a mere 3 or 4 percent alcohol by volume. On a hot summer day, with the sound of thunder booming in the distance, there's nothing quite like sitting out on the porch with a glass of cool sparkling cider, a salad of fresh-picked lettuce, and a thick slice of good whole-grain bread. To accompany such a light repast, beer seems out of place, and wine is best saved for later, when the day's work is done and, as Pindar puts it, "the troublesome cares of humanity / drift from our hearts, and on seas of luxury streaming in gold / we swim together,

and make for a shore that is nowhere." (Employers these days tend to frown on midday swimming to nowhere.) Of course, as with anything else, one can overindulge in cider, but for many people a couple of glasses serve to heighten rather than dull the senses. It offers a more civilized, pleasant, and healthful alternative to the proverbial three-martini lunch.

Perhaps the best way to educate your palate and discover the many kinds of cider that are available is to host a cider tasting for friends, neighbors, and fellow enthusiasts. Not only is this a good excuse for a party, but it also allows you to gather valuable and interesting opinions from many people at one time. This chapter introduces some of the criteria used in evaluating cider, but the final determination, of course, will involve your own individual senses, your personal likes and dislikes.

Organizing a Cider Tasting

Ideally, a successful cider tasting should include three distinct classes of people: cider neophytes, cider aficionados, and cidermakers. The first type, neophytes, is easy to find; especially in the U.S., almost everyone has friends who rarely, if ever, have tasted real hard cider but who are keen to try it. The second group, the aficionados, are people who have had some exposure to cider; they aren't necessarily experts, but they may have tried different styles of cider and generally they "know what they like." Third, there are those people who make their own cider, which gives them valuable insight into why a particular brand of cider is good, bad, or indifferent. Another reason to invite a few cidermakers is that they invariably will bring along a bottle or two of their "best stuff," which can be either entered and scored as part of a blind tasting (if they don't mind constructive criticism) or sampled before or after the judging (if they're sensitive souls).

Any number of people can participate in a tasting, though having a critical mass of at least ten guests tends to make things more lively, and the final results more significant. The purpose of inviting lots of people with varying degrees of "cider literacy" is to cancel out the more extreme tastes and judgments on either side of the equation. For instance, in the first tasting that I held, many of the first-time cider drinkers showed a preference for the sweeter types of draft cider, while the cidermakers and aficionados generally preferred ciders with a sharper profile or fuller body, even tolerating those with a pretty funky or unusual aftertaste. Combining the scores from all the participants helped to level the playing field. In practical terms it meant that not many of the ciders sampled received an overall score very near the top (10) or very near the bottom (0).

Collecting Ciders for Your Tasting

Which styles or brands of cider should you include in your tasting? It depends very much on what's available in your area. In most parts of the country, it's easy to find a few nationally distributed brands of draft cider, usually sold in six-packs at beer and wine outlets. Woodchuck, Cider Jack, Hard Core, and Hornsby's are familiar brand names, and each of these companies markets several styles (typically a basic draft cider; a "black" or "dark and dry" that is sweetened with caramelized sugar; and various specialty ciders like apple-cranberry and apple-raspberry). These national brands, to me at least, are all fairly similar in terms of taste and quality. My first tasting consisted of many of these draft ciders, but after that I included just a few of the drafts that had scored best the first time around. Another alternative is to seek out draft ciders produced by smaller companies,

ones that have more of a regional distribution. In the West or Northwest this might mean a brand like Ace, Wyder's, or Spire Mountain; in the East, Harpoon Brewing Co. started marketing a new draft cider in 2007. The company says that Harpoon Cider is made from fresh-pressed Vermont apples (not from concentrate), and contains no preservatives, artificial colors, or sweeteners. The debut edition was apparently made chiefly from surplus McIntosh apples. Overall, the draft cider market, though strong and growing, is also quite volatile; aside from the national brands, you'll just have to see what's available in your area.

Regional cideries and wineries represent the next level of sophistication in terms of different and more interesting styles. For instance, one of the best small cideries in the country, West County Cider in Colrain, Massachusetts, produces a broad range of ciders throughout the year, enough to justify an entire tasting on their own. West County uses some classic European cider apples, like Reine de Pomme and Dabinett, but also makes several varietal ciders made predominantly from heritage American apples like Baldwin, Golden Russet, and Redfield. Owners Terry and Judith Maloney, who come from a winemaking background in California, use only their own homegrown apples and those from local orchards, in the best tradition of European artisanal cidermaking.

The good news is that more and more orchardists around the country are actively planting or grafting classic European cider apples, or experimenting with good old American varieties. At Farnum Hill Ciders in Lebanon, New Hampshire, cidermaker Stephen Wood has grafted lots of uncommon dessert apples and English bittersweets alike onto his family orchard's old McIntosh trees, as well as planting nearly forty new acres to classic cider apples. In the 1980s, as New England land values

Chapter 6: Tasting and Evaluating Cider

were increasing and the prospects for small wholesale orcharding began to look grim, Wood took the plunge and decided to specialize in these apples that, as he says, "nobody would ever want to eat." Today he is regarded as something of a visionary and an American cider pioneer, and his Poverty Lane Orchards is selling a large surplus of cider apples that Wood can't use himself to other cidermakers, large and small—for prices that are far better than the base price for surplus and ungraded dessert fruit. And similar tales could be told from all around the country, from Diane Flynt's heritage orchard at Foggy Ridge Cider in rural southwest Virginia, to Richard Anderson's European apple plantings at Westcott Bay Cider in Friday Harbor, Washington.

The bad news is that not everyone lives within easy driving distance of such farmhouse cider mills and small-scale wineries. What's more, various antediluvian state liquor laws (a patchwork of rules that followed the repeal of Prohibition) currently limit the amount of mail-order business these cideries can do. Fortunately, with the resources of the Internet at our disposal, it only takes a little searching by key words (your state, or the names of neighboring states, and "hard cider" usually does the trick) to find the closest cidery to your location. As local artisanal cider becomes increasingly visible, it will also become easier to find it at state or private liquor stores. Sometimes store managers don't quite know where to put it ("Next to the Boone's Farm or the sake?"), but this situation is beginning to improve as well.

Homemade ciders—either your own or those made by other tasters—are always welcome at a tasting, of course, regardless of the style they represent (see chapter 5). Imported ciders, from Canada and from Europe, are also worth seeking out, and in my experience can be found in some of the larger liquor outlets, especially those near major cities. For comparison with American draft ciders, it's worth tracking down a few bottles of a commercial English draft cider, such as K or Dry Blackthorn (made by Gaymer's), Woodpecker and Strongbow (from H. P. Bulmer), or Magner's (made by Bulmers, Ltd. in Ireland). And although real Spanish *sidra natural* is at present almost impossible to find in the U.S., there are a few examples of more sophisticated ciders from France (Bordelet, Comte de Lauriston, Drouin, and Dupont are all good choices) and the UK (Gwatkin and Sheppy's are sometimes available). The problem with finding good, representative British ciders in this country is that most of the typical "farm" ciders of the West Country are never bottled for export and are sold, well, at the farm gate, typically in one- or two-litre plastic bottles. I recall flying home from London a few years ago with a quart of Somerset cider in my carry-on. (Thanks to international terrorism, those days of relatively care-free travel are probably a thing of the past.

Canada, though, offers an easier option for Americans than trans-Atlantic smuggling. The number of small farm cideries in Quebec is truly impressive, and I am always amazed at the excellent ciders they produce from apple varieties that are okay but unspectacular as cider apples down in the U.S. (McIntosh, Cortland, Lodi, Spartan, et al.). Other provinces, notably British Columbia, Ontario, New Brunswick, and Nova Scotia, can boast some good small cideries that are well worth checking out. Encourage your cider-loving friends to bring back bottles from their trips up north.

The total number of ciders in the tasting is partly a function of how successful your scavenger hunt has been and partly limited by the patience and palates of your guests. My first tasting featured 27 kinds of cider, which is far too ambitious, especially for cider novices. Since then I have tried to limit my offerings to around 12 to 15 varieties at most. Also, in that first venture I included as many ciders as I could find, regardless of style. That's not a bad idea for your first tasting; however, as you learn more about cider, it's possible to organize subsequent tastings to emphasize, for instance, single-variety ciders, or European versus North American ciders, compared head-to-head within the different styles.

Props and Procedures

Keeping a few basic tips in mind helps to ensure a smooth and successful cider tasting. First, use transparent glasses or cups, so that tasters will be able to evaluate the color and general appearance of the cider. Some people recommend using glassware only, letting guests rinse their glasses with water after each sample. For a large group of tasters, I prefer the ease and economy of small clear plastic cups. A large supply costs only a few dollars, so a fresh cup can be used for each new cider sample. In the end, the choice is a personal and aesthetic one. Some experts claim that plastic can affect the flavor of cider; others maintain that a thin film of dish detergent on glass will do the same. I haven't encountered problems with either glass or plastic.

Every taster will need a pen or pencil and a score sheet with space enough for brief comments on each cider. The form I now use (see the Sample Cider Tasting Score Sheet on page 105) is a very simplified version; you can make yours much more involved if you prefer. For a friendly, informal tasting I prefer to keep things uncomplicated and so use a scale of 0 to 10, which relates to overall quality and drinkability. The most important criteria for judging a cider's quality are discussed in the section "Evaluating Cider," on page 103.

Because the cider tasting is also a social occasion, it's good to have some kind of food on hand. Cheese is a simple and natural accompaniment to cider, so long as it is mild-flavored; a strong-tasting variety like Stilton or extra-sharp Cheddar will overwhelm the delicate taste of most ciders. But soft cheeses like Camembert and Pont l'Évêque, both of which come from Normandy, will complement cider nicely. The same goes for all other hors d'oeuvres you serve or ask people to bring to the party: A yogurt or sour cream dip for raw vegetables is fine; garlicky hummus is not. Sliced baguette rounds or unsalted crackers work well as a foundation for cheese, pâté, or some other spread, or even eaten plain as a way to clear the palate between tastings. Similarly, it's good to keep a pitcher of water on the table and another, empty pitcher for people to use when they want to dispose of an uninspiring (or undrinkable) cider sample.

Speaking of cheeses, for the past several years I have had the honor of leading cider and cheese pairings along with some of the nation's top cheese authors and cheesemongers. These tastings are rather different than those focused exclusively on cider, because the object is to find the best matches between ciders and cheeses. In general, strong cheeses, especially blue types, pair well with sweeter ciders, or even fortified dessert wines like pommeau or ice cider (see chapter 8). Otherwise, this is not an exact science, since ciders and cheeses from individual producers vary so much. You might try a fruity cider with a fresh chevre, but a more acidic or sparkling cider with an aged goat cheese, for instance. For a party tasting, I suggest buying four or five different types of cheese (sheep, cow, or goat's milk; young and aged styles), and then having guests try a sip of each cider with a bite of each cheese, then scoring them and seeing which make the best pairings. For a good book on American artisan cheeses, I recommend Jeff Robert's *The Atlas of American Farmstead Cheese* (Chelsea Green, 2007), which profiles cheesemakers all across the U.S. and describes the cheeses they make, as well as giving suggested pairings with cider, beer, and wine.

Chapter 6: Tasting and Evaluating Cider

The best and fairest way to rate different ciders is by the method known as blind tasting. This involves covering over the labels on the cider bottles with plain sheets of paper, assigning a number to each one, and keeping the names of the brands or cidermakers a secret until after the tasting and the scoring are over. This way there's less chance that judges will, for instance, subconsciously knock a commercial draft cider in favor of a small artisanal one. After all, in a tasting what you're rating is the cider itself—not its packaging, origins, or reputation.

The number that you assign to each cider will reflect the order of the tasting. The order is up to you: Most authorities recommend serving lighter, lower-alcohol ciders first, then following up with the stronger, more full-bodied examples. In my first tasting I divided the twenty-seven types of cider into unequal halves (fourteen and thirteen), with an "intermission" for people to catch their breath and clear their palates. The first half I devoted mainly to dry and semisweet ciders; the second half was for sweeter and specialty types. Whenever possible, I put two or more similar styles of cider one after the other in the order of tasting. For instance, I lumped together two "dark and dry" draft ciders at the end of the evening, which allowed guests to compare them head-to-head without overwhelming the ciders that preceded them.

One of my pet peeves is when "experts" rounded up by a newspaper conduct a cider tasting and publish their results, after tasting a sweet, carbonated commercial draft cider, for example, against a bone-dry, still cider from a small craft cidermaker. If these same experts were asked to taste a bunch of Rieslings alongside a few big California cabernets they would refuse, for obvious reasons. But the number of brands of cider that are widely available in the U.S. is still limited, and it's often difficult to focus a tasting to compare "apples to apples." This is

okay; just do it for fun at home, and don't read too much into the advice of the experts; the fact is, we are all in the process of rediscovering cider in this country, and you are probably as much of an expert as anyone. Another natural, but common, error is to fault a cider for not "tasting like apples." After all, no one complains that wine doesn't taste like table grapes, or that beer doesn't taste the same as raw barley. Typically, the original flavors of any fresh-pressed juice are metabolized or lost during the fermentation process, and they're replaced by new flavors that are formed by the yeast acting on compounds in the juice. Sometimes the flavors in the finished cider are the same or similar to those that were lost in fermentation, but it certainly doesn't follow that a cider will taste the same as the apples it is made from. Understanding this makes it easier to get "beyond the apple," and to enjoy the complex flavors and aromas that a well-made cider can possess, from fresh citrus fruits to leather and smoky bacon.

Following the tasting, reveal all of the cider labels and let people compare notes as the party breaks up. Offer some dessert and a full glass of a nice sparkling cider or perry. Collect the score sheets and then, in the next day or two, tote up the results—first totaling all the scores for each cider and then dividing by the number of tasters who rated it. Then compile a list showing which ciders scored best and worst (see "Sample Cider-Tasting Results" on page 106 for an example) and send these results out to everyone who participated in the tasting.

It's interesting to note that a cider that may not seem all that impressive in a tasting against other ciders can taste very different when enjoyed with food. So after the tasting party is over, don't throw away that bottle of cider that no one especially liked. Set it aside in the refrigerator for a day or two, then try it again with a meal. Some ciders, like some wines, just are just better as a complement to food than they are for contemplative (or competitive) sipping.

In my experience, the ciders that tend to score the highest are well-balanced ones that appeal broadly to the entire group of tasters, but that do not necessarily have the most character or "personality." Among neophytes or fans of very sweet, fruit-forward cider, one of the draft types that has a lot of sugar added after fermentation or a French *cidre* will probably do well. For a person who prefers dry white wine, an austere, fairly dry, still cider will rank high. The overall winners, though, tend to be well-made consensus favorites, and this in itself is significant.

Evaluating Cider

The three most important characteristics to consider when judging any cider are appearance, aroma, and flavor. Each of these individual components contributes to the overall quality and drinkability of the cider, and each should be taken into account when you evaluate it.

Wine connoisseurs have their own vocabulary for describing various vintages and styles, often comparing the wine's flavor to other suggestive descriptors like vanilla, blackberries, pineapple, and so on. Cider tasters have a similar shared vocabulary, though it tends to be much more basic and a lot less highfalutin than that used by wine fanciers. The taste or smell of cider may be acidic (sharp), acetic (vinegary), astringent (high in tannin), or any one of numerous other adjectives: chemical, fruity, musty, sulfuric, sweet, woody, yeasty. (For definitions of some common descriptors, see "Common Cider-Tasting Terms" on page 107.)

The appearance of a hard cider is evident as soon as it is poured into the glass. The most basic distinction is between *still cider* (without carbonation) and *sparkling cider* (with either natural or forced carbonation). Naturally sparkling cider will foam up as it hits the bot-

tom of the glass, and the bubbles that swirl up to the surface are smaller and longer-lasting than those in an artificially carbonated cider. Clarity is another aspect of a cider's appearance, and it is usually described as brilliant, clear, slightly hazy, hazy, or cloudy. Most cidermakers strive to make a drink that is brilliantly clear, or nearly so, but there is nothing inherently wrong with a slight haze, especially in a homemade or unfiltered farmhouse-style cider or perry. Just be sure not to shake up a bottle before decanting it if you see that it has a bottom sediment of yeast—this will spoil the cider's appearance. Finally, the color of cider can range from pale straw to rich golden yellow, from delicate salmon or apricot to medium amber, or even darker, depending on the varieties of apples used as well as certain adjuncts like caramelized sugar. For example, the classic Harrison cider apple makes an especially rich, dark-colored cider. Some ciders are naturally tinged pink like a rosé wine because they're made with red-fleshed apple varieties such as Redfield and Red-Veined Crab. However, a green, gray, or orange-red cast to a normal cider may indicate a serious problem, such as excessive oxidation or cider sickness (see page 78).

A hard cider's aroma or bouquet usually comes from the percentage of fragrant apple varieties that were used in the original cider blend—ones like McIntosh, Red Delicious, and Cox's Orange Pippin. Yeasts, both natural and cultured, plus other fruits, spices, or adjuncts (like honey in cyser) can also contribute to the complex aroma of a good cider. To evaluate the aroma, put your nose near the top of the glass and take a good whiff; the cider's bouquet should be a preview of its flavor. If it smells bad or is excessively sharp or vinegary, don't even bother tasting the cider.

Flavor is the most complex, and important, part of a cider's character and will determine ultimately how drinkable it is and how well it rates with you. When evaluating a cider, it's a good idea to "chew" it a bit with your head tipped back slightly, incorporating some air into your mouth and warming the cider. Most good ciders will continue to release a pleasant bouquet. Another thing to note as you roll the cider around in your mouth is its body, or lack of same. A full-bodied cider will have a heavier, richer mouthfeel than a lighter style with a lower alcoholic content. Both can be good; a cider that is thin or watery, however, won't measure up in terms of taste or quality.

Other components of flavor to mention include a cider's sweetness or dryness, which should be obvious, and its balance, which is when all the elements that go into making the cider are in harmony and none of them overshadows any of the others. Particularly important is the balance between sugars and acids. When there is a good balance, the cider will have just the right amount of sweetness for the style, and the acids will lend it a zest or briskness that stimulates the palate and contributes to a pleasant, lively taste. Malic acid is the primary acid in cider, but as we've seen in chapter 4, the malolactic fermentation that often takes place after primary fermentation can convert some of the malic acid to lactic acid, which helps cut the sharpness of an acidic cider and lends it a smooth nuttiness. The other important aspect of balance is that between the alcohol in a cider and the tannins. In a cider with a higher alcoholic content, such as a New England style, it's important that the alcohol doesn't create a "hot" taste in the mouth—something that the astringency of tannins helps to counter.

Various authors over the years have attempted to define what constitutes a perfect glass of cider. One of the fullest and best descriptions was made by J. M. Trowbridge in *The Cider Maker's Handbook*, originally published in 1890:

A pure article of cider, skillfully made from select fruit in perfect condition, should have perfect limpidity and brightness, even to sparkling in the glass; it may vary in color from a delicate straw to a rich amber color, more or less deep, but should never be bright red, nor, indeed, show much of a roseate tinge. It should be fragrant, so that when a bottle is freshly opened and poured into glasses an agreeable, fruity perfume will arise and diffuse itself through the apartment, "with a benison on the giver." It should be tart, like Rhine wine, and by no means sharp or harsh. It should have a pleasant, fruity flavor, with aromatic and vinous blending, as if the fruit had been packed in flowers and spices. It should have a mild pungency, and feel warming and grateful to the stomach, the glow diffusing itself gradually and agreeably throughout the whole system, and communicating itself to the spirits. It should have a light body or substance about like milk, with the same softness or smoothness, and it should leave in the mouth an abiding agreeable flavor of some considerable duration, as of rare fruits and flowers.[1]

However, despite all the variables that come into play when you are evaluating a great cider, the final determining factor is always your own taste, and individual preferences can vary widely. I have seen results of tastings, published in newspapers or magazines, in which a panel of judges extols some brand of cider that I've tried myself and wouldn't drink again on a Halloween bet. The important thing is not to feel intimidated by the terminology of cider tasting: The words are there merely to help you express what your senses are already trying to tell you. As Thomas Hobbes once wrote, "Words are wise men's counters, they do but reckon with them; but they are the currency of fools." At the end of the day, the best cider is, simply, the one you like the best. *Vive la différence.*

SAMPLE CIDER-TASTING SCORE SHEET

The following cider score sheet is similar to ones I have used at my tastings. For people who are new to the terminology of cider tasting, I recommend handing out a list of common descriptors (see pages 107–108) before the tasting, to give them a point of reference for their own comments. The sample notes and scores for the ciders below suggest that certain ciders (usually the really good and the really bad ones) elicit the most comments.

Name:_____ Date: _____

Please evaluate and characterize the appearance (color, clarity), aroma, and flavor of each entry.

Assign ratings for drinkability and overall quality on a scale of 0 to 10.

Code No. Notes (Appearance, Aroma, Flavor)   Score

1 slightly sweet, balanced but bland. 3
2 sherry-like aftertaste; still, slight haze 6
3 ruity; nice carbonation; a bit too sweet 7
4 semisweet; medium amber color; tiny bubbles. 5
5 woody; tobacco-like aftertaste; not enough acid 5
6 good apple flavor; smooth. 8
7 light taste; vegetal aroma; good balance 7
8 unpleasant, harsh taste like sulfur or fuel oil 2
9 strong clovelike flavor and aroma; like mouthwash 3
10 balanced bittersweet; highly flavored. 9
11 bland taste; lacks character; too sweet 3
12 clean, crisp apple flavor; nice finish; fine bubbles. 7
13 musty, chemical, sulfur taste; needs acid; slightly green 2
14 very spicy, more like an apple wine; slightly medicinal 5
15 bland; sulfur aftertaste; not enough carbonation 4
16 still; undistinguished 3
17 citrusy; aftertaste like a pineapple Lifesaver 3
18 refreshing; very attractive color; lacks astringency 5
19 pretty good cranberry flavor, but too sweet. 2
20 very sweet; not much flavor 2
21 nice apple flavor; sweetness balanced with acid 5
22 slightly sweet; refreshing apple flavor; sugary aftertaste 6
23 woody, smoky, earthy, strong, unpleasant 2
24 very sweet, cloying 1
25 strong medicinal taste; like chewy cough syrup 2
26 caramel flavor; like root beer. 3

Chapter 6: Tasting and Evaluating Cider

SAMPLE CIDER-TASTING RESULTS

To determine the overall score for a cider, add the individual scores together, then divide by the number of people rating it. The following are the top-scoring ciders from a private tasting I held in 2001.

Rank	ID No./Order	Brand/Producer/Location	Ave. Score
1	11	Tremlett's Cider (5.2% abv) West County Cider, Colrain, MA	7.346
2	9	Redfield Cider (4%) West County Cider, Colrain, MA	6.231
3	16	Vermont Sparkling Cyder (9.5%) Flag Hill Farm, Vershire, VT	6.142
4	2	K Draft Cider (6.9%) Matthew Clark Brands, Bristol, UK	5.833
5	8	1999 Esopus Spitzenburg Cider (9.2%) Farnum Hill Ciders, Lebanon, NH	5.769
6	1	Gale's Hard Cider (7%) Thomas Family Winery, Madison, IN	5.692
7	10	New England Cider (7%)—sl. sweet Russell Orchards, Ipswich, MA	5.654
8	12	White Oak Cider (6.8%) White Oak Cider, Newberg, OR	5.385
9	15	Green Mountain Mac Cider Wine (11%) Putney Mountain Winery, Putney, VT	5.115
10	14	Cider & Perry (7%) Russell Orchards, Ipswich, MA	4.615
11	6	1999 Ashmead's Kernel Cider Farnum Hill Ciders, Lebanon, NH	4.538
12	17	Heirloom Cuvee Cider Wine (11%) Putney Mountain Winery, Putney, VT	4.385
13	3	New England Cider (7%)—dry Russell Orchards, Ipswich, MA	4.333
14	5	Reine de Pomme Farm-Style Cider (6.7%) West County Cider, Colrain, MA	4.292
15	7	2000 Cote des Blancs Still Cider Ben Watson, Francestown, NH Ben Watson, Francestown, NH	4.192
16	4	Cidre Bouche Doux (3%) Gerard Maeyaert, Milly-sur-Therain, Haut-Normandie, France	3.417
17	13	Savannah Dry Premium Cider (6%) Stellenbosch Farmer's Winery, Stellenbosch, Capetown, South Africa	2.654

COMMON CIDER-TASTING TERMS

The following definitions were adapted from a cider score sheet once used by judges in the National Homebrew Competition, sponsored by the American Homebrewers Association (see "Resources"). Obviously, there are many more adjectives and comparative terms that can be used to describe the appearance, aroma, and flavor of a cider. However, even highly creative or imaginative tasters will benefit from reading these definitions before judging, if only to develop some general frame of reference. I also recommend reading the Cider Guidelines and Style Categories for cider and perry that are used currently by the Beer Judge Certification Program (www.bjcp.org).

Acetic—A smell and sharp taste like vinegar, solvent, or acetone/nail polish remover; a distinct fault in cider, caused by acetic or lactic acid bacteria.

Acidity—The presence of malic acid, which balances sweetness and is responsible for the briskness or zing in cider.

Alcoholic—The general effect of ethanol and higher alcohols. The taste is warming.

Astringent—A drying sensation in the mouth, similar to sucking on a tea bag. Due to excess tannin and acceptable only in a young cider.

Aftertaste—The lingering taste in the back of the throat. Ideally long and pleasant.

Balanced—No component of the cider overpowers another. An alcoholic cider is balanced by tannin, a sweet cider by crisp acidity.

Body—The "middle" of a mouthful of cider. Good body will feel heavy in the mouth.

Bouquet—Also known as the aroma, smell, or nose.

Carbonation—Naturally carbonated cider has small, beading bubbles. An artificially carbonated (force-carbonated) cider has large, uniform bubbles.

Clarity—The visual aspect of cider, described as brilliant, clear, slightly hazy, hazy, or cloudy.

Clean—Free from apparent "off" odors or flavors.

Diacetyl—Aroma and flavor described as buttery, butterscotch, or toffee; in moderation, and in certain regional styles, can contribute to flavor; in large concentrations, it's a fault.

Dry—A sensation on the tongue that indicates a lack of residual sugar. Dryness varies from bone-dry to dry, off-dry, and semidry.

Estery—Sweet-solvent, chemical, banana or tropical fruit flavors; artificial fruity-floral aroma.

Fruity—May indicate fruitiness in flavor and/or aroma.

Hot—An unpleasant taste sensation due to excess alcohol content.

Light—Refers to the body and is descriptive, not negative, as opposed to "thin."

Metallic—A tinny or coppery taste caused by exposure to certain metals; not a good thing.

Moldy (or musty)—An unpleasant smell sometimes compared to damp cardboard or sherry. Due to oxidation or overfiltration of cider.

Mousy—A cider disorder caused by lactic acid bacteria. The cider smells and tastes like the bottom of a rodent's den.

Oxidized—The chemical oxidation of stored cider or perry in contact with air or containing high levels of dissolved oxygen; color can be dark golden brown; aroma and taste described as stale, leathery, caramelized, or sherry-like.

Phenolic—A plastic taste and smell caused by some wild yeasts and bacteria. Also sometimes described as smoky, pitchy, medicinal, barny, or leathery.

Sparkling—Having carbonation.

Still—Lacking carbonation.

Sulfuric—A smell or taste like burnt matches. Due to fermentation at high temperatures or excessive use of sulfites.

Sweet—The basic taste associated with sugar; appropriate to certain styles of cider.

Thin—Lacking body.

Woody—A taste or aroma usually caused by cider aging for an extended length of time in oak casks or in contact with wood chips.

Yeasty—A breadlike aroma caused by a cider sitting on its lees (spent yeast) for an extended period.

Young—A cider with components that have not yet matured into a balanced whole.

DEUTSCHE POMOLOGIE   I.30

CHAMPAGNER REINETTE

Gem. v. W. Lauche   Verlag v. Wiegandt, Hempel & Parey in Berlin

7. PERRY, OR PEAR CIDER

PEARS AND APPLES ARE CLOSELY RELATED POME FRUITS, and along with quince, medlar, hawthorn, and other fruits are members of the large Rose Family (Roseaceae). Yet perry—either the fresh or fermented juice made from pears—is not nearly as well known as cider. That's a shame, because well-made perry is a lovely drink, one that more people should definitely seek out and try. As America redevelops its taste for good cider, though, can perry be far behind?

This chapter is far from a definitive guide to the subject of perry, but the fact is that very little has been written on the subject in recent years. The classic work on the subject, *Perry Pears,* edited by Luckwill and Pollard and issued in the 1960s by the now-defunct Long Ashton Research Station in England (see Bibliography), is a good basic overview of British history and traditional perry pear varieties. However, even that book is dated and wanting in terms of the kinds of detail that a modern grower or prospective perry-maker would want.

What follows here is a brief historical sketch of pears and perry, plus an overview of perry-making today, with some general and technical notes on how perry differs from cider in terms of the processes we've already discussed in chapters 3 and 4.[1]

A Short History of Perry

The wild ancestor of the modern European pear *(Pyrus communis)* is native to central Europe and northern Asia, and has been cultivated almost as long as the apple. The Greek botanist Theophrastus around 300 B.C.E. wrote about cultivated pear varieties, and by imperial Roman times many writers and naturalists were discussing the best varieties and uses of pears. Pliny the Elder mentioned that Falernian pears were the best for making pear wine, and Palladius in the fourth century A.D. described how to ferment pear juice, which was then called Castomoniale and apparently was esteemed more highly than apple wine by the Romans.

Not surprisingly, then, the Romans appear to have spread the cultivation of pears into Gaul (France) and probably Britain, as the historian Tacitus suggests; however, there is no definitive written record of pears in England until after the Norman Conquest of 1066. Pear culture was already well established in France, however, and during the thirteenth century many French varieties were imported into England. The first significant English pear variety, the Wardon, was introduced by a Cistercian order of monks at Wardon in Bedfordshire. These pears, like many of the time, were primarily intended for culinary use and were widely used to make "Wardon pies."

During the sixteenth century pears were again introduced into England from France, along with apples and other fruits, by Richard Harris, fruitier to Henry VIII (see chapter 1). Gerard's *Herball* in 1597 refers to more than a hundred pear varieties, a few dozen of which he considered superior types. He also mentions wild pears that grew in hedgerows and were harsh-tasting and astringent; this might refer to either wild common pears or perhaps the snow pear (*Pyrus nivalis),* but in any case it's possible these sorts of inedible pears could be the progenitors of traditional English perry pears. This proliferation of pear varieties continued throughout the seventeenth and eighteenth centuries, with more varieties introduced to Britain from France and Belgium.

In 1770 one of today's most important commercial varieties was bred by Mr. Stair, a schoolmaster in Berkshire. Named the Williams Bon Chretien, it was introduced to the United States in 1797 by James Carter of Boston. In 1817 an Enoch Bartlett took over the estate in Dorchester, Massachusetts (now a neighborhood of Boston) where these pears were growing, and he sold them under his own name. Today "Bartlett" is still the most widely grown variety in the U.S., accounting for about three-quarters of all pears produced in this country.

The centers of perry production are similar to those for traditional cider: the West Country of England (primarily the three counties of Gloucestershire, Herefordshire, and Worcestershire), plus Monmouthshire and the Welsh Marches; and the southern part of Normandy, especially the *department* of Orne, where very bittersharp perry pears like the classic Plant de Blanc are grown in the countryside around Domfront and either made into traditional *poire fermier* or distilled to make the unique Calvados Domfrontais, which by rule must contain at least 30 percent pears (see chapter 8).

In fact, one of the limitations to the spread of perry culture probably involves the requirements of the pear trees themselves. Pears are somewhat less adaptable than apples, and fussier about the climate and soils in which they can be grown. They grow best in very temperate climates: warm, dry summers and cold (but not too cold) winters. Also, the trees prefer somewhat heavier soils than apples, ideally a deep loam, though they also tolerate other soil types, so long as they are deep enough and have adequate drainage. Add to this that many European pear varieties are highly susceptible to fireblight, a bacterial infection that makes branches blacken and look scorched, and this further limits possibilities for pear growers here in North America. At present, the vast majority of commercially grown pears in the U.S. come from the West Coast states, with Washington the top producer, followed by California and Oregon.

Another important factor for pear growers is the relatively long period of time it can take for trees to produce. The old saying is "Plant pears for your heirs," indicating just how much of a commitment a pear orchard can represent, especially if the trees have been grafted onto *Pyrus communis* or other seedling rootstocks. The tradeoff here is longevity and production over time. It might take a standard pear twenty-five or thirty years to become productive, but after that the large trees generally crop heavily; the famous Holme Lacy perry pear tree that was photographed for *Perry Pears* grew on the banks of the River Wye and was reported around 1790 to have covered three-quarters of an acre and to have yielded an annual crop of five to seven *tons* of fruit. Standard pear trees can have an incredible lifespan, in some cases up to three hundred years. In southern Normandy a late December storm in 1999 blew down many of the grand old perry pear trees; although some trees could be saved, this one event had an enormous and long-lasting impact on the farmers of that region.[2]

Despite all these limitations, though, there has been increasing interest in traditional perry pears among cidermakers and orchardists, both in the U.S. and England. By grafting pear scions onto semidwarfing rootstocks like the Old Home x Farmingdale clonal series and traditional dwarfing rootstocks like quince, growers can reduce the time between field planting and first harvest to a reasonable five to seven years.

Perry pears are similar to European cider apples in the respect that they are typically high in tannins and far too astringent for fresh eating. English perry pear varieties typically have short, matter-of-fact handles (Butt, Gin, Pint, Rock, Sack) or humorous and descriptive folk names that suggest their intoxicating or other qualities (Bloody Bastard, Clipper Dick, Dead Boy, Merrylegs). One Gloucestershire variety, Stinking Bishop, even lends its name to a raw-milk cheese made by perry expert Charles Martell. The cheese's rind is washed in Stinking Bishop varietal perry, and its powerful aroma and exquisite flavor resulted in its winning the honor of Best British Cheese at the 2001–02 World Cheese Awards.

A good illustration of just how inedible perry pears really are comes from Stephen Wood, the master cidermaker and orchardist at Farnum Hill Ciders in Lebanon, New Hampshire. A few years ago, Steve eagerly harvested his first bin (about fifteen bushels) from the trees he had planted several years earlier. Both of us were excited and interested to try our hands at pressing these unknown varieties. But one morning Steve came into the ciderhouse and found that hungry squirrels had gotten into the bin of pears and had eagerly chewed almost every last one. Then they had, quite methodically, eaten all of the pear seeds and spit out all the flesh on the concrete floor. That, to me, is the definition of inedible— when even the squirrels won't eat it.

In terms of style, English perry tends to be drier and stiller (noncarbonated) compared to French *poire*, which is considerably sweeter and undergoes some fermentation in the bottle. This gives it a natural carbonation that is generally somewhere between *petillant* (lightly efferves-

Chapter 7: Perry, or Pear Cider

cent) and truly sparkling or *bouche*. Due to limited production, nearly all perry tends to be consumed locally in the regions where it is made. In the U.S., though, French *poire* is sometimes available from specialty wine stores (Eric Bordelet and Christian Drouin are the two producers most often represented) and English perries made in Herefordshire (Gwatkin and Oliver's) are beginning to get distribution. Also, not all real perry made in England is dry by any means; examples ranging from sweet to medium-sweet to dry are easy to find.

Slow Food's International Ark of Taste has recognized a Three Counties Perry Presidium (producers group) that has been formed in England's West Country to help preserve old perry pear varieties (there are perhaps a hundred or more that are maintained in the National Perry Pear Collection at Malvern) and support the handful of traditional perry-makers who keep this centuries-old tradition alive. In addition, the Welsh Perry and Cider Society was founded in 1999 to revive and improve perry and cider production in Wales.

A few years ago I had the opportunity to attend the annual London Drinkers Festival, which is sponsored by the Campaign for Real Ale (CAMRA; see Resources). Despite their focus on real ale, CAMRA also has a commitment to real cider and real perry, and there were dozens of barrels of both at the event. Traveling to France or Britain on a vacation remains the best way to sample the genuine product, whether that's traditional farm cider or perry. CAMRA's *Good Cider Guide* (see Bibliography) is one good place to look up producers and pubs, but there is also other information online, particularly in France, which promotes a "cider trail" of recommended producers and outlets that welcome visitors.

In terms of the United States, several small wineries have experimented with perry pears. In the Pacific Northwest, Oregon State University and the USDA's

National Germplasm Repository at Corvallis have helped to some extent to introduce virus-tested true European perry varieties to this country. And at least two nurseries, Raintree and Cummins, offer at least a few grafted perry pear trees to orchardists. (For descriptive information on some of the English varieties that are available, see the table on page 115) Alan Foster, who planted traditional apple and pear varieties at his orchard in Newberg, Oregon, made some wonderful experimental batches of perry for his White Oak Cider company, which is sadly no longer in operation. Other producers use mainly or exclusively dessert varieties of pears, such as Comice, Bosc, and Conference. Shawn Carney at Blossomwood Cidery in Colorado currently makes a commercially available perry, as does Mike Beck at Uncle John's Fruit House Winery in Michigan. Charles McGonegal of AEppelTreow (pronounced "apple true") Winery in Wisconsin has done a lot of experimenting with pears and always has a perry on offer, but a few years ago he produced a test batch of a remarkable dessert wine that he called Poirreaux, made from a blend of dessert and perry pears. In the hands of these and other skilled cider-makers, there is hope for perry's future in this country—for now we simply have to be patient and drink what we can find.

In addition to the small, artisan wineries making perry, there are a few draft ciders that are labeled as "pear cider." When buying these products, check the label and make sure that what you are buying is actually made partly from fermented pear juice. As often as not, the ciders merely contain pear flavoring (natural or artificial), which is hardly the same thing, and certainly doesn't represent what real perry is all about.

Making Your Own Perry

Although I have made perry on a very small, experimental scale at home myself, I certainly do not consider myself an expert. Fortunately, though, you don't need to acquire much more knowledge beyond the cidermaking basics we have already discussed in chapters 3 and 4. However, apples and pears are somewhat different in respect to their chemical composition, the way they are harvested and pressed, and the fermentation process. And it's important for anyone who wishes to make good perry to understand these distinctions.

First let's examine the issue of ripeness. In chapter 3 we talked a little about how to know when an apple is ripe, and some tricks for determining that, including the starch iodine test (see page 53). Pears are a bit more complicated because not all varieties ripen uniformly from the core outward. This makes it harder to gauge exactly when to harvest and press them. Dessert pears are usually picked before they are fully tree-ripe, because they will continue to ripen and soften gradually in storage. Most perry pears, on the other hand, stay hard and fibrous and then ripen quickly and turn brown and soft. Descriptions of perry pears generally include the time

frame in which you have to press them (see table on page 115). As Shakespeare wrote, "And so from hour to hour we ripe and ripe,/And then from hour to hour we rot and rot,/And thereby hangs a tale." In processing pears, timing is everything. In any case, it's doubtful you will be using genuine perry pears, unless you happen to be growing them yourself; more likely you will be either pressing dessert pears or purchasing fresh juice from an orchard.

Dessert pears should be pressed just as they are beginning to ripen and become aromatic, because overly soft fruit can be messy and difficult to mill and to squeeze, generally clogging up the grinder and the press cloths. Charles McGonegal and other cidermakers who press pears report that ripe Bosc are among the worst to deal with; he uses a high proportion of rice hulls, much as you might if you were pressing slippery pomace from Golden Delicious or other overly ripe apples. Still, you

should not expect to get anywhere near as much of a juice yield from pears as from apples. Most people agree that pears will yield one gallon or less per bushel of fruit.

Once pressed, fresh dessert pear juice oxidizes quickly, turning cloudy and deep brown in color much sooner than fresh cider. Juice from true perry pears, on the other hand, remains lighter and clearer, because it contains much more acid and a good deal of tannin; they don't present the same problems with grinding and pressing as dessert varieties, but they do benefit from maceration for a few hours between milling and pressing.

As mentioned above, pears differ somewhat from apples in their chemical makeup. For one thing, more of their acidity comes from citric, not malic acid. With relatively low-acid dessert pears this isn't that much of a problem, but with perry pears the acids are high enough so that in storage they can be turned into ethyl acetate by lactic acid bacteria. To prevent this, it's a good idea to treat fermented perry with extra metabisulfite, both pre-fermentation and post-fermentation, before bottling or bulk storage (about 50 parts per million SO_2 *each time* more than what is recommended for cider of the same pH level; see the sulfite chart on page 77 in chapter 4). The extra pre-fermentation sulfite is recommended because pear juice contains larger amounts of acetaldehyde than apple juice, and this binds up more sulfur dioxide during the fermentation process.

Pears contain a bit more sugar than most apples, so the Brix/specific gravity of your must (juice) may be a few points higher as well. You can almost tell this by "feel" and taste, because juice from dessert pears seems thicker and "deeper" than most ciders, except for those made from high-sugar varieties like Golden Russet. Pears also contain sorbitol, an unfermentable sugar not found in apples. This means that even a "dry" English-style perry should have a perceptible roundness in the mouth-feel, and the final gravity of the perry will be higher than that of a fully fermented cider, anywhere from 1.000 for dry styles to 1.020 for sweet ones.

I have made a "pider" using half apple and half pear juice, and have also tasted one or two commercial examples of the same. The general rule of thumb in the UK is that apples and pears can be mixed together, but that something sold as cider can contain a maximum of 25 percent pears, and something called perry can have up to 25 percent apples.

Thus far, I confess I've been underwhelmed by my own experiments with fermenting juice from dessert pears. The resulting "common perry" is drinkable enough, but seems rather thin and innocuous compared to the excellent traditional perries that are made from European bittersharp pears. However, some of the sweeter commercial perries and pear wines available in the U.S. do retain much of the flavor and aroma of the fruit. To me, they taste uncomplicated and appealing, very pleasant to sip well-chilled in the summertime or to enjoy with a bit of cheese or dessert.

The fact is, aside from some really expert perry producers in the UK and France—most of whom are themselves pear growers and who use time-honored methods to get the best out of their fruit—not many people in the U.S. can claim to know all that much about what we're doing—not yet. Following the example of artisan cidermaking, as more good fruit becomes available to both hobbyists and commercial producers, and as we learn more about what makes a good perry, both the quality and availability of this wonderful beverage should improve.

English Perry Pears Grown in North America[3]

Variety	Harvest	Mill Within	Growing Notes/Vintage Quality
Sweet (low to moderate acid, low tannin)			
Barnet	early-mid	1–3 weeks	small fruit, orange-red flush and russet; biennial; flowers late; little scab; average
Red Pear	mid	3 weeks	small red fruit; firm, dry flesh; heavy crops; biennial; flowers late; some scab; average
Medium Sharp (medium acid, low to medium tannin)			
Blakeney Red	mid	1 week	small to med. fruit with red cheek; slow to bear, but reliable crops; dual-purpose for perry and eating; average
Brandy	mid	4 weeks	small fruit with red cheek; bears early; heavy crops; biennial; flowers mid to late; some scab; dark-colored, aromatic, mild juice; average
Gin	late	3–5 weeks	small, broad green fruit flushed with orange; heavy crops; biennial; some scab resistance; good
Hendre Huffcap	mid	2 weeks	small fruit; scab-resistant; flowers early; good
Taynton Squash	early	2 days	small fruit with reddish brown flush; white, sweet/acid flesh; heavy crops; biennial; flowers early; scab-prone; fruit breaks down quickly; average
Thorn	early-mid	1 week	small yellow fruit; slow to bear but good crops; scab-prone; good
Winnals Longdon	mid	1 week	small fruit with red blush; heavy crops; biennial; scab-resistant; adaptable to dwarfing quince rootstock; good
Yellow Huffcap	mid	1 week	small fruit with thick stem and yellow-green flesh; high acids; slow to bear, but heavy crops; biennial; flowers early; excellent
Bittersharp (high acid, high tannins/astringency)			
Barland	early-mid	3 days	small, dull-colored fruit; possibly triploid, needs pollinator; bears early; fragrant blossoms; scab-prone; flesh breaks down quickly; fruity flavor; average
Butt	late	4–10 weeks	small, bright yellow fruit; coarse, yellowish flesh; slow to bear; heavy crops; biennial; keeps well

> Cider smiles in your face,
> and then cuts your throat.
>
> —Seventeenth-century English proverb

8. STRONGER WATERS: CIDER VINEGAR AND SPIRITS

S O FAR WE HAVE BEEN LOOKING AT HARD CIDER as if it represents the final stage in the natural evolution of fresh-pressed apple juice. It can, so long as it is fermented and bottled with care and drunk within a reasonable period of time. Yet when natural hard cider is exposed to air and left to its own devices, various organisms begin to oxidize the ethyl alcohol and convert it into acetaldehyde, and eventually into acetic acid. In other words, it turns to vinegar.

Something entirely different happens to hard cider when it is distilled. Evaporating and then condensing the cider separates its various chemical constituents and yields a liquid with a much higher alcohol content, one that can taste as young and raw as moonshine or as smooth and mellow as the finest Cognac, depending upon how well it was made and how long it has been aged. In this way, humble hard cider undergoes a kind of metamorphosis, from a light, low-alcohol drink that quenches the thirst on a hot summer's day to a volatile, intoxicating liquid that warms the heart and fires the soul in the dark watches of a winter night. These kinds of cider-based spirits answer to a variety of names: apple brandy, applejack, Calvados, and *eau-de-vie de cidre*.

Apple brandy and cider vinegar, although very different in their natures, do share certain qualities when it comes to their uses—whether medicinal or culinary. Both have been identified for centuries as having health-promoting properties. Of course, that was the excuse for many alcoholic spirits in their earlier days: In more repressed or puritanical societies, no one wanted to admit that they were drinking just for the sheer bibulous pleasure of it. Cider brandy was touted as being "of special good use to expel melancholy," as one author put it, and a nineteenth-century French doctor, Édouard Denis-Dumont, spent his career conducting clinical experiments with cider in Normandy. Based on his findings, Denis-Dumont maintained that the strong Norman constitution was due in part to a prodigious consumption of cider, which helped prevent kidney stones, gallbladder disease, diabetes, and urinary complaints.[1]

Similarly, the various medicinal claims for cider vinegar have been known and exploited for centuries. Even today, tabloid headlines routinely trumpet the startling "new" information that a dose of cider vinegar is nothing short of a miracle cure for whatever ails you. Whether your trouble is obesity, hypertension, headaches, fatigue, or arthritis, chances are that someone, somewhere, has been treating the condition with a spoonful of cider vinegar, often with some success. As folk remedies go, it's one of the most revered and reliable.

In the kitchen, too, brandy and vinegar have served similar functions, mainly as preserving agents for other fresh foods. In the days before refrigeration, pickling with vinegar was one of the few techniques available for preserving fresh vegetables and other foods for winter consumption, and brandies were used in much the same way to preserve fresh fruits. Modern-day home canners still rely on commercial cider vinegar, though "pickling" fruits in apple brandy or Calvados is much less common

a practice in America, as brandy made from grape wines is better known and more widely available than apple brandy. (See chapter 9 for some traditional recipes using Calvados.)

Unlike hard cider or apple wine, making your own applejack or apple brandy at home is considered illegal by the U.S. government. However, you can still find good information on stovetop distilling in books like *Cider*, by Annie Proulx and Lew Nichols (see Bibliography). Rather than tempt the wrath of the revenuers, this chapter will focus mainly on the cultural history of applejack and apple brandy, and on the traditional methods of making them. Cider vinegar, on the other hand, is not only a legal product, but also one that is easy to make at home, and likely to be healthier and better-tasting than any mass-produced commercial vinegar you can buy.

Apple Brandy (Calvados)

The first reference to the manufacture of distilled spirits from cider comes from 1553, when Gilles de Gouberville, the "seigneur of Mesnil-au-Val," reportedly set up an alembic (otherwise known as a still) at his manor house and began producing apple brandy. By 1606 the production of such spirits had apparently become widespread, so much so that the provincial parliament in Normandy endorsed the establishment of a closed guild of distillers. (In those days, in order to legally manufacture products such as vinegar, brandy, and even mustard, a person had to belong to the appropriate professional guild.)

The name Calvados became officially linked to French apple brandy during the nineteenth century, much as the regional name Champagne had become synonymous with Dom Perignon's sparkling white wine more than a century earlier. Calvados is one of the five *départements* of Normandy, a green, rolling region that borders on the Baie de la Seine, lying across the Channel from Portsmouth, on England's southern coast. Its largest city is Caen, which for many centuries has served as the capital of the French cider industry. Locals claim that the *département's* name is a corruption of *Salvador,* the name of a Spanish man-of-war that was reportedly wrecked on the Normandy coast when the English defeated the Armada in 1588. True or not, it makes for a dashingly romantic etymology. Another, perhaps more plausible interpretation, is that the name Calvados derives from the Latin root word *calva,* meaning 'bald scalp,' and that it appeared on early maps of the Norman coast, referring to some distinctive "bald" rocks that sailors used as reference points.

Just as real champagne is controlled by French law (it can come only from the Champagne region, it has to be made from Chardonnay and/or Pinot Noir grapes, and it must get its fizz and sparkle from a secondary in-bottle fermentation, the so-called *méthode champenoise*), so for an apple brandy to be called Calvados it must be produced either in Calvados itself or in one of the other four *départements* of Normandy: Eure, Manche, Orne, or Seine-Maritime. In the famous pear-growing region around Domfront, in the Orne and adjacent areas, a special kind of spirit, Calvados Domfrontais, is made from cider fermented from a mix of apple and pear juice (pears must comprise 30 percent or more of the blend).[2]

Calvados is distilled from fermented hard cider, sometimes in small pot stills as it was traditionally made, but increasingly in modern continuous-column stills. The most highly regarded Calvados is produced in the Pays d'Auge, the famous cidermaking region that lies on either side of the Touques River Valley, running some 60 kilometers south into the French countryside, from Deauville and Honfleur on the coast through Pont

l'Évêque and Lisieux. In this area Calvados continues to be made in pot stills, gleaming copper vessels with graceful swanlike necks through which the vaporized alcohol passes into a condensing coil.

The cider is distilled twice, as the first pass through the still results in a liquor that is only about 30 to 40 percent alcohol. The French call this first run *les petites eaux,* or "little waters," which is the same thing whiskey distillers refer to as "low wines." Revaporizing these low wines in the still doubles their strength and produces a clear, rough apple brandy of around 140 to 150 proof (70 to 75 percent alcohol). The second distillation also ensures that the brandy, after aging, will have sufficient body and bouquet. At the end of each run, the first and last drippings from the still (the "heads" and the "tails"), which contain impurities like aldehydes and fusel oils, are either discarded or redistilled to extract more of their ethyl alcohol. At this point the brandy is clear and can be sold unaged as *eau de vie de cidre,* which has a clean, fruity palate and can be drunk ice cold or used in mixed drinks. (For some recipes, see the little bilingual book, *Normandy Cocktails,* mentioned in the Bibliography).

Like good whiskeys, Calvados loses much of its rough, raw edge during storage. It is always barrel-aged in wood, preferably in oak casks that have previously been used to age brandy. Newer, smaller casks are generally used only for the youthful spirit, to pick up the tannins from the wood. Calvados must be aged for at least two years at a storage temperature around 55°F (a *cave,* or wine cellar, is the traditional location, with its constant and naturally cool temperatures). Like good Scotch or bourbon, apple brandy improves with extra cask time, and some of the best Calvados has been aged for twenty years or even longer. Unlike other *eaux-de-vie* (nongrape fruit brandies), which are bottled colorless and crystal-clear right out of the still, most Calvados takes on a golden straw or light amber hue during its long-term tenure inside the oak cask. A cellar-master *(maitre de chai)* regularly checks the contents of the barrels and ultimately blends them to balance their desirable qualities. Before bottling, the brandy is sometimes cut back with distilled water to a final strength of between 80 and 100 proof (40 to 50 percent alcohol).

Many drinkers and connoisseurs maintain that a well-made Calvados is every bit the equal of, or even superior to, an excellent grape brandy or Cognac. For instance, in his book *Normandy Revisited,* the American journalist A. J. Liebling observed:

I have never wavered in my belief that old Calvados has a more agreeable bouquet, a warmer touch to the heart and a more outgoing personality than Cognac. It is less precocious, but that is only a confirmation of its more profound character. The barrel of Calvados laid down at an infant's birth matures with him; he is unlikely to need it until he is at least 11, and by that time it will be passable. If the boy is to drink Calvados at its best, however, it is better to lay down several barrels, so he will still have some when he is 50.[3]

This passage reminds me of another old Norman custom, in which a drop of Calvados is touched to a baby's lips at his or her christening. I have no idea how prevalent this practice may be today, but it says a lot about the reverence for apple brandy in the land where it, too, was born and brought to its greatest perfection.

In 2006 I had the pleasure of meeting Christian Drouin, the second of three generations of cider and Calvados makers, whose Domaine Coeur de Lion is located near Pont l'Eveque in Normandy. In a small flight of tastings, we sampled some old vintage Calvados from his cellars. My expectation going in was that the older vintages *(millesimes)* would be drier and more austere than the younger editions, but this was decidedly not the case. In fact, the Calvados dating back to the late 1960s and early 1970s was much fruitier than those from recent years. The roundness and complexity of the decades-old spirits came as no surprise, but the intense fruitiness of the older brandy did. This might have been due to the fact that Drouin has bought in cider and Calvados from different farm producers over the years; whatever it was, it was a fascinating and educational exploration, and I envied Christian the task that he performs every summer, when he samples each and every barrel on the estate, to gauge each one's character and evolution.

Although available in the United States in most high-end and specialty liquor outlets, real Calvados is not always easy to find. Laird's Applejack, a longtime American product, consists mainly of grain-neutral spirits, which are flavored with about 30 percent apple

MAKING A VINEGAR STARTER WITH POMACE

An alternative method for making a vinegar starter culture, or mother, is to use fresh apple pomace after you have pressed your cider. Transfer some pomace into a bucket or shallow vat and move it away from the press area to a warm location out of direct sunlight. Sprinkle the pomace if necessary to keep it moist, and let it ferment for several weeks. Once the pomace begins to smell vinegary, squeeze and strain it through a muslin (cheesecloth) bag. Then place the expressed liquid, which is full of acetobacter organisms, in a jar and cover with cheesecloth. It will quickly develop a gelatinous mother on its surface.

Chapter 8: Stronger Waters: Cider Vinegars and Spirits

brandy. The result is a smooth-drinking alcohol, but by no means is it the same thing as a good Calvados. In recent years, though, as interest in both hard cider and specialty spirits has increased, many microdistilleries around the country have begun to produce increasingly drinkable cider brandies made from American apples. A few years ago Ian Merwin of Cornell University told me about some apple brandies that were made as part of a demonstration project at the New York State Agricultural Experiment Station at Geneva. In this case, the apples were crushed but not pressed into cider for their primary fermentation (in much the same way that other fruits are handled when making eaux-de-vie). The prolonged contact between the juicy pulp and the skins of the fruit infused the final clear, distilled apple brandy with the delightful fresh bouquet of the apple variety from which it was made. So perhaps in the not-too-distant future we will be lifting our cordial glasses to savor a Cox's Orange Pippin or Jonagold varietal apple brandy, produced in some new, as yet unheralded, American cider region. The Pays de Sheboygan? Stranger things have happened.

DEUTSCHE POMOLOGIE

CARMELITER REINETTE

Pommeau

Pommeau is a lightly sweet, reddish amber liqueur (16 to 18 percent alcohol by volume, or about the strength of a fortified wine). It is made by blending Calvados or clear apple brandy into fresh sweet cider, usually at the ratio of one part brandy to two parts juice. The high alcohol of the brandy prevents fermentation of the fresh juice, which retains its fruity character. After blending (*mutage*), pommeau is aged in oak for eighteen months or more before bottling. It's especially good served as an aperitif with different kinds of pâtés or cheeses, but is also useful as a dessert wine and in cooking.

Historically French farmers made pommeau for their own consumption, but beginning in the 1980s it began to appear for sale. In 1991, an official appellation was created for Pommeau de Normandie, followed in 1997 by a new AOC for Pommeau de Bretagne. Currently there are around sixty producers in Normandy and around ten in Brittany, most of whom also make apple brandy. In the U.S. Christian Drouin, Etienne Dupont, and other brands are most commonly available.

Because of its official designation, it's no longer legal to call something "pommeau" that isn't made in the designated regions of France. The few American cidermakers who have made a similar product (like Mike Beck at Uncle John's Fruit House Winery in St. Johns, Michigan) generally sell it as an "apple dessert wine" (see also Ice Cider, page 123).

However, pommeau is easy to make at home (where you can call it whatever you want) using your own fresh-pressed cider and some cider brandy or clear apple eau-de-vie). Use a sweet, fruity cider as the base; late-season russet apples and European bittersweets are particularly nice to include in the sweet cider blend. The proof, or percentage alcohol, of the brandy doesn't matter much; I have used cider spirits ranging from 40 to 65 percent alcohol (80 to 130 proof). Use the winemaker's formula for fortifying wines, known as the Pearson Square (see sidebar), to calculate how much brandy you will need to add to create a pommeau with the alcohol content you want; shoot for 15 to 18 percent, since making it much stronger will result in a "hot" alcoholic flavor that will detract from the fruitiness of the sweet cider.

The only problems I've ever noticed with homemade pommeau are that every so often a bottle of it will start to ferment and get somewhat funky-tasting (not enough brandy), and, more frequently, it will drop a light sentiment to the bottom of the bottle. One way to avoid this sediment problem, and make a brighter, clearer pommeau, is to treat the sweet cider with pectic enzyme and let it precipitate before blending with the brandy. I usually put my pommeau into glass bottles that have a metal and rubber "Grolsch-type" closure, so that I can decant or rack again later if needed.

Applejack

Applejack, sometimes called cider oil, is the familiar American term for apple brandy. As with the commercial brand known as Laird's Applejack, the name may refer loosely to spirits made by the distillation of cider, as described earlier. However, traditional applejack is something very different, produced not with fire but with ice. Once a common practice throughout the New England countryside, making applejack involves setting a barrel of hard cider outdoors in the dead of winter. There, in the frigid temperatures (the colder the better), the 75 to 90 percent of the cider that is water begins to freeze. During the day, warmer temperatures allow the alcohol to drain out of the ice, which then refreezes at night, causing greater and greater separation between the increasingly pure water ice and the increasingly concentrated liquor at the "heart" or core of the barrel. This process is known as *fractional crystallization*—a fancy way to say "freezing."

According to Sanborn C. Brown, whose *Wines & Beers of Old New England* offers the best, most detailed information on traditional 'jack-making, real honest-to-goodness applejack can't be made in areas where night-time temperatures in midwinter don't reliably dip below 0°F. That's because lower temperatures produce a stronger, higher-proof liquor. At 0°F, Brown estimates that the finished applejack would reach about 28 proof (14 percent alcohol by volume), which is akin to a forti-fied wine. In fact, in 1817 William Coxe compared the strength of applejack to that of Madeira (between 19 and 25 percent), and described the liquor as "an excellent, vinous, strong, pure liquor; free from any spiritous taste; of twice the ordinary strength of good cider, and prom-ises with age to improve to a high degree of strength and perfection."[4]

Coxe lived in the Middle Atlantic region, where win-ter temperatures are not nearly as extreme as they are in northern New England. Brown's figures show that really cold temperatures, around -30°F, will produce a very strong applejack of 65 proof, whereas relatively warm winter lows, around 5°F, will yield a liquor that measures only 20 proof, or 10 percent alcohol. In other words, a difference in climate can mean the difference between an applejack that approaches brandy on the one hand and one that merely achieves the potency of apple wine on the other. Yet another reason to curse global warming.

The main drawback to applejack has always been its legendary kick, which long ago earned it the affectionate nickname "essence of lockjaw." Overimbibing results in a hangover of epic proportions, and in chronic drinkers can even cause a condition known as apple palsy. No doubt this was one reason that hard cider—such a mild, temperate drink at heart—came to be so reviled by nine-teenth-century temperance groups in America. Cider could be, and often was, bolstered with rum or brandy or made into applejack, which turned some cider drunks into nasty, abusive slobs. And so hard cider suffered guilt by association.

The thing that gives applejack its bad reputation isn't so much the alcohol it contains; although it can vary greatly, its proof is always lower than twice-distilled liquors like Calvados, whiskey, and many other spirits. No, the problem lies in the *way* it is made, by freezing instead of distillation by heat. The distillation process separates out the various components of a fermented liq-uid such as hard cider or sour mash, and the distiller's goal is to save the pure ethyl alcohol while discarding most of the other impurities, or "fractions," that are usu-ally present in the first or last parts of the run of liquid from the still. But applejack is made by freezing, and there is no similar separation of these "heads" (methanol, acetaldehyde) and "tails" (fusel oils). They all end up in the liquor that is contained in the core of the barrel. In other words, as the ice crystals on the outside of the barrel grow purer and clearer, the applejack becomes not only stronger in proof, but also more con-centrated with fusel oils and other impurities. A very

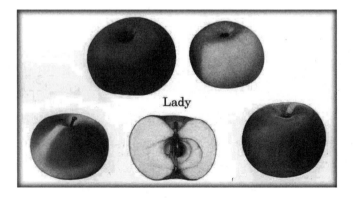

Lady

small amount of these substances is necessary in liquor to give it character and flavor. Too much of them, though, can prove very unhealthy for the liver.

Even though it is not distilled in the traditional sense of the word, it is still illegal to make applejack at home in the United States. However, it is also a lot easier to keep a single, innocent-looking barrel in the barn (or a container full of hard cider in the freezer) than it is to hide a working still. In the 1500s, during the reign of Ivan the Terrible, Russian peasants used to make illegal vodka (which was, even then, a state-owned monopoly) by freezing grain beer outdoors, and independent New England farmers were no doubt doing the same thing to turn out applejack during the dark days of Prohibition.

If you have enough of your own hard cider to spare—say four or five gallons—manufacturing a small batch of applejack might make an interesting experiment (for purposes of historical research only, of course). Using the current season's cider may not be practical; because applejack is best made during the coldest part of the year, the cider that you started in mid to late fall probably will not be completely fermented in time. Instead, use still, dry cider made the previous year, or petite cider made from late-summer and early-fall apples, which should be fully fermented by Christmas.

Wooden casks are traditionally used for making applejack, but an even better option today is to get a five-gallon plastic carboy, which lets you keep close tabs on the freezing process. When the weather gets really cold, put the container outside to freeze. Once you notice that a very white ice layer (one inch or more) has formed inside the container, siphon off the unfrozen liquid into another carboy, leaving the ice behind. (In the old days, 'jackmakers would bore a hole through the ice with an auger or a red-hot poker to reach the liquid heart of the barrel.) Continue this process, moving from carboys down to gallon and then half-gallon jugs. Eventually you will be able to pour off the liquid rather than siphoning it.

The applejack is ready to bottle when the liquid no longer freezes at a temperature of 0°F or below. At this point, the applejack will represent only a small fraction of the hard cider you started with—as little as one-tenth the original volume. Bottle the applejack cold. It will be quite dry and can be sweetened if you like; Sanborn Brown recommends adding 4 tablespoons of sugar to each pint bottle, along with 1 tablespoon of activated charcoal, to help the liquor age. Cap the bottles and put the applejack away to age for at least two years before attempting to drink it. I've also found that the applejack can in time deposit a light sediment on the bottom of the bottle; if this happens, simply rack it off or filter it into another bottle and recap or recork.

Ice Cider

Ice cider (*cidre de glace*) is a very recent introduction to the cider world. In terms of taste, it's akin to French pommeau, though a bit less alcoholic and much sweeter. In terms of production, it's more like applejack, because it is made during the coldest time of the year in North America.

The Canadian province of Quebec is the birthplace and the cradle of ice cider, specifically the Eastern Townships, a large agricultural area just east of Montreal and north of the U.S. border. Around 1989 or 1990 a transplanted Frenchman named Christian Barthomeuf decided to try making something out of local apples that would resemble ice wine made from frozen grapes: the naturally concentrated juice would be fermented to create a sweet, dessert-style wine. The first commercial ice cider appeared on the market in 1996, and in 2000 Barthomeuf started making the product for Domaine Pinnacle in Frelighsburg, which lies close to Vermont's northern border. In 2001 the market for ice cider was still very small, but by 2007 around half a million bottles were being produced by 50 or so producers, most of them based in southern Quebec.[5]

There are two basic methods for making ice cider: cryoconcentration and cryoextraction. The first involves freezing fresh cider pressed from apples in the dead of winter, with large containers left outside to naturally separate the ice and the concentrated sweet cider (again, much like applejack). The second method, cryoextraction, involves leaving the fruit on the trees until January, when temperatures plummet to -8°C to -15°C (16°F to 5°F). They are then harvested and pressed, still partially frozen. In practice, since few apple varieties will hold that long on the trees naturally, the vast majority of ice cider is produced by holding apples in cold storage until midwinter, then moving them outdoors when the temperature is right and freezing them that way.

Aside from freezing the fruit (or fresh juice) by natural means, the Quebec production standards for ice cider require that the sugar concentration of the cider before fermentation be at least 30 degrees Brix, and that the finished product have a residual sugar level of at least 130 grams per liter. The final alcohol level has to be between 7 and 13 percent.

I'm not a big fan of sweet wines, but I must admit that the best ice ciders aren't cloyingly sweet to my taste. This is because the apples contribute a nice acid balance to the high sugars. The ice cider itself has a rather full and syrupy mouthfeel, again like ice wine, which makes it ideal for serving with fruit desserts or as a foil to blue-veined or other aged or assertive cheeses.

According to Charles Crawford, the owner of Domaine Pinnacle, it takes 80 apples to make just one 375 ml. bottle of ice cider, which is only one reason it is so expensive. The harvest, pressing, and eight- or nine-

ROYAL CIDER

The term *royal cider* refers to a fermented cider or apple wine that has been fortified by adding apple brandy or other distilled spirits. A typical ratio is one part brandy to four parts hard cider, mixed together and poured into sturdy champagne bottles, which are then fitted with crown caps or wired-down corks and stored in a hot place, like an attic, all summer long. This period of warm storage allows the flavors of the two liquors to meld. Another traditional way of making royal cider is to add apple brandy to apple wine in a barrel and place the barrel in the hot sun, which produces a drink very much like sherry.

Bottles used for royal cider were often tied up in apple trees in the springtime, when the fruits were very small and could fit through the necks. These bottles then hung in the tree all season long, with the neck plugged up with cotton to shed rainwater and keep out pests. The apples grew to their full size inside the bottles, which were "harvested" in the fall along with their fruit and filled with royal cider.

month fermentation are all labor-intensive, and producers use special wine yeasts and must stop fermentation to leave just the right amount of residual sugar.

I've tried making ice cider at home, from frozen Baldwin and late-harvested Red Delicious apples. My advice is to leave it to the pros. Put aside the obvious question of how to produce a natural ice cider in, say, San Diego or Tampa (the freezer is your only option here). More than that, unless you can effectively stop fermentation, your ice cider will ferment way too dry and at best turn into a very strong example of what Quebecers call *cidre fort*. This can be good in its own right, but it's not at all the same thing as commercial ice cider. Fortunately, in addition to some excellent Canadian producers (including Quebec's Domaine Pinnacle and La Face Cachée de la Pomme, and TideView Vintage Cider in Nova Scotia), there are a few cideries in the northern U.S., particularly New York State (Eve's Cidery in Ithaca and Slyboro Cider House in Granville), who are making dessert wine that they can't market as ice cider (remember pommeau?) but that is every bit as tasty.

Cider Vinegar

So much of a cidermaker's time and care is spent in trying to *prevent* cider from turning into vinegar that intentionally trying to make it at home can seem at first strange, then strangely liberating. Homemade vinegar is even easier to make than cider, and it has a thousand and one uses, many of which you probably won't discover until you have your own supply on hand. As the old saying goes, "To a man with a hammer, the world is full of nails."

Early American settlers certainly valued cider vinegar highly, especially as the only alternative was the expensive wine vinegar imported from Europe. In fact, cider vinegar played such a central role in the farm and domestic economy that at one time it commanded a price almost three times greater than that of regular hard cider. As William Coxe wrote in 1817: "The superiority of vinegar made from strong well-flavored cider, over the ordinary wine vinegar imported from Europe, is generally acknowledged. The manufacture of vinegar has become an important branch of rural economy among many of our respectable farmers, who are from principle opposed to the practice of distillation of ardent spirits."[6] Coxe also reported that the demand for cider vinegar was especially high among "our seafaring citizens" and in "our white-lead manufactories," which required a steady supply of vinegar for making lead carbonate, a white powder once used in paint pigments.

Today, almost all commercial cider vinegar is made quickly and cheaply in an acetator, an industrial-scale fermenter with forced aeration and a large population of acetobacter. These legions of microbes convert the cider into vinegar in a matter of hours, after which it is diluted

Genuine cider vinegar is wonderful for cooking, preserving, and for a thousand other uses. *Rich Stadnik*

Chapter 8: Stronger Waters: Cider Vinegars and Spirits

to the desired strength (typically a 5 percent acetic acid solution), then pasteurized or preserved with chemicals to prevent the growth of molds and other undesirable organisms. By contrast, the home vinegar-maker needs very little equipment to get started. In fact, the only real prerequisite is patience: It can take anywhere from several weeks to several months for the natural population of acetic acid bacteria to produce a good, strong, natural cider vinegar.

Of course, good cider is essential for making good vinegar, and it is important to start with a fully fermented dry or "still" cider that has an alcoholic content of at least 5 percent. Using a hydrometer, check the fresh cider after you press it or purchase it to determine its potential alcohol before fermentation (see chapter 4). Most cider blends should have no trouble reaching the 5 percent threshold for potential alcohol. However, if your juice tests low, you will want to add some sugar to raise its specific gravity to the appropriate level.

Don't add sulfites to your fresh cider before fermenting it if you intend to turn it into vinegar. That's because sulfur dioxide can inhibit the conversion process of alcohol to acetic acid. Pitching the cider with a commercial yeast strain as you normally would is fine, though, as is adding a yeast nutrient—both of which steps help ensure a quick, complete fermentation.

Once the cider has fermented completely to dryness, transfer it to the container in which you are going to make vinegar. *Never*, under any circumstances, use the same containers or equipment for making hard cider as you do for making vinegar. In fact, it's best to keep your cider and vinegar operations in completely separate areas to guard against possible cross-contamination from acetobacter, which can ruin a good batch of cider.

A wooden barrel or cask is the traditional container used for making vinegar, although a large ceramic crock or plastic food-grade bucket is even easier to use. If you use a crock, make sure that it isn't cracked or chipped, as the acetic acid in vinegar can sometimes react with substances underneath the fired clay. The object here runs contrary to all good cider-making practice: In this case, we want the fermented cider to be exposed to as much oxygen as possible, because the acetobacter operate in aerobic conditions, unlike the yeasts that turn sugars into alcohol. So, in the case of the barrel, fill it about three-quarters full with dry cider and leave the bunghole open to the air, but covered with a double layer of cheesecloth to keep out flies and other uninvited guests. The same goes for crocks and buckets, which have some advantage over the barrel in that they have a larger aperture through which air (and acetobacter) can pass. In general,

MAKING VINEGAR FROM SWEET CIDER

It is entirely possible to turn sweet cider into vinegar, as anyone who has ever left a jug sitting around too long can attest. Simply cover a container of fresh cider with cheesecloth and allow it to ferment in the presence of air—first into alcohol, then into vinegar.

However, this is more of a hit-or-miss proposition than is fermenting the cider to dryness as you normally would, then using that hard cider to make vinegar. Various bacteria and other organisms can contribute to cloudiness or unpleasant off-flavors in the finished vinegar. Fully fermenting the sweet cider before exposing it to the air is the best way to avoid these problems and to ensure a consistently good quality of cider vinegar.

the larger the surface area of liquid exposed to the air, the easier it is for the acetobacter to gain a quick foothold in the cider.

Set the barrel, crock, or bucket in a warm location (as high as 85°F, if you have such a place) out of direct sunlight. A cellar is most convenient for many people, and the cooler temperatures found there really aren't a problem; they just slow down the process a bit.

Now sit back and wait. The cider won't need any further attention as it begins its conversion into vinegar. Under ideal conditions, the alcohol in cider turns into vinegar at the rate of about 1 percent per week. So a fairly typical dry cider at 6 percent alcohol would take a couple of months to become a fairly strong vinegar. Don't be alarmed when the vinegar begins to foam or cloud up. The gelatinous mass that forms is called the mother (short for "mother of vinegar"), and it indicates that the vinegar is almost ready. Check the vinegar in about two weeks and either bottle the vinegar if it seems strong enough, or let it age awhile longer for a stronger, sharper-tasting product.

An acid-testing kit comes in handy if you want to adjust the strength of your finished vinegar. Most natural ciders (those without added sugar) will produce a vinegar with 5 to 7 percent acetic acid. Five percent is the most common strength used for preserving and pickling, in salad dressings, and for other kitchen needs. If your vinegar seems too sharp, add distilled water to dilute its strength.

Using the so-called Orleans process is the best way to ensure a continuous supply of vinegar. When you draw or pour off the finished vinegar, leave at least a quart of the vinegar behind, along with the cloudy mother as a starter for your next batch. Then simply add more fresh or hard cider to the container. Just like the starter culture that is used in making sourdough bread,

Pierre Gingras in his cider orchard, Rougemont, Quebec. Gingras makes an artisanal "balsamic-type" cider vinegar that is aged over three years in oak barrels and then bottled unfiltered and unpasteurized. *Rich Stadnik.*

the presence of the mother from the get-go will greatly speed up the conversion of alcohol to acetic acid.

It is also possible to make your own mother beforehand by covering a pint jar full of still, hard cider with cheesecloth, then placing it in a warm, dark place to work. In a few weeks time the mother will form on top of the liquid. Transfer the mother and the liquid to a bottle and cap it tightly. Then, whenever you start a full batch of vinegar in a crock or barrel, pour the reserved mother into the cider to get things working fast.

Whether to pasteurize or add preservatives to your cider vinegar is a personal decision. If all the sugars have been fermented completely in the cider that you use to make vinegar, you should not have mold or other stor-

Chapter 8: Stronger Waters: Cider Vinegars and Spirits

age problems over the short to medium term. Usually the worst thing that will happen to your vinegar is that it will develop a haze in the bottle after storage. If you do decide to pasteurize your vinegar, though, one authority recommends funneling it into canning jars or bottles (leaving a 1/2-inch headspace in the jars, 2 inches in the bottles), then covering the sealed containers with water and processing in a 150°F water bath for three minutes. Adding ascorbic acid powder (vitamin C) or one crushed Campden tablet (50 ppm) per gallon before bottling will also inhibit the growth of unwanted organisms that can cause spoilage. However, like sweet cider, unpasteurized vinegar is perfectly safe to use. Many people, myself included, prefer its taste to vinegar that has been processed or chemically treated, and believe that, when taken as a tonic, it is a more natural and healthy product than the pasteurized version.

Once you have made your first successful batch of cider vinegar, you might want to try varying it with different natural flavorings. Flowers, herbs, spices, berries, and other fruits are all possibilities. Most people who make specialty vinegars at home add these ingredients to a jar and then steep them for several weeks in a finished vinegar. If you are making your own cider vinegar, though, you can add these ingredients right to the crock or barrel while it is working. Raspberries, chive blossoms, sprigs of rosemary—the number and variety of gourmet cider vinegars you can create is limited only by your imagination.

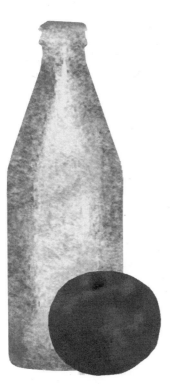

9. COOKING WITH CIDER

CONSIDERING THE SIMILARITY THAT EXISTS between good cider and good wine, it should come as no surprise to learn that cider, like wine, is a wonderful accompaniment to many foods and an essential ingredient in a wide variety of dishes, both main courses and desserts.

With their centuries-old tradition of cidermaking, the people of Normandy have thoroughly incorporated cider and cider brandy into their cooking, so much so that it now typifies the cuisine of northern France. Open up almost any classic French cookbook and you will find recipes for sole or pork à la normande, chicken or veal Vallée d'Auge, or tripe or rabbit prepared "à la mode de Caen." These place-names all correspond to the premier cidermaking towns or regions, and are a sure tipoff that the recipe that follows will call for cider and/or Calvados as one of its main ingredients. Visit one of the "crêpe houses" commonly found throughout Normandy and Brittany, and you will find delicate crêpes that have a sweet or savory filling cooked in cider. To wash them down, you can take your pick from among the perhaps twenty or so different ciders that the restaurant stocks.

Given the relatively undistinguished quality of Norman wines, cider came to be regarded there as the best and most widely available cooking liquid, useful in any recipe that would otherwise call for a white wine. The sweeter kinds of cider are a great substitute for a recipe that calls for a Sauternes or champagne, whereas a "still" cider, one fermented almost completely to dryness, pinch-hits nicely for the drier white wines, and when paired with some foods accompanies them even better than wine. A not-so-obvious affinity exists between ciders and most Asian cuisines, especially ones like Thai, Vietnamese, and Szechuan foods that bring a lot of freshness, flavor, and heat to the table.

Normandy, like Herefordshire and Devon in England, is as famous for its dairy industry as it is for its cider. In fact, the two agricultural traditions grew up together, with orchards featuring large, standard-sized trees planted on wide spacings; between the trees animals could be pastured on the grassy sod. In addition, the spent pomace from the cider press makes a good livestock feed, and some authors have even remarked that the meat of hogs and other animals fed on apple pomace has a particularly fine flavor. Traditional breeds like the

Milking Devon cow and Gloucestershire Old Spot pig (a.k.a., Orchard Hog) are now making a comeback in both Europe and America, thanks to a collaboration among small-scale farmers, visionary chefs, and businesses and organizations that bring them together like Heritage Foods USA, Slow Food, and the American Livestock Breeds Conservancy (ALBC). In the early 1970s, one of England's oldest native cattle breeds, the Gloucester, came perilously close to extinction. Only through the heroic efforts of local conservationists, like Gloucestershire perry and cheese producer Charles Martell, did the breed survive. Thirty-five years ago there was one Gloucester herd; today there are around one hundred breeders who maintain the breed.

In the kitchen, too, cider matches up well with dairy products like butter and crème fraîche, which figure so prominently in classic French cuisine. Crème fraîche is a thickened, cultured heavy cream that, unlike regular cream, resists curdling even in the presence of wine. Paired in a sauce with a good hard cider or Calvados, it provides the distinctive texture and flavor common to many Norman meat and fish dishes.

Dry or slightly sweet ciders are also a good accompaniment for all kinds of cheeses, whether they are served as snacks before dinner or alongside fruit as a dessert course. Camembert, Pont l'Évêque, and Livarot are the classic cheeses from Normandy, named after the towns that first produced them; not surprisingly, all three match up well with cider. A mild Cheddar or a Port Salut is another likely partner. And a sparkling, champagne-type cider provides a ideal finish to a dinner party or an evening's entertainment with friends. In fact, a well-made sparkling cider can be every bit the equal of champagne. There's a story about one less-than-ethical nineteenth-century American hotelier who would substitute domestic sparkling cider for French champagne after

GRAVENSTEINER

Cider, Hard and Sweet

the first round of toasts at wedding receptions, charging the same price for the cider as for the imported bubbly, with no one apparently the wiser.

As for cider brandy, or Calvados, the French outside of Normandy refer to it as *le trou normand,* or "the Norman hole," because a small glass of it was traditionally consumed between courses at a large meal to aid digestion, or, in other words, to open a "hole" in the stomach. (It can also be used to flavor a sorbet that does much the same thing, refreshing the palate and aiding the digestion.) Calvados is also used in rural France for preserving fruits such as peaches, cherries, and pears (see the recipe on page 153). Though it is widely available in America, Calvados is still relatively little known and appreciated except among the cider cognoscenti (a society to which you, dear reader, now belong), and it is normally consumed, like cognac and other brandies, as an after-dinner drink. However, its usefulness in cooking—for making sauces, deglazing pans, and flaming desserts, among other things—makes it as welcome an addition to the kitchen cupboard as other, more familiar cooking spirits like Marsala and sherry. A young Calvados, or a clear, unaged cider brandy or eau-de-vie, is the best choice for most cooking purposes or in mixed drinks where you would use vodka or white rum; it is far less expensive than long-aged Calvados and will contribute a fresh, clean, lightly fruity character. As with most spirits, save the really good, expensive stuff for contemplative sipping and special occasions with friends. Well-aged Calvados is famous for how well it accompanies a good after-dinner cigar or cup of coffee. After finishing the coffee, Normans pour their Calvados into the still-warm cup, which helps to open up its flavor and aroma even more.

Cider in American Cooking

In the case of cider, the leap from haute cuisine to home cooking is not a large one. As fancy as the names of classic French dishes sound, it's important to remember that the use of cider in cooking is, at heart, a peasant tradition—using the foods that are grown or produced on the land. And in America, as we have seen, the apple was the quintessential homestead fruit, from the time of the first settlers right through the nineteenth century. Putting down barrels of cider to ferment in a cool cellar was the most efficient way to preserve the bulk of the apple harvest, yet other cider-based products were also important additions to the farm pantry.

Cider vinegar was perhaps the most important of these farm products, as it was essential for preserving other types of fresh foods. Fresh, or sweet, cider, however, could also be used for recipes and preserves, either by combining it with quartered apples and spices and cooking it down to make apple butter or by evaporating and reducing the cider alone, which turns it into boiled cider and, eventually, cider jelly.

For all of the recipes and instructions that follow, I recommend using fresh, unpasteurized sweet cider that contains no preservatives. Buy from a local orchard or cider mill if you can, and freeze some cider for use throughout the year. Whatever the arguments for pasteurization might be, there is absolutely no reason to buy cider that is adulterated or processed in any way, when you will be heating it yourself in the sanitary conditions of your own kitchen. Any potentially harmful organisms will be eliminated in the cooking process.

Boiled Cider

Boiled cider is similar to maple syrup in terms of its consistency and its role in the kitchen. A dark brown, intensely apple-flavored sweetener, it has at the same time a definite "snappiness" that keeps it from being too cloying. Little known outside New England, boiled cider can be used on top of pancakes or hot cereal; stirred into yogurt; added to a pot of New England baked beans; used to sweeten baked squash (see recipe on page 146); and in most baking or dessert recipes calling for apples. Not quite as versatile and certainly not as delicately flavored as fancy-grade maple syrup, it is more akin to the Grade B syrup that comes from the later runs of maple sap: Both sweeteners have a strong, assertive flavor that holds up well in cooking.

In *The White House Cookbook* (1935), the authors describe boiled cider as being "indispensable to the making of a good 'mince pie,' adding the proper flavor and richness, which cannot be substituted by any other ingredient," to which I say amen. They also claim that 1/2 cup of boiled cider added to fruitcake makes it better, moister, and longer-keeping. I haven't tried this yet, but anything that can improve fruitcake is, to my way of thinking, a godsend.

Boiled cider is still made in parts of New England, where it is sold in pint bottles at some of the better orchard stores and specialty or regional food shops. One long-time producer is Wood's Cider Mill in Springfield, Vermont, a family farm that has been making boiled cider and cider jelly since 1882. You can now order both items from their Web site (www.woodscidermill.com). Yet even here, in its traditional stomping grounds, it remains one of the many traditional and versatile food products that are either unknown or little regarded by today's mass market culture. That's a shame, because boiled cider makes a nice change from the more familiar maple syrup and costs less per pint than Grade A medium amber syrup.

Fortunately, it's easy to make boiled cider yourself at

DEUTSCHE POMOLOGIE

PRINZENAPFEL

home. Given the current retail price of fresh sweet cider, I estimate that you could make your own batch of boiled cider as described below for around three dollars a pint. Of course, if you press your own fresh cider, the cost would be virtually nothing. What's more, if you could sell enough boiled cider to justify buying an evaporator, like the ones used for maple sugaring, you might have a nice little home business. It certainly is easier, if less romantic, than lugging sap buckets out of the woods in February or March—easier even than tapping the trees and stringing plastic tubing through your sugarbush.

If you can boil water, you can make boiled cider in small batches right at home, on top of the stove. Pour 5 quarts of fresh sweet cider into a heavy-duty, nonreactive kettle. Bring to a boil and simmer slowly, until the cider is reduced in volume to about 1 quart. Meanwhile keep an eye on things and stir to make sure the cider heats evenly and doesn't scorch. Ladle the hot boiled cider into sterilized pint glass canning jars, leaving a 1/4-inch headspace, and process in a boiling-water bath for 10 minutes. Remove the jars and let them cool on a rack; then check to make sure the lids are sealed well and don't pop up when pressed with your thumb. Store the boiled cider for use as needed. This recipe makes 2 pints.

The reduction ration used in the instructions above is 5:1 sweet cider to boiled cider. Willis Wood at Wood's Cider Mill concentrates his boiled cider in an evaporator even further, in a 7:1 reduction. How much you reduce your homemade boiled cider depends on your personal preference; experiment with a batch, and adjust the above instructions to 7:1 if you like. Any thicker than that and you will be well on the way to making cider jelly (see below).

Cider Syrup

Boiled cider is the real, unadulterated cider syrup—a natural product that contains nothing but cider, sweetened only by natural reduction and the concentration of fruit sugars. In fact, its only real drawback is its appearance: murky, dark brown, and opaque. When it's being used in baking or cooking, looks are unimportant, but for people who like a more attractive, amber-colored syrup for table use, there's another good alternative that goes under the name of cider syrup. This product is made by adding some granulated sugar to the reduced cider just before it's finished.

DEUTSCHE POMOLOGIE

PARISER RAMBOUR REINETTE

The late Vrest Orton, in his *American Cider Book,* includes a lot of great traditional cider recipes, and among them also gives instructions for making cider syrup. Orton calls for boiling 1 quart of cider for 25 minutes, then adding 2 1/2 cups of sugar and boiling another 3 minutes to make a medium syrup (or 5 minutes for a heavier syrup). This recipe yields about 1 1/2 pints. To make cinnamon cider syrup, Orton recommends adding 1 tablespoon of cinnamon drops with the sugar; however, I prefer to boil a couple of cinnamon sticks with the fresh cider to impart a warm spicy taste. In any case, can and store the resulting syrup just as you would boiled cider.

Cider Jelly

Another little-known but useful apple product is cider jelly, which is boiled cider taken to its logical conclusion. My friends Michael and Nancy Phillips, who run Heartsong Farm in northern New Hampshire, make what they call a "fully puckered" cider jelly from their own cider, which is pressed from their organically grown fruit. Use it on biscuits, muffins, or toast; as a glaze for meats; or in the Phillipses' recipe for cider pie (see page 149). The taste of cider jelly is intense and snappy. I defy anyone not to perk up and feel a little more alive after eating it.

Making your own cider jelly is easy, as it involves no other ingredients except fresh cider; the fruit sugars and pectin from the pressed apples will cause the mixture to jell naturally. Pour 1 gallon of sweet cider into a heavy, nonreactive pot and boil it down as rapidly as possible, adjusting the heat and stirring as necessary to avoid scorching or boiling over. (Boiling quickly will make the color of the finished product lighter than slowly simmered jelly, and helps it to retain more of the apple bouquet.) When the temperature of the reduced cider reaches the jellying stage (around 220°F on a candy thermometer, or 8 degrees higher than the temperature at which water boils at your altitude), it should run off a spoon in a sheet. Remove from the heat and ladle the jelly into hot sterilized canning jars, leaving a 1/2-inch headspace. Process jars in a boiling-water bath for 5 minutes to seal the lids. One gallon of cider makes about 2 cups of cider jelly.

Using Cider in Recipes

One of the highlights of researching this book had to be trying all kinds of sweet and hard ciders from a variety of orchards and wineries. The first cider tasting I ever hosted (see chapter 6) was a resounding success, with only one problem facing me after the guests had gone home and the dishes were washed and put away. What was I going to do with all of the half-opened bottles of hard cider that I now had tucked away in my refrigerator? Drinking them was the most obvious answer, and I did quaff quite a bit over the next few days. But hard cider begins to lose some of its natural effervescence after opening, and, quite frankly, a few of the ciders at the tasting didn't appeal to me at all, being either too sweet or somehow off-tasting.

And so began my culinary adventures with hard cider. I began to seek out new recipes that called for cider, and to adapt some old favorites to include it as an ingredient. As a result, I discovered that even a less-than-drinkable cider can be just fine for cooking. I had heard the oft-quoted line from chefs that "I wouldn't cook with any wine I wouldn't drink," and that was true in my case, too. However, my standards for hard cider weren't quite so high: I found that even an indifferent cider can come in handy in a recipe, especially for marinating or braising meats. (As mentioned in chapter 4, even the lees, or sediment left over from fermentation, can be useful as a braising liquid or for other uses.) The

acids in cider help to tenderize meat, and the more assertive the meat's flavor (rabbit, pheasant, duck, venison, and Cornish game hens come to mind), the less it matters how wonderful the original cider tasted. In short, my advice for cooks using cider is to save the best stuff for drinking, and, unless you're adding the cider to a delicately flavored food or fancy French dish, stick with the cheaper and more commonly available draft ciders for cooking purposes.

Of course, this calculus changes somewhat once you begin to make your own hard cider. For instance, my neighbor and fellow cider enthusiast Roger Swain makes a lot of wonderful sparkling cider every fall—more, in fact, than he can easily give away or drink with his friends and family. As a result, he uses this ambrosial liquid with a free hand to perk up the most pedestrian dishes, including as a steaming liquid for mussels and a variety of vegetables.

By the same token, fresh cider that has just begun to ferment and has passed its drinking prime can be used in any recipe that calls for either hard or sweet cider. The natural sweetness of fresh cider means you can substitute it in recipes that call for a sweet wine. It also makes a great sweet-and-sour marinade when paired with soy sauce (see page 141).

The following recipes are by no means the alpha and omega of cider cuisine. I've tried to include only a few of my favorites, recipes that I have made and served with good results. If you enjoy cooking, it's fairly simple to experiment and develop new recipes. Cider is terrific for marinating, braising meat and vegetables, adding flavor to sauces, steaming vegetables and shellfish, and a hundred other culinary uses. For more ideas and inspirations, spend some time looking through French cookbooks for regional recipes from Normandy and Brittany or poke around on the Internet. The possibilities are limitless.

RECIPES

Old-Fashioned Apple Butter

It is possible to make apple butter with nothing more than sweet dessert apples and fresh cider, but most recipes call for some sugar as well as spices to perk it up. I've also made apple butter for a friend whose diet doesn't include sugar, by substituting a 12-ounce can of apple juice concentrate for the sugar.

24 medium apples, peeled, cored, and
quartered (about 6 pounds)
2 cups sweet cider
3 cups sugar (or less, depending on the sweetness of the apples)

1 1/2 teaspoons cinnamon
1/2 teaspoon cloves

In a heavy, nonreactive pot, cook the apples in the cider, simmering slowly until tender. Process the cooked apples through a food mill, or press through a sieve.

Return the apple pulp to the pot and add the sugar and spices. Simmer slowly, uncovered, stirring frequently as the mixture thickens. When it is very thick and rounds up on a spoon, transfer the hot mixture to sterilized canning jars, leaving a ¼-inch headspace. Process in a boiling-water bath for 10 minutes.

Yield: about 3 pints

Hot Mulled Cider

This is the classic spicy, warming drink for late-fall and winter festivities. Mulled cider mixes are available, both as bulk spices and in tea bags, but it's fun and easy to make your own. Feel free to experiment and vary the spices according to your own taste.

1/2 gallon sweet cider
4 to 6 cinnamon sticks
6 cardamom pods, crushed
1 whole nutmeg, cracked open
10 to 12 whole cloves

6 allspice berries (optional)
4 to 6 star anise pods (optional)
Zest of 1/2 lemon or 1/2 orange, cut into thin strips
Orange slices for garnish

Put the cider, spices, and lemon or orange zest in a large, nonreactive pot and bring to a boil over medium heat. Reduce the heat and simmer gently for 15 minutes.

Line a colander with a square of cheesecloth and pour the hot cider into another pot or large bowl, straining out the spices. Return the mulled cider to the pot over very low heat. Add the orange slices and serve hot.

Some people add about 1½ cups of rum or brandy to the mulled cider after straining, then return it to a boil before reducing the heat. I prefer the nonalcoholic kind, but by all means try it both ways.

Serves 8 to 10

Cider Wassail Bowl

The word wassail *derives from the old Anglo-Saxon toast,* Waes haeil, *meaning "Be whole" [well]. It's like saying "To your health," and it gave its name to the custom that took place throughout Britain around Christmastime, when revelers carried a wassail bowl made of ash or maple and festooned with ribbons from house to house, expecting the bowl to be filled with refreshments and in turn blessing the occupants. The traditional wassail punch is made from ale and sherry, sugar and spices, and topped with toasts and roasted apples.*

Wassailing the apple trees is an old Twelfth Night ritual, too, and so it seems only fitting to include a recipe for a cider-based wassail cup.

1/2 gallon sweet cider

1/2 cup dark brown sugar

10 to 15 allspice berries

8 to 10 whole cloves

2 cinnamon sticks

1 whole nutmeg, cracked in half

Pinch of salt

1 cup dark rum

1/4 cup Calvados or other apple brandy (optional)

1 lemon, halved and sliced thin

1 or 2 oranges, halved and sliced thin

4 to 6 squares toasted bread (optional)

4 to 6 small roasted apples (optional; see note)

whipped cream (optional)

In a large, nonreactive kettle, mix the cider and sugar. Tie up the spices in a square of cheesecloth and add to the pot along with the salt. Bring to a boil, stirring to dissolve the sugar. Reduce the heat and simmer for 15 minutes. Remove from the heat.

Remove the spice bag and add the rum (and optional apple brandy) and the lemon and orange slices. Place over medium heat and stir for 2 to 3 minutes. Garnish with toasts and roasted apples if desired, or pass a bowl of sweetened whipped cream to add in dollops to the individual cups, along with a grating of fresh nutmeg.

Note: *A traditional variety is the ancient French apple called the Pomme d'Api, better known in America as the Lady apple, which is commonly found in specialty food markets around the Christmas season.*

Yield: 15 to 20 servings

Chapter 9: Cooking with Cider

Pork Chops Braised in Hard Cider

Braising pork chops in a liquid like cider ensures that they will be moist and flavorful. This is one of my favorite cider recipes, which I adapted from Judy Gorman's wonderful cooking primer, The Culinary Craft *(Yankee Books, 1984).*

3 tablespoons vegetable oil
4 center-cut pork chops
1 large onion, sliced into rings
1 1/2 cups hard cider
2 teaspoons caraway seeds

Salt and freshly ground black pepper
1 pound sauerkraut, undrained (use the good-quality variety available from the deli or a natural foods store, or homemade)

Place the oil over medium heat in a large, heavy skillet or Dutch oven. Add the pork chops and cook, turning frequently, until they are lightly browned. Remove the chops to a platter.

Add the onion rings to the pan and toss to coat. Reduce the heat to low and cover the pan. Cook for 8 to 10 minutes, or until tender. Remove the onions with a slotted spoon and arrange over the chops. Drain the fat from the pan.

Pour the cider into the pan and bring to a boil over high heat. Return the pork chops and onion slices to the pan and sprinkle the caraway seeds over them. Season with salt and pepper to taste and turn down the heat to its lowest setting.

Arrange the sauerkraut over the chops so that the chops are completely covered. Cover the pan and cook for 20 to 30 minutes, or until the meat is tender.

Serves 4

Chicken Breasts Vallée d'Auge

This classic French recipe is named for one of the great cider-making regions of Normandy, the Pays d'Auge. Not coincidentally, some of the best apple brandy in the world also comes from that region. The combination of sweet cider and Calvados, finished with thickened crème fraîche, makes this a spectacular dish.

6 tablespoons butter

3 boneless chicken breasts, halved lengthwise
   and trimmed of fat

2 to 3 shallots, peeled and finely chopped

Salt and freshly ground black pepper

1/4 cup Calvados (apple brandy)

1 cup sweet cider

8 ounces small white mushrooms, wiped clean,
   trimmed, and sautéed over medium heat in
   2 tablespoons butter for about 5 minutes

1 cup crème fraîche, either store-bought or
   homemade (see recipe on page 140)

Finely chopped parsley (for garnish)

In a large, heavy skillet or Dutch oven, heat the butter and sauté the chicken breasts and shallots over medium heat until the chicken is golden brown. Season with salt and pepper.

Warm the Calvados in a small saucepan. Using a long kitchen match, ignite the Calvados and pour it over the chicken. Allow the flame to die, then add the cider and sautéed mushrooms. Reduce the heat under the pan to low and cook the chicken, covered, for 30 minutes, until the meat is tender. Transfer the chicken breasts to a heated platter.

Increase the heat under the pan to high and cook to reduce the liquid, about 3 minutes. Reduce the heat to low and whisk in the crème fraîche, being careful not to let the sauce boil. Spoon the sauce over the chicken, garnish with the parsley, and serve hot.

Serves 6

Crème Fraîche

A thickened, cultured cream, the slightly sour crème fraîche not only is useful for finishing sauces, as in the preceding recipe, but also can be whipped and dolloped (or simply poured as is) over fresh fruit and other desserts as a topping. You can find crème fraîche in some specialty food markets, but it's also easy to make at home using sour cream, buttermilk, or yogurt as the culturing agent.

1/2 cup sour cream (or 1 tablespoon buttermilk or yogurt)
1 cup heavy cream

Blend the ingredients by stirring them with a fork or wire whisk. Pour into a glass jar.

Cover the jar and set out at a warm room temperature (around 75°F). Use a thermos bottle rinsed out with either hot or cold water to compensate for a too-cool or too-warm room temperature, respectively.

Check the mixture after about 8 hours. If it hasn't thickened and begun to have a slightly sour taste, stir it and cover the jar or thermos again for another couple of hours. Continue checking every few hours, until the mixture is thick and tangy.

Refrigerate crème fraîche in a covered glass jar and use as needed. It will keep for 7 to 10 days.

Yield: 1 to 1½ cups, depending on the culturing agent

Apple Cider Marinade

This is a recipe I picked up from Libby Hillman of Whitingham, Vermont, when I was editing her cookbook, The Best from Libby Hillman's Kitchen *(The Countryman Press, 1993). Libby recommends it for marinating pork spareribs and poultry, to flavor and tenderize the meat before it goes on the grill.*

1 cup sweet cider

2 tablespoons soy sauce

2 tablespoons maple syrup (or boiled cider)

1/2 teaspoon dried mustard

Salt and freshly ground black pepper to taste

Mix together all the ingredients in a bowl that is large enough to accommodate the meat.

Marinate the meat for at least 1 hour before barbecuing, or refrigerate overnight.

Before grilling the meat, be sure to wipe off any excess marinade, since substances like soy sauce will burn readily at the temperatures needed for grilling.

Yield: 1½ cups

Fish Poached in Cider

This quick recipe takes about twenty minutes to prepare and works well with almost any kind of white-fleshed fish: cod, haddock, halibut, monkfish, snapper, or sole. In Normandy and Brittany, the sauce is traditionally made quite rich, finished with extra butter and crème fraîche, as in the recipe for Chicken Breasts Vallée d'Auge, on page 139. To preserve the delicate flavor of the fish, try this somewhat lighter version of this recipe first; you can always make it richer the second time around.

1 1/2 to 2 pounds white-fleshed fish (cod, haddock, sole, etc.)
2 to 3 tablespoons butter
1/2 cup minced shallots or onions
1 cup chopped mushrooms (button mushrooms, portobello, crimini, or other types)

Salt and pepper to taste
1 cup dry sparkling hard cider
1/4 cup Calvados (optional)
1 cup crème fraîche (optional)
2 tablespoons butter (optional)

Cut the fish into two or four equal-sized pieces if necessary, so that they fit comfortably into a large frying pan or skillet.

Melt the butter in the pan and sauté the shallots or onions over medium-low heat until they are translucent. Season the fish with salt and pepper and arrange the fish pieces in the skillet. Cook a few minutes more, then add the mushrooms. Pour in the cider (and the Calvados, if you're using it) and turn up the heat to bring the liquid to a simmer. Cover and cook for 8 to 10 minutes.

Transfer the fish pieces to a deep serving dish. Continue heating the cooking liquid in the uncovered pan to reduce it slightly. Taste and season as necessary. At this point, if you want to make a richer sauce, you can add the optional crème fraîche and butter.

Pour the sauce with the mushrooms over the fish and serve. Garnish if you like with parsley and chopped fresh chives; croutons; and oysters, mussels, or crayfish poached in stock or white wine. Another way to prepare this dish is to preheat the oven to 500°F and rub about half a tablespoon of butter over the bottom of an ovenproof skillet or casserole. Season the fish pieces with salt and pepper and place in the middle of the pan, sprinkling the shallots and mushrooms around the sides. Pour the cider over the fish and bring to a boil on the stove. Then transfer to the oven and cook, covered, for 8 to 10 minutes, depending on thickness. Remove and sauce with the cooking liquid, or reduce further as described above.

Serves 4

Onion Cider Relish

My friends Stephen Wood and Louisa Spencer own Farnum Hill Ciders in Lebanon, New Hampshire, and use a wide variety of classic European and American apples to make well-balanced, distinctive ciders that aren't overly sweet and pair especially well with food. Their onion cider relish makes not only a nice spread for crackers or crisped pita toasts, as described below, but can also be used on grilled meats or as a flatbread or pizza topping.

1/4 cup canola or olive oil
2 red onions, peeled and sliced
4 white onions, peeled and sliced
1 bottle (750 ml.), minus one glass (or two!)
   semi-dry or extra-dry cider

Salt and freshly ground black pepper to taste
6 medium-sized pita breads for toasting

Heat the oil over medium heat in a heavy saucepan. Saute the onions in the oil, stirring occasionally, for about 10 minutes, or until the onions begin to soften. Add ½ cup of cider and continue to cook, stirring, over medium-low heat. After the cider is absorbed you can continue to add more cider by half-cup increments, until the flavor is to your liking. Season to taste with salt and pepper.

To serve on pita toasts, cut each pita in half, then cut each half into four triangular pieces. Separate the triangles along their outside edge. Place on a cookie sheet and brush each triangle lightly with olive oil. Sprinkle kosher salt on the oiled pieces and place in a 450°F oven for about 5 minutes or until lightly browned.

Serves about 4–6 people as an appetizer

Red Cabbage Braised in Cider

Both sweet and hard cider are wonderful for steaming or braising vegetables such as carrots, cauliflower, and many others. This is one of my favorite fall recipes, and a great way to cook red cabbage. Crunchy and slightly sweet, it makes a nice side dish for most meats, but as a former vegetarian I also like serving it alongside a grain-based dish like kasha varnitchkes.

4 tablespoons butter
1 medium head red cabbage, cored and
  shredded finely
1 1/2 cups sweet cider

1 teaspoon sugar
Pinch of salt
Freshly ground black pepper

Melt the butter over medium heat in a large, heavy skillet or Dutch oven. Add the cabbage and toss it with a slotted spoon to coat. Increase the heat to high and keep tossing until the cabbage starts to wilt.

Pour the cider into the pan, then mix in the sugar, salt, and pepper. Cover the pan and reduce the heat to its lowest setting. Cook until the cabbage is tender but still crunchy.

Using a slotted spoon, transfer the cabbage to a heated serving bowl. Increase the heat under the pan and cook the cider liquid until it has thickened slightly into a sauce. Pour over the cabbage and serve warm.

Serves 4

Harvest Stuffed Squash

Willis and Tina Wood operate Wood's Cider Mill in Springfield, Vermont, a family farm that has been making traditional boiled cider and cider jelly since 1882. This recipe from their Web site (www.woodscidermill.com) combines several seasonal fall favorites in this one terrific side dish, which goes well with roast pork or poultry.

2 or 3 Butternut, Buttercup, or Acorn squash
1 large apple, peeled and chopped
1/4 cup boiled cider
1/2 cup walnuts, chopped into pea-sized pieces

1/3 cup brown sugar or maple syrup
1/2 cup fresh or frozen cranberries
1/4 cup raisins (optional)
2 tablespoons butter

Preheat the oven to 400°F. Wash the squash, slice in halves, and scrape out the seeds. Place cut side down on a baking sheet and bake until the squash halves are very tender when pierced with a fork. Keeping the skin intact, scoop out the squash halves and put the flesh in a mixing bowl. Mash to a smooth consistency.

While the squash is baking, combine the chopped apple, boiled cider, walnuts, sugar or syrup, cranberries, and raisins in a saucepan. Simmer over low heat for about 10 minutes, or until the apple pieces are fork-tender.

Add the apple mixture to the mashed squash and gently mix together. Scoop the squash/apple mixture back into the original squash shells. Put a tab of butter on top of each and return to the oven for 5 minutes, or until heated through.

Serves 4 to 6

Pears Poached in Cider

Apples and pears, which are close botanical cousins, match up well in the kitchen, too, as this simple but elegant dessert demonstrates. I first learned about this classic combination from Terence Janericco, a Boston-based chef who wrote what is still one of my favorite cookbooks, Fabulous Fruit Desserts *(Yankee Books, 1986).*

6 pears, peeled, with stems left on
1 lemon, cut in half
2 1/2 cups sweet cider
1/2 cup sugar
Strip of lemon peel

1 vanilla bean, split
1 cinnamon stick
1 1/2 cups heavy cream
1 1/2 tablespoons Cognac

Rub the pears with the lemon halves and trim their bases so that they will stand upright. In a saucepan, simmer the cider, sugar, lemon peel, vanilla bean, and cinnamon stick for 2 minutes. Add the pears and poach them until tender. Let the pears cool in the liquid. Discard the cinnamon stick.

Whip the cream in a bowl and blend in the Cognac. Set aside.

Transfer the pears to a serving dish. Bring the poaching liquid to a boil and reduce it to a syrup, then pour over the pears.

Serve the pears, passing the cream separately.

Serves 6

Caramel Apple Gelato

This recipe comes from Mike Webb, the chef de cuisine at Pearl Restaurant and Oyster Bar in Peterborough, New Hampshire. One autumn, when he was looking for new flavors for Pearl's house-made gelato, Mike made some of his own New England boiled cider and decided to try it as a sweetener. The results were amazing.

16 large eggs
13 ounces granulated sugar
5 cups heavy cream
1 1/2 cups boiled cider

1 tablespoon vanilla extract
1/2 teaspoon ground cinnamon
2 cups whole milk

Separate the eggs, placing the yolks into a heat-safe mixing bowl (save the whites for the lemon meringue pie you'll make tomorrow). In a saucepan bring water to a boil, and make sure you have a thermometer close to hand. Place the mixing bowl over the simmering water and begin carefully whisking the egg yolks. You don't want to get too much yolk on the sides of the bowl because the yolks there will overcook and flake into your mixture. Checking the temperature frequently, heat to 180°F, then remove the bowl from the stove and add sugar. Transfer to the bowl of an upright mixer, or whisk by hand until the egg mixture turns pale yellow and begins to get fluffy. Set aside.

In a large saucepan, heat the cream, boiled cider, vanilla, and cinnamon until the mixture reaches the simmering point. Then ladle 2 cups of the hot cream mixture into your sugar/egg yolk mixture, whisking rapidly at the same time. (This can be tricky by yourself; if there's no one around to help you, place a damp towel under your mixing bowl for stability.) Once blended thoroughly, pour this mixture back into your hot cream on the stove. Whisk over medium to high heat until the mixture begins to thicken, and remove from the stove when the thermometer once again reads 180°F. Pour in the milk and mix to blend thoroughly. Place in the refrigerator and, when completely cool, transfer to an ice cream maker and follow the manufacturer's instructions.

Yield: Makes about 1 gallon

Cider, Hard and Sweet

Lost Nation Cider Pie

Lost Nation is a rural enclave in the North Country of New Hampshire, way up near the Canadian border. It's where my friends Michael and Nancy Phillips have their farm and tend an apple orchard and cider mill down the road. Every year they host a wassail party around Twelfth Night, and kids and grown-ups alike sing and dance around the biggest apple tree, then shoot off fireworks and make a hellacious racket in the cold, dark January night. Afterwards, it's back to the warmth of the farmhouse for some hard cider and a slice of this amazing pie, which is made with cider jelly (see page 133 for how to make your own). (Note: This recipe is adapted from The Apple Grower: A Guide for the Organic Orchardist *by Michael Phillips, Chelsea Green Publishing, 2005. Used by permission.)*

3/4 cup sugar
3 tablespoons cornstarch
Pinch of salt
1 cup cider jelly (see page 133)
1/2 cup boiling water

1 egg, lightly beaten
1 tablespoon butter, melted
2 cups sliced apples

Pastry for a two-crust 9-inch pie

Preheat the oven to 425°F. In a bowl, combine the sugar, cornstarch, and salt. Add the cider jelly and water and mix well. Add the egg and melted butter.

Arrange the apple slices on top of the bottom crust in the pie plate and pour the filling over them. Place the top crust on the pie, crimping the edges around the rim and slashing cuts in the top to allow steam to escape. Bake for 40 minutes or until the top crust is golden. Serve topped with a slice of sharp Cheddar cheese or with a scoop of vanilla ice cream on the side.

Serves 6

Tarte aux Pommes (Apple Tart)

This is another traditional recipe from Normandy. As with pies, the best apples to use are the tart, high-acid cooking varieties. Early varieties I like for pies and tarts include Gravenstein and Mantet; excellent later apples include Esopus Spitzenburg, Newtown, Pippin, and Calville Blanc d'Hiver, an old French variety that reputedly has the highest level of vitamin C of any apple.

One 9-inch pie shell, pricked with the tines of a
   fork and baked in a 450°F oven for 12 minutes,
   until golden brown (see following recipe for
   Pâté Brisée or use your own crust recipe)
6 large apples, peeled, cored, and cut into
   eighths

3 tablespoons butter
6 tablespoons sugar
1/2 cup Calvados (apple brandy)
1/2 teaspoon cinnamon
Scant pinch of salt

Combine the sliced apples in a saucepan with the butter, 3½ tablespoons of sugar, ¼ cup of the Calvados, and the cinnamon and salt. Cook the mixture over medium heat for about 8 minutes, stirring gently, until the apples are tender but still retain their shape.

Arrange the apples in the baked pie shell. In another saucepan, combine the remaining 2½ tablespoons of sugar and the rest of the Calvados. Warm the liquor, stirring until the sugar is dissolved; then ignite and pour over the apple slices.

Serve the tart warm, passing a bowl of whipped cream or crème fraîche (see page 140) separately.

Serves 6

Pâté Brisée

Here's a quick-and-easy recipe for a one-crust tart or quiche, made in the food processor. (For quiche, the shell does not need to be prebaked before filling.)

1 1/3 cups unbleached white flour

1/4 cup cold butter

1 teaspoon salt (or less, if you're using
   salted butter)

1 tablespoon sugar (optional)

1/4 cup ice water (slightly more if needed)

Preheat the oven to 450°F. Place the flour, butter, salt, and sugar into the bowl of a food processor fitted with a steel blade. Process until the mixture has the consistency of coarse meal. Add the ice water a little at a time, until the dough gathers together in a ball on top of the blade. (The entire process takes only a few seconds.)

Now you're ready to roll out the crust and bake the pie shell. Line a pie plate with the dough and prick it with the tines of a fork all over its surface. You can also place another pie plate of the same size on top of the dough, to ensure that it doesn't rise or bubble up while baking. Bake for about 12 minutes, until the shell is golden brown.

Yield: a single crust for one 9-inch pie or tart

Chapter 9: Cooking with Cider

Boiled Cider Apple Crisp

Boiled cider gives an extra tang and concentrated apple flavor to this apple crisp. If you can't find boiled cider for sale in your area, it's easy to make your own from fresh sweet cider (see pages 131–133), or substitute real maple syrup.

8 medium to large baking apples, peeled, cored, and sliced (look for baking or pie varieties that will hold their shape in cooking)
2 tablespoons unbleached white flour
1/2 to 3/4 cup granulated sugar
1/2 cup boiled cider
1 teaspoon ground cinnamon
1/4 teaspoon ground or freshly grated nutmeg
1/4 teaspoon ground allspice
1/4 teaspoon ground mace (optional)
1/4 teaspoon ground ginger (optional)

Topping:
1 1/2 cups oatmeal
1 1/2 cups unbleached white flour
3/4 cup light brown sugar
1/2 cup boiled cider
12 tablespoons butter, melted
1 teaspoon baking soda
1 teaspoon baking powder

Preheat the oven to 350°F. To make the filling, thoroughly mix together the apples, flour, granulated sugar, boiled cider, and spices in a large bowl. Transfer to an ungreased 9 x 13-inch baking dish.

Now combine the topping ingredients and mix thoroughly. Spread evenly over the apple mixture. Bake, uncovered, for 40 minutes, or until the topping is lightly browned. Serve warm with vanilla ice cream, or pass a container of light cream to pour over the crisp.

Serves 12

Pears Preserved in Calvados

One Christmas I gave these brandied pears to friends and family, in widemouth quart canning jars with tricolored raffia tied around their necks. Calvados, like other brandies, is terrific for preserving various kinds of fruits, especially peaches, pears, and cherries. Follow instructions in canning guides, substituting Calvados for grape brandies.

3 to 4 pounds pears (select firm, slightly under-ripe fruits; I like the small, sweet Seckel variety)

1 cup sugar

2 1/2 cups water

Juice and zest of two fresh limes

2 star anise pods

1 cinnamon stick

4 to 6 cardamom pods

6 to 8 allspice berries

2 1/2 cups Calvados (apple brandy)

Peel, core, and cut the pears in half. Place the sugar and water in a pan over low heat and stir until the sugar dissolves. Add the pears, lime juice and zest, and spices. Simmer for about 10 minutes. (Depending on the size of your pan, the pears may not all fit in one layer; if they don't, cook them in batches until just tender and transfer to a bowl while you finish simmering the rest.)

Lift the pears out with a slotted spoon and continue cooking the syrup for about 10 minutes more, until it thickens. Remove from the heat and add the Calvados.

Pack the pears into sterilized pint or quart canning jars and pour the hot syrup over the pears to cover. Pour in additional Calvados if necessary to cover fully, and, using a wooden utensil, remove any air bubbles.

Process for 15 minutes in a boiling-water bath to seal jars. Store in a cool location.

Yield: about 2 quarts

Chapter 9: Cooking with Cider

> The Apple being so closely connected with our wants and enjoyments, is entitled to the first notice in the catalogue of our fruits. The apple orchard is in truth the vineyard of our country; and the delicious beverage that can be obtained from some of the varieties of this excellent fruit being calculated to cheer the invalid, as well as to strengthen the healthy, entitles it to high consideration.
>
> —Thomas Bridgeman, *The Young Gardener's Assistant,* *7th edition* (1837)

10. CIDERMAKING: BEYOND THE BASICS

CHANCES ARE, BY THE TIME YOU ARE READING THIS CHAPTER you have already digested the information on the basics of the cidermaking process (chapters 3 and 4), and perhaps even made a batch or two of your own. Like most hobbies, making cider can be as simple or as complex a pursuit as you decide to make it. It's entirely possible to produce a very drinkable cider at home with virtually no equipment, for little more than the cost of the fresh cider, or the apples if you are pressing your own. Basically, you can make good cider if you remember only two things:

1. Use the best-quality cider apples you can find, or buy fresh juice from an orchard that grows and presses these varieties (see chapter 2).

2. Yeast needs oxygen to get fermentation started, but after things have settled down, you need to protect the cider from contact with air.

These two points summarize and greatly simplify the whole cidermaking process, but essentially that's all you need to know: all the specialized winemaking aids and equipment can be helpful, but they aren't necessary to the basic process. Fresh cider wants to ferment and to become hard cider, and eventually, unless we control the conditions, hard cider wants to turn into vinegar. It helps to think of your sweet cider as a kind of complex ecosystem, a veritable parade of microbial life. All we are really doing is controlling, and sometimes manipulating, the conditions in which these critters operate, in an attempt to keep hard cider from going any further along in the process, or to produce a particular style of cider.

No one book, and no one person, can give you every conceivable detail about cider, or can trouble-shoot every aspect of the process and make it completely foolproof. I still occasionally field questions from people whose problems I cannot diagnose with complete certainty. "Why didn't my cider work?" is the most basic question I hear, but the answer might be far from basic, and could involve any one of a thousand variables, including—sometimes—simple impatience or inexperience. Beginning cidermakers tend to be overly anxious and hover over their carboys like a mother hen sitting on eggs; while this in itself isn't necessarily bad, one obvious reason why people don't like the taste of their own cider is because they try and drink it too soon. My friend from Quebec, Claude Jolicoeur, and I are alike in that we almost never take our cider out of bulk storage and bottle it until at least nine months after we have started fer-

mentation, and often we leave it to develop and age even longer. It's a myth that a well-made cider needs to be drunk very young, within the year. After all, we don't pour bottles of white wine down the drain because they're a couple of years old. Neither should we do that to the cider that we've so carefully crafted from good apples.

This chapter isn't intended to give you a complete tutorial in intermediate or advanced cidermaking practices, but merely to address some of the most common points that might interest you after you've made a few batches of cider and are looking to expand your horizons or scale up your operation. The key is to enjoy the process (as well as the end result) of making cider. If you do, it can become a rewarding lifelong pursuit, as it has with me. Every autumn gives me another opportunity to try something a little different, or to use what I've learned to improve upon the previous year's cider. The best advice is to learn from experience, including the successes and failures of other cidermakers: two excellent ways to do that are to join an online community like the Cider Digest or to attend a festival like the annual CiderDays event in western Massachusetts, where hobbyists and professionals alike come to attend workshops and tastings (see Resources). Also, anyone who has any ambitions about "turning pro" and making a commercial cider should consider taking a course like the one offered by Peter Mitchell, a noted British cider consultant. Titled "Principles and Practice of Cider Making," Mitchell's course is a multi-day affair that focuses in part on sensory evaluation, so you can gain a deeper understanding of what's really going on in your cider and how to encourage (or discourage) it. These courses are offered periodically at either Cornell or Washington State universities, and they tend to fill up quickly. (Advance notice is usually available through the Cider Digest.) The price for this kind of course is certainly not out of line if you are intending to get really serious about your cider. Others in the U.S. are also becoming engaged in cider education and improvement, including Vintage Virginia Apples, which holds an annual Cidermakers Forum at their orchard facility near Charlottesville.

Scaling Up

The first thing to consider is what additional pieces of equipment might prove useful if you want to increase or improve your cider production. I tend to be more of a Neo-Luddite than a gadget-lover, preferring simple methods and low-tech tools whenever possible. However, there are a few useful items that you might want to acquire as you get deeper into cidermaking, either to keep closer tabs on your cider, or to make life easier as you produce more and larger batches. Most of this equipment can be purchased either through home-brewing and winemaking suppliers (see Resources), or by doing a quick Internet search to locate a product's manufacturer, who often will provide useful technical information as well.

Measuring Instruments

A **refractometer** is a good instrument to use out in the orchard or vineyard to check the sugar levels of fruit or juice. The handheld model is about 4 inches long and measures sugar based on the refraction of light. By putting a bit of juice extracted from crushed fruit onto a glass prism at one end and reading the scale through a lens at the other end, you can see the sugar level expressed in degrees Brix. (Typically the scale measures between 0 and 30°B.) Once you know the Brix, you can find the corresponding specific gravity and potential alcohol of the fruit juice (see the table in the Appendix). This handheld model of refractometer generally costs around fifty dollars.

You can also check your pressed sweet cider with a refractometer, though if that's all you're using it for, I'd save my money. After pressing, it's easy to measure specific gravity with your hydrometer and a sample jar full of juice. The only advantage of the refractometer here is that you only need a few drops of juice.

Measuring acid levels in cider can be important for a couple of reasons. First, it helps determine how much or little SO_2 you'll want to add to your juice before fermentation, and perhaps later, in the form of metabisulfites (see the table on page 77). Second, for cidermakers who press European bittersweet apples, especially those who ferment them separately, it's important to know the pH of the juice, since these varieties are very low in acid, which can encourage unwanted microbial infection.

We've discussed this a bit in chapter 4, and I have found that some cidermakers use narrow-range pH strips, and find them adequate, while others think that they are worthless and swear by some form of **pH meter,** a device that is essentially a voltmeter connected to an electrode and sealed, so that it displays not the measured potential, but the ready pH value. A good pH meter, when used correctly, will be accurate to plus or minus 0.01 unit of pH (as opposed to a margin of error on the order of 0.5 to 1.0 unit for pH test strips); however, the meter will probably set you back around three hundred dollars. Then, too, you will need to buy buffer solution, electrode cleaning solution, and eventually a replacement electrode.

In my opinion, the expense isn't worth it if you are only testing the occasional small batch of cider, though there is a less expensive model of pH meter available called a Checker, which retails for around fifty dollars. Still, my feeling is that, if you are pressing a good mixture of dessert, culinary, and cider apples (see chapter 2), then you should have plenty of acidity in your blend and

Winesap

needn't worry that your acid level is too low. Or, if your fermented cider has especially high acidity, that often mellows naturally with time. For example, Steve Wood at Farnum Hill Ciders in New Hampshire occasionally makes a single-variety cider from Ashmead's Kernel. When first bottled it will practically take the enamel off your teeth; after a couple of years in the bottle, though, it becomes very nice indeed. And of course there are other post-fermentation techniques for reducing malic acid, such as introducing a malolactic culture (see chapter 4). In other words, high acidity in cider generally isn't as much of a problem as low acidity.

Tannins are the third and final consideration. Here, I definitely wouldn't waste my time or money measuring them if you are just making cider for yourself and your friends. You either have them (mainly because you're pressing either European apples or wild or crab apples), or you don't. Tannins add structure and interest to cider, but you can make a perfectly drinkable cider without them. One important point about tannins that we didn't discuss in earlier chapters is that the U.S. government doesn't allow the use of grape tannin powder (the most widely available kind) in commercial ciders. Oak tannins (also known as *ellagitannins*) are okay, though, which makes sense, since wine and cider producers often ferment or age in oak barrels (see page 160).

Keep in mind that your mouth is your most valuable and sensitive measuring instrument (and it comes free, as standard equipment!). There is no substitute for putting your teeth into a wide variety of apples, because that will give you the firsthand experience that's necessary to decide which kinds of fruit will contribute to a good cider blend. Chomp into a Red Delicious or a Pound Sweet. Not much acidity there. Now bite into a tree-ripe Ashmead's Kernel or Bramley's Seedling and see if you can keep one eye from squinching up. It won't take long before you become a good judge of sugar and acidity. The only thing that takes a bit of practice is determining

Chapter 10: Cidermaking: Beyond the Basics

TRADITIONAL SPARKLING CIDER

One cidermaking practice that we haven't addressed is how to make a sparkling or "champagne-style" cider. It is identical to the *methode traditionnelle*, or the old artisanal process of making champagne. The goal is to give the cider a dosage of sugar and then rack it into sturdy champagne bottles and apply a crown cap of the appropriate size (see chapter 4, page 71) or a hollow plastic cork secured with string or a wire cage. (Crown caps are the least expensive option at this stage, because you will be removing the caps and resealing the bottles during the process.) Determining how much sugar to use depends on how sparkling you want the cider; a sturdy champagne bottle can withstand 6 "atmospheres" of CO_2 pressure (equivalent to bottling a cider at 1.010 specific gravity), but it's always wise to err on the side of caution. Figure on a dose of roughly 2 teaspoons sugar per bottle, a bit less than 1/4 cup per gallon (about 50 grams), and 2 rounded cup or 1 1/4 cup for a 5-gallon batch of cider. This obviously isn't rocket science, and using any approximation of this amount, between 1 and 1 1/2 cups per 5-gallon batch, should be fine. Go easy on your first try, then increase the dosage the next time around if you feel that the cider should have more carbonation.

Allow the yeasts to do their secondary fermentation work and bottle-condition the cider; then leave the cider to sit on its lees for several months in the bottle. The next step is what's called riddling, or *remuage* (literally 'shaking') in French, and it involves placing the bottles with their necks inverted, so that the lees will dislodge and fall into the neck of the bottle behind the cap or cork. The French traditionally used an A-frame wooden rack called a *pupitre* with holes cut in both sides to accommodate the bottles. During riddling, the *remueur* twists the bottles to help dislodge the sediment. It's a good idea to wear heavy gloves and eye protection when doing this, just in case a bottle has a flaw and decides to burst on you.

Once the lees have settled behind the caps or corks of the bottles, the bottles need to be inverted again, this time with their necks plunged into a tray containing rock salt and ice. This solution freezes the lees into a solid pellet. The bottles are then turned right-side up and opened, and, ideally, the frozen pellet flies out along with the top. This step is known as *dégorgement*.

Finally, the bottles are topped up with reserved cider of the same batch or with an additional dosage of sugar in solution, and recapped or fitted with champagne corks and wire cages.

Sound like a lot of work? It is, and frankly I only know of a few commercial cidermakers in the U.S. who go to all this trouble. They at least can recoup some of their time and effort by charging a higher price, but I don't recommend it as a method for home cidermakers, unless you have a lot of time on your hands. For while riddling and disgorgement do eliminate the heavy sediment from the bottle, this process really doesn't improve the drinking quality of homemade sparkling cider, which can be carefully decanted off its lees and enjoyed as the simple country wine that it is.

how much sugar is in a "high-flavored" or "sprightly" apple like Ashmead's or Esopus Spitzenburg. When tree-ripe, the acids can dominate and mask the sugars in the fruit. But wait a couple of months and taste the same apple that's been in cold storage; the flavor will be much more mellow and fully developed, though the fruit will still have good acidity.

Tannins are even easier for most people to pick up. Some European cider apples have "soft" tannins and are almost good enough to eat out of hand; a good, ripe Kingston Black is a little dry, but not unpleasant. Other varieties like Dabinett and Chisel Jersey have "hard" tannins and are very astringent. Again, tasting is your best bet. The good thing is that tannins, in moderation, won't be a problem, even if you are only making sweet cider; in fact, they contribute body without much bitterness and give fresh cider a desirable "chewiness."

Fermentation Vessels and Supplies

Most home cidermakers won't be making anything approaching the 200 gallons per household allowed by the federal government. I like cider, but I'm not drinking it morning, noon, and night—nor am I using it to pay thirsty farmhands or bartering with the neighbors (although that's not a bad idea). My point is, for most of us, plastic fermentation pails and glass carboys work just fine; the largest reasonable size to lug around is 6.5 gallons, which currently runs less than twelve dollars (for a new bucket) or roughly twice that for a glass carboy, which with reasonable care will last you practically forever.

However, if you intend to scale up your operation, you will probably want to consider other, larger vessels for primary fermentation and/or bulk storage. Commercial cidermakers often use stainless steel tanks, but these are really expensive unless you can buy one used from a dairy operation, brewery, or winery. Another option is high-density polyethylene (HDPE) barrels. These come in a wide range of sizes (9, 15, 30, 55 gallons, for example) that make it easy to match your capacity needs. They are also available used, but be very careful what was in them previously before you start filling them up with your good sweet cider; like all plastic they retain flavors, and you probably don't want your delicate cider tasting like tamari soy sauce or even orange juice concentrate. Also, the price differential between new and used HDPE barrels is not that great; a used one might cost twenty-five dollars, and a new one perhaps twice that much.

HDPE barrels come in different thicknesses. If you can find ones that are 1/4-inch thick (so-called closed-head drums or Dixie drums) they are better than the thinner, usually blue-colored juice barrels that have a wall thickness of only 1/8 inch.

Another issue with the thinner-walled HDPE barrels is that, like wooden barrels, they "breathe" and allow some air exchange between the cider inside the barrel and the outside world. This isn't a problem during primary fermentation, because the cider is outgassing CO_2 and protecting itself. But it can become an issue during bulk storage. One low-tech solution would be to swathe your barrels in plastic wrap.

One commercial cidermaker I know uses the thicker-walled Dixie drums extensively. The lids are of his barrels are fitted with airlocks and the barrels stored upright in an insulated room in his barn for long, slow fermentation. The only piece of equipment he needs to move the barrels around is a sturdy hand truck. At the end of the season, after racking or bottling the cider, he puts a cup of bleach in each 30-gallon barrel and fills them with water. Then he leaves them in a hot, sunny spot for a couple of weeks before rinsing them out once or twice with water. The barrels are sanitized and set aside for the next season; before use, though, he does rinse them out once more. He has used these sturdy plastic barrels for about five years now, and plans to get five more years service out of them.

A third option is fermenting in stainless steel kegs. Cornelius kegs are most often used for kegging beer and cider as well as carbonating and filtration, and we'll discuss them below under "Kegging, Filtration, and Bottling Equipment." For now, suffice it to say that Corny kegs, if you can pick one up used, for a reasonable price, also make perfectly good primary fermentation tanks (the one disadvantage being that you can't visually monitor the cider). They come in a variety of sizes ranging from 2.5 to 15 gallons (with 5 gallon being a popular size) and they are certainly versatile, useful, and more movable and manageable for the home operation than either stationary metal tanks or large wooden barrels.

Fermenting and Aging in Oak Barrels

Last but certainly not least, there are wooden barrels. Barrel fermentation in oak is traditional, but there are definitely pluses and minuses to using wood. First and foremost is the issue of cost. It will run you about two hundred dollars for a new 5-gallon (20-liter) American oak barrel, and about three hundred for a French oak barrel of the same volume—and the prices go up from there. Used wine barrels are an option, if you can find them; Steve Wood at Farnum Hill Ciders bought "played-out" Chardonnay barrels when he started fermenting and aging in oak, ideally ones that had been used three or four times, after which much of the oak's fresh tannins had been leached out into the wine. Compared to most wines, cider is a low-alcohol, delicate

drink, and using a new, untreated oak barrel would give you a product with all the insouciant charm of a two-by-four. Obviously, barrels that have held red wine don't work well, either. An old American custom is to ferment cider in used whisky barrels (preferably just emptied, and with a bit whisky still inside). This method makes a fiercely interesting specialty cider, but you certainly wouldn't want to use it for a cider where you wanted to emphasize fruitiness and subtle delicacy of flavor and aroma.

Oak, when used judiciously, can add a complexity and structure to cider, just as it does to some white wines. However, much like a pet, once you acquire an oak barrel you have to take care of it. In particular you will need to treat a new barrel before use, filling it with water for a week or so before pouring in cider. It also helps to leach out some of the tannins before use by filling the barrel half-full with very hot water, then adding soda ash dissolved in hot water (2 ounces for every 3 gallons barrel capacity), and topping up the barrel with more hot water. Bung the barrel tight and roll it around over a 24-hour period. Then empty it and rinse it out thoroughly with several changes of water.

Clean out barrels thoroughly after each use, and in between uses fill them with a storage solution, adding 1 teaspoon citric acid and 1 teaspoon potassium metabisulfite for every 10 gallons of barrel capacity, then filling the barrel with water and bunging it tight.

Never, ever use a barrel that has contained vinegar for making cider; the acetobacter will remain in the pores of the wood no matter how thoroughly the barrel has been cleaned and sanitized. (The same is true of HDPE barrels; I would never considering reusing one that had previously held anything that was pickled or otherwise was made with acetic acid.)

In addition to pretreating and good sanitation, there

are a couple of other issues related to wooden barrels. First, wood "breathes," and once primary fermentation is over and you've bunged up the cider in another barrel for aging, you will need to check the barrel periodically and top it up as liquid evaporates through the wood. (The blank air space, which you don't want sitting above your cider, is called the *ullage,* and the lost liquor is often referred to as "the angel's share" by distillers.)

All of this brings up a key question: Do you want to do your primary fermentation in wooden barrels, or just put the fermented cider in wood to condition it and give it some oaky character? Fermenting cider in oak is certainly romantic and rather fun. Leaving the bung open at the beginning, the incredible froth and foam that issues forth as the cider cleanses itself is truly impressive. And once things slow down and you've fitted a stopper and fermentation lock into the bung, the steady glub-glub of CO_2 escaping is a cheery sound in the cider house. However, unless you have a number of barrels at your disposal—some for fermenting and some for aging cider—and unless your cider room has enough space to accommodate the requisite carriages or racks for seating the barrels on their sides, plus a strong concrete slab with good drains and maybe outdoor access (you will be doing a lot of washing and sanitation), then I recommend using another kind of vessel as your primary fermenter and then racking the fermented cider into the wooden barrels for aging. That, after all, is what you are after—the contribution that oak makes to taste and body, not a lot more work that can make a hobby seem more like a career.

If you are using wooden barrels for aging and conditioning, then it's important to consider the size (volume capacity) of the barrel, and the newness or amount of tannin that is in the oak. Smaller barrels (especially the 5-gallon size) have a higher surface-to-volume ratio than larger barrels. This means that cider in a smaller barrel will pick up oakiness more quickly than cider in a larger barrel, assuming the barrels have been used for roughly the same amount of time and contain similar amounts of tannin. For this reason, and because wood is porous and you need to top up the cider in the barrel due to evaporation, barrels are not a good long-term means of storage for regular cider (though the French age pommeau in wood for eighteen months, and Calvados for two years or longer). As soon your cider has picked up the desired amount of oakiness, it's best to either bottle it (ideally), or rack it into another container for further bulk storage. Just remember that every time you rack cider, no matter how carefully, you are introducing some air and potentially reawakening the yeast; to discourage this, it's often wise to add sulfites. However, the total amount of sulfites you use, from pre-fermentation through final bottling, should not exceed a maximum of 200 parts per million, except in extreme circumstances. Generally less is more, and one should use as little SO_2 as is practical, based on the pH of the cider.

A final word about oak conditioning. If you want to use wooden barrels for traditional cidermaking or nostalgic purposes, that's great. But for most hobby (and even commercial) cider producers, it's far less expensive and time-consuming to get your oak character by using oak cubes, chips, sticks, or spirals, which are available from almost any winemaking supply store or online outlet. These small chunks of wood, which are often made from old barrels themselves, are fire-treated to a light, medium, or heavy "toast." They are much more efficient than whole barrels for imparting an oaky character to wine or cider, because they have a much greater surface-to-liquid ratio than even the smallest barrel. Like barrels, oak chunks or chips can be used either during primary fermentation or, more often, in the aging/conditioning

Chapter 10: Cidermaking: Beyond the Basics

period after fermentation is complete. Before introducing them to your cider, you will need to sterilize these wooden chunks or chips by boiling or steaming them for ten minutes. Suspending a sterilized muslin bag containing the chips in your carboy or other vessel makes it easy to extract the wood whenever you think it's appropriate; otherwise place the chunks or sticks in the carboy first and then rack or transfer the cider into the vessel. Once again, keep in mind that a little oak goes a long way, particularly with something as delicate as cider, so use them sparingly and follow instructions from the producer or ask your winemaking supply retailer for advice.

Kegging, Filtration, and Bottling Equipment

We've mentioned Cornelius (or Corny) stainless steel kegs earlier, and many small-scale brewers and cidermakers use them effectively for fermentation (primary or secondary), storage, or even dispensing, if you have the appropriate draft system. They are also useful if you decide to filter your cider to remove the yeast and stop fermentation, and for force carbonation and bottling. The kegs themselves are expensive if purchased new (up to several hundred dollars), but it's generally easy to find reconditioned 5-gallon kegs for a fraction of that price (usually forty dollars or less), especially from soft drink bottling plants, which don't use them any longer and generally have a good supply, Make sure if you are buying a used Corny keg that you clean it out very thoroughly and replace all the O-rings or seals as well as any parts that contain plastic, since it's virtually impossible to get these completely clean and sanitized after years of contact with the sticky, concentrated syrups used to make soft drinks.

It's beyond the scope of this chapter to discuss all of the hardware and accessory parts you'll need to do kegging and filtration. Hoses and fittings, a regulator, an aluminum CO_2 tank (plus the CO_2 that goes into it, which you can buy from a local welding shop), and an aeration stone for quick carbonation—all these are necessary to get the most out your kegging system. E. C. Kraus and other homebrew and winemaking suppliers carry complete systems, plus all of the components (see Resources).

Bottling equipment is associated with kegs because the main tool for small producers (aside from the low-tech but time-honored racking tube) is the counterpressure bottle filler, which purges a bottle with CO_2 gas and then gently transfers the cider to the bottle, creating a minimum amount of foaming. Handheld models of stainless steel fillers cost around seventy dollars, but as with kegs, you need to spend a little more to buy the requisite hoses and connectors. This technique of filling bottles is what's referred to as forced carbonation, as opposed to the natural carbonation we've already discussed that takes place during secondary fermentation, when some form of sugar is added to cider and it's sealed in a closed keg or bottle; the activity of the remaining yeast cells releases carbon dioxide into the liquid, pressurizing the contents of the bottle or tank a bit and filling any airspace at the top of the container. Even if you carbonate your cider naturally in a keg, though, it's good to use a counterpressure filler when bottling, so that you don't lose any of the fizz. The alternative is to use a gravity-feed bottle filler, which is relatively inexpensive and easy to use, though you will lose some carbonation in the bottling process. For some people, this is a perfectly acceptable tradeoff.

Filtration equipment is used by some cidermakers to help stop fermentation while the cider still contains some residual sugar. This is usually accomplished by transferring

A countertop bottling setup, showing cider being transferred from a Cornelius keg into bottles using a counterpressure bottle filler and CO_2 tank. *Ben Polito*

the cider from one keg into another, under CO_2 pressure, through a sterile filter pad or series of pads. Anything larger than the size of the pores in the filter (typically 0.45 or 0.5 micron) gets excluded, including yeast cells.

Keeping Things Sweet

The ultimate goal for many cidermakers involves keeping their cider from "going all the way" to dryness. However, there is no easy way of retaining residual sweetness in cider. You are fighting an uphill battle against a determined legion of microorganisms, particularly yeasts that want to feed on sugars, reproduce, and in the process produce alcohol and burp carbon dioxide. And as usually happens when we work against Mother Nature, we end up devising complex and not always effective ways to thwart her will.

In chapter 4 we mentioned that the wild yeast populations, which naturally start the fermentation process (*Kloeckera*, et al.), do not tolerate high concentrations of either sulfur dioxide or alcohol. They are suppressed when we add sulfites to the juice or must, and even if we don't these early-succession yeasts die out as the alcohol level rises. Other wild yeasts, including *Saccharomyces* strains (the same types as packaged wine and beer yeasts) take over the fermentation, and these yeasts, under normal circumstances, consume nearly all the available sugars (a process otherwise known as "complete attenuation") and produce a dry, fully fermented cider.

Before we discuss some of the options for keeping a cider sweet, let me make a pitch for keeping things simple. When you are first starting out as an amateur cidermaker, it's important to learn to like your own dry cider. It is true that most humans have a sweet tooth, and some of us still struggle with the popular notion that "cider should taste like apples," which we've already dismissed as poppycock. Yet dry, still ciders, in my humble opinion, are not only more drinkable and interesting in many cases than sweet or overly carbonated ciders, but you can taste more in them, and learn much more from them. By that I mean that the true nature of the fruit shines through more clearly in a cider fermented to its logical endpoint. A classic cider variety like Golden Russet or Baldwin often shows you what it's capable of, and so too do other apples that might be great in a blended cider. Also, dry ciders tend to be far more versatile than sweet ones whenever they are served with food.

If you do decide to make a cider with some residual sweetness, though, try to resist the urge to make something that tastes like liquid apple candy or "glucose wine." There are plenty of commercial products out there on the market that are probably just as drinkable as anything you can make along these lines. Six-pack

Chapter 10: Cidermaking: Beyond the Basics

"draft" ciders are generally as sweet as wine coolers and are back-sweetened with concentrate, pasteurized and stabilized. If you have a sweet tooth, eat some cake; if you enjoy cider, drink it at least a little dry. As a sweet apertif, try pommeau; for dessert, I recommend a sip of ice cider (see chapter 8).

There are several methods that cidermakers employ to halt fermentation and produce a sweeter style of cider.

Passing cider under pressure through two ganged sterile micropad filters is one way to remove yeast cells and help stabilize a cider that has not completely fermented to dryness. *Terence Bradshaw*

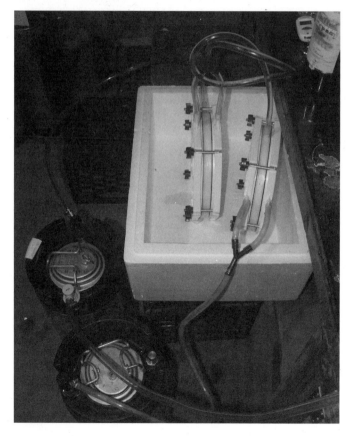

One of them (keeving) is a traditional European technique. The others are modern and include cold shocking, filtering, and in-bottle pasteurization, usually combined with the use of sulfites and sorbate to discourage re-fermentation in the bottle.

Keeving

Keeving is a procedure that strips nitrogenous nutrients out of a juice or must that is being fermented. The object is to produce a cider that retains some natural residual sugar, by essentially "starving" the yeasts so that fermentation stops at a higher specific gravity than usual. (The French term for this process is *défécation*, but since that sounds a bit earthy to most Anglophones, we'll stick with the British word *keeving*.)

Undernourishing yeast flies in the face of almost every good cidermaking tenet that we discussed in chapter 4, and many producers are in fact not enthusiastic about keeving their cider, believing instead that fermentation should always be as strong and complete as possible—even when it's done more slowly at a colder temperature. They make the case that when wild yeasts (which aren't really capable of fermenting a cider to dryness anyway) are starved for nutrients, they often produce a cider with funky or "off" smells, most often a sulfurous emanation like rotten eggs (hydrogen sulfide or H_2S).

On the other hand, keeving has been practiced for centuries in the traditional cidermaking areas of northwest Europe. Even before modern knowledge of fermentation chemistry, this was possible because apple orchards were not fertilized with agricultural chemicals, and the large standard-sized trees were widely spaced, to allow room for domestic animals to graze the orchard floor. Both the absence of high-nitrogen fertilizers and the fact that the animals were removing nitrogen from the

Cider, Hard and Sweet

ground (in the form of grass) ensured that less nitrogen actually wound up in the apples and in the juice pressed from them.

Keeving takes place when positively charged amino acids and other nitrogenous substances like thiamin bind to negatively charged pectinate anions that are generated by an enzyme (pectin methyl esterase, or PME) that occurs naturally in apples. In less technical terms, the pectin acts like a matrix to remove the nutrients from the juice, forming a gelatinous mass and eventually a frothy *chapeau brun* (brown cap) on top of a layer of very clear, nutrient-poor juice and a heavy bottom sediment. This middle portion of clear juice is then racked off into another vessel and primary fermentation is allowed to continue until it stops naturally, usually well short of dryness at a high final specific gravity.

The enzyme PME should not be confused with pectinase, which is a common winemaking aid whose only function is to clarify a juice or must. Only for the past twenty years or so has a commercial PME enzyme been available to cidermakers, and they now use it, along with small amounts of calcium chloride salt ($CaCl_2$) or calcium carbonate ($CaCO_3$), more commonly known as precipitated chalk. Roy Bailey of Lambourn Valley Cider in Berkshire, England, reports that he uses about 6 ounces of a crystalline form of calcium chloride to 50 gallons of juice, which works out to roughly 1 tablespoon per 5-gallon batch.

Another common practice associated with keeving is maceration (see box on page 61). If, after grinding or milling the apples, you leave the pomace for 24 hours before pressing, more pectin will diffuse out from between the cell walls and will become soluble in the juice. According to British cider guru Andrew Lea, it also helps if the apples themselves are fully mature and thus already rich in soluble pectin. This underscores the

The "brain-in-a-bottle" appearance in the carboy indicates that a keeved cider is separating nicely. It is now time to rack off the very clear juice in the center layer into another vessel and allow it to complete primary fermentation. *Terry Bradshaw*

importance of either "sweating" the apples (see chapter 3) or storing them until they are completely ripe and full of sugar.

If you want to try your hand at keeving, know that there are a lot of variables involved and that it isn't invariably successful. The best idea is to try a batch in a 5-gallon glass carboy, where you can clearly see what's happening with the cider. Fill the carboy with juice about halfway, and then add the calcium chloride and the PME separately. In my keeving experiments I've used only 1.4 milliliters of PME per 5-gallon batch, as per manufacturer's directions. (Or, as a rough estimate, multiply 0.24 times the number of U.S. gallons in the batch to get the number of grams, or milliliters, to add to the

Chapter 10: Cidermaking: Beyond the Basics

juice.) Then continue filling the carboy with fresh cider, but only up to the top of the straight portion, leaving the entire "shoulder" of the vessel as head space. This is because, once the brown cap starts to form, it can easily sink and dissolve back into the cider if it doesn't have enough room. (Some cidermakers refer to the appearance of a successful keeve as "the brain in a bottle.")

The amount of time it will take the brown cap to form can vary considerably, depending on the temperature of the juice. At around 60°F (15°C–16°C) it might take less than one day; at 50°F (10°C) it might be more like five days, or correspondingly longer at even lower temperatures. Because of this uncertainty, you'll need to keep a close eye on the cider so that you can rack off the clear juice immediately after the brown cap has risen. Top up the keeved cider in the new fermenter with fresh juice and let it ferment as usual.

Test the specific gravity of the cider as it ferments slowly. Knowing when to bottle takes a bit of practice. In general, a successfully keeved cider will ferment to a specific gravity somewhere around 1.035 and will then stabilize and slowly "finish up" at around 1.020 S.G. by the end of the summer, at which point you should plan to bottle it. If you intend to carbonate naturally in the bottle and produce a sparkling cider, you should bottle at an even higher point, perhaps around 1.030 or a few points higher. Once again, erring on the side of caution and bottling at a lower S.G. is recommended, at least for your first time around.

Clearly, keeving is something that only the real cider aficionado will attempt. If it works well, though, you can make a remarkable-tasting, medium-sweet cider that should impress your friends and fellow cider enthusiasts. At worst, if it fails, you can usually still produce a regular batch of cider.

For more information on keeving, I recommend reading up in old cidermaking texts, or getting instructions on how to do it from PME suppliers or on the Internet.

Cold Shocking, Filtering, and Stabilizing Cider

Cold shocking—subjecting partially fermented cider to very cold temperatures to halt all yeast activity—is a relatively simple way to bring things to a crashing halt. Different strains of yeast will continue working down to different temperatures, with some champagne yeasts (*Saccharomyces bayanus*) plugging away slowly but surely down into the lower forties.

Moving a carboy into a walk-in freezer or leaving it outside or in an unheated garage when the temperatures are reliably below freezing, say in the twenties, should do the trick. Your goal should be to reduce the temperature of the juice without actually freezing it solid. Obviously this will take longer and be easier to control with a large batch (5 gallons) rather than a small 1-gallon test batch. Be aware that a sudden drop in temperature can suck the contaminated sanitizing solution out of the airlock and into the cider. So it's a good idea to replace the lock with a newly filled one containing fresh sulfite solution before you bring the cider into the cold.

Cold shocking, though, only halts the fermentation; it doesn't kill the yeast or prevent refermentation. For this, most cidermakers fine their cider with a wine clarifier and rack it or, better yet, filter it using a little CO_2 pressure through a sterile pad system into another container, such as a Cornelius keg. (Using a 0.45 micron pad won't guarantee a sterile product, though it will reduce yeast counts substantially.) The cider should remain at a cold temperature, and then, before bottling, you'll need to add potassium sorbate, a little less than

200 ppm, to guard against refermentation. It's also a good idea to use an additional 50 ppm of SO$_2$ at bottling time as well, since this seems to make the sorbate more effective and also suppresses any microbial activity. The downside is that people will be more sensitive to sulfites when added at this late stage, and both they and the sorbate can affect the final flavor of the cider—adversely, according to some tastes.

The yeast most frequently recommended for ciders that will be cold-shocked is Côte des Blancs (formerly known as Epernay 2; see the box on page 82). This yeast also tends to give some fruity and floral quality to the cider, which is in keeping with a sweeter style.

All of this effort strikes me as way too much of a hassle for the amateur cidermaker, although I do know people who cold-filter their cider to stabilize it. A much more practical solution, and one that doesn't involve preservatives, is to stabilize the cider after bottling by pasteurizing it, bottle and all.

DEUTSCHE POMOLOGIE.

RÖTHLICHE REINETTE

In-Bottle Pasteurization

At first blush it may appear ironic, or at least incongruous, that I should argue so strongly in favor of unpasteurized sweet cider (or at least the option of not pasteurizing it), yet describe here the method of pasteurizing hard cider, bottle and all, to stabilize it. In fact, I'm not fanatically for or against pasteurization—just for using it in its place. I wouldn't conceive of making apple juice without stabilizing it, and in-bottle pasteurization is just the equivalent of that process as it applies to hard cider. The good news is that, since unfermented juice and alcoholic cider are different, you don't need to heat the latter to as high a temperature or for nearly as long. This is because in the case of juice we are targeting mainly bacteria and spoilage organisms, whereas in the case of hard cider we are mainly trying to stop the yeast from starting up, or continuing to ferment in the bottle.

To do bottle pasteurization, you will need to use a sturdy champagne-type bottle, one that can withstand at least 6 atmospheres of pressure; this is true whether or not you are making a still or sparkling cider.

Ferment the cider to dryness, and allow it to rest in bulk storage for a few months. Next, add some reserved fresh juice to the fermented cider. (This is why it's good to freeze several gallons of cider every fall, to have on hand for just such an occasion.) Add the juice gradually and keep testing with a hydrometer until the specific gravity of the mixture reaches 1.010, or just a few points higher if you want to let the mixture carbonate in the bottle before pasteurizing.

Bottle the cider and apply crown caps. Allow the cider to bottle-ferment until the desired level of carbonation has been achieved. You'll need to open up a bottle and check this every few days. Depending on the ambient temperature and other variables, this might take only

Chapter 10: Cidermaking: Beyond the Basics

a few days, or as long as two or three weeks. Don't let the fermentation go too far; pasteurizing too soon is far better than doing it too late.

For small batches, it's probably easiest to do the pasteurizing in a large kettle on the stovetop, or in a metal tub or livestock trough that's set over a propane burner outdoors. Place the capped bottles in the water bath; the water should come up to the fill line on the necks. Fill one bottle with water that's at about the same temperature or cooler than the cider, and leave it uncapped, with a thermometer (or the temperature probe of a digital thermometer) inserted in it.

Heat the water in the tub or kettle until the thermometer in the test bottle reads 150°F (65°C). Then turn off the heat and hold the temperature of the water bath above 140°F (60°C) for 10 to 20 minutes, covering the tub or kettle with an insulating blanket if necessary. The bottles may start leaking gas around their caps and hissing; this is fine and isn't cause for concern.

Remove the bottles carefully and cool them slowly to minimize any risk of breakage. (Wear protective goggles, gloves, and a heavy sweatshirt or jacket while you are doing this.) Don't set the bottles onto a cold countertop or splash cold water on them while they are warm; this only increases the risk of shattering.

If held above the specified temperature, all of the yeasts should be killed, and the cider will remain stable and can be stored for months or even years with no signs of refermentation.

The one downside of bottle pasteurization is that some people claim they detect a "cooked" taste to the cider. I haven't found this to be a major problem in the commercial samples I've tried. In fact, if done correctly, this method is probably the simplest and best way to stabilize a sweet cider without the use of preservatives.

A Final Thought

Some people are frustrated mechanics; others love nothing more than to play with their chemistry sets. I myself am a plant geek, and my idea of "scaling up" has been to start learning the ancient arts of grafting and orcharding, so that I can find and grow the fruit that I want to use for my own future cider. My point is that we all have our passions and our interests. Together perhaps we can learn from one another—our successes and failures, our triumphs and tribulations. I hope that as you venture further into the culture and craft of cidermaking, you too will discover much that you can share with the cider community, and with future generations, who will learn from us. Keeping these traditions and techniques alive is what this book is all about.

DEUTSCHE POMOLOGIE

KAISER ALEXANDER

APPENDIX

Brix/Specific Gravity/Potential Alcohol Table

(for use with hydrometers calibrated for measuring liquids at 20°C/68°F)

Note: Many hydrometers are calibrated to a different temperature, typically 60°F (15.6°C). Check the instructions that come with your instrument, or use the equivalent scales below as a fairly close approximation. Take the specific gravity reading from the bottom of the liquid's convex curve (meniscus) inside the sample jar.

Degrees Brix (°B)	Specific Gravity (S.G.)	Potential Alcohol (% abv.)
0	1.0000	0.00
1	1.0039	0.58
2	1.0078	1.15
3	1.0117	1.73
4	1.0156	2.30
5	1.0196	2.88
6	1.0236	3.45
7	1.0277	4.03
8	1.0318	4.60
9	1.0359	5.18
10	1.0400	5.75
11	1.0441	6.33
12	1.0483	6.90
13	1.0525	7.48
14	1.0538	8.05
15	1.0610	8.63
16	1.0653	9.20
17	1.0697	9.78
18	1.0740	10.35
19	1.0784	10.93
20	1.0829	11.50
21	1.0873	12.08
22	1.0918	12.65
23	1.0963	13.23
24	1.1009	13.80
25	1.1055	14.38
26	1.1101	14.95
27	1.1148	15.53
28	1.1195	16.10
29	1.1242	16.68
30	1.1290	17.25
31	1.1338	17.83
32	1.1386	18.40
33	1.1435	18.98
34	1.1484	19.55
35	1.1533	20.13
36	1.1583	20.70
37	1.1633	21.28
38	1.1683	21.85
39	1.1734	22.43
40	1.1785	23.00

Temperature Adjustment: For Hydrometers Calibrated for 20°C (68°F)

Note: Add or subtract the factors in the chart below from the readings observed in the juice/liquid being measured for specific gravity. If your hydrometer is calibrated for a different temperature, refer to the instructions that come with your equipment.

°C	°F	15°B	20°B	25°B	30°B	35°B	40°B

Correction factor to be subtracted from observed hydrometer reading:

°C	°F	15°B	20°B	25°B	30°B	35°B	40°B
15	59	0.26	0.28	0.30	0.32	0.33	0.34
16	60.8	0.22	0.23	0.25	0.26	0.27	0.28
17	62.6	0.16	0.18	0.19	0.20	0.20	0.21
18	64.4	0.11	0.12	0.13	0.13	0.14	0.14
19	66.2	0.06	0.06	0.06	0.07	0.07	0.07
20	68	0	0	0	0	0	0

Correction factor to be added to observed hydrometer reading:

°C	°F	15°B	20°B	25°B	30°B	35°B	40°B
21	69.8	0.06	0.06	0.07	0.07	0.07	0.07
22	71.6	0.12	0.12	0.13	0.14	0.14	0.15
23	73.4	0.17	0.19	0.20	0.21	0.21	0.22
24	75.2	0.24	0.26	0.27	0.28	0.29	0.30
25	77	0.31	0.32	0.34	0.35	0.36	0.38

RESOURCES

Web Sites

Beer Judge Certification Program (BJCP)

www.bjcp.org
Publishes style guidelines and descriptions for cider and perry.

The Cider Digest

www.talisman.com/cider
A free, informative, and well-run online forum created in 1991, with contributions from both amateur and commercial cidermakers. As of 2008, nearly 1500 issues of the Digest had been published to the online mailing list, and back issues are accessible in the Archives section. Email issues are sent out about once or twice a week. An invaluable source of information, and a great forum for asking questions about anything related to cider.

Lost Meadow Orchard and Cider Mill

www.lostmeadowvt.com
Terry Bradshaw is a serious amateur cidermaker with an impressive home setup. His Web site and blog are well worth checking out, especially for anyone looking to scale up their own cider operation.

Old Scrump's Cider House

www.ciderandperry.co.uk
An amalgamation of two former British cider Web sites; offers general information on cider and perry history and cidermaking, plus lists of producers in the UK.

The Three Counties Cider and Perry Association (TCCPA)

www.thethreecountiesciderandperryassociation.co.uk

The UK Cider Page

www.ukcider.co.uk/wiki/index.php/Main_Page
Lots of articles on cider and perry, plus an online discussion forum for subscribers; a guide to cider pubs, festivals, and events; and information on cider and perry producers in the UK, Europe, and around the world.

The Welsh Cider and Perry Society

www.welshcider.co.uk

The Wittenham Hill Cider Portal

www.cider.org.uk
The most thorough and useful Web site for small-scale cidermakers. Dr. Andrew Lea is an enthusiastic hobbyist who has a background in food science and he contributes much in-depth and relevant information on every aspect of cidermaking.

The Winemaking Home Page

http://winemaking.jackkeller.net
Lots of good information on home winemaking, updated regularly. The page "Strains of Wine Yeast" briefly describes the characteristics of many commercially available yeasts.

Home Cider Presses and Orchard Equipment

Correll Cider Presses

24791 Warthen Road
Elmira, OR 97437
541-935-3825
Handmade wooden cider presses in several sizes and models; write or call for price list.

Happy Valley Ranch

16577 West 327th Street
Paola, KS 66071
913-849-3103
www.happyvalleyranch.com
Wood and cast-iron cider and wine presses in a variety of styles, from the Pioneer Jr. and Harvester (single-tub) to the double-tub American Harvester; also carries grinders, press bags, and other accessories.

Lehman's

Mailing address: 289 Kurzen Road N., Dalton, OH 44618
Store address: 4779 Kidron Road, Kidron, OH 44636
888-438-5346
www.lehmans.com
Carries cider-making equipment, plus a whole line of nonelectric appliances and tools.

Orchard Equipment Supply Co. (OESCO)

P.O. Box 540
Conway, MA 01341
413-369-4335; 800-634-5557 (toll-free)
www.oescoinc.com
Supplier of hand tools, equipment, and orchard supplies.

Peach Ridge Orchard Supply, Inc.

8405 Fruit Ridge Avenue
Sparta, MI 49345
800-452-6748 (toll-free)
www.peachridge.com

The Phoenix Foundry

Box 68-L
Marcus, WA 99151
509-684-5434
Sturdy, custom-made, single- and double-tub hand-screw presses that come with a five-year warranty.

Vigo, Ltd.

Dunkeswell Airfield
Honiton, Devon EX14 4LF
England
01404-890-262
www.vigoltd.com

Organizations and More

American Homebrewers Association

P.O. Box 1679
Boulder, CO 80306-1679
303-447-0816
www.beertown.org
A nonprofit organization dedicated to providing information to its 20,000 members and the general public on the art and science of homebrewing. Sponsors the annual National Homebrew Competition, which includes a cider category.

Campaign for Real Ale (CAMRA)

230 Hatfield Road
St. Albans, Herts AL1 4LW
England
44-01-727-86-7201
www.camra.org.uk
CAMRA operates a subgroup called the Apple and Pear Produce Liaison Executive (APPLE). APPLE publishes the Good Cider Guide, *which lists pubs in Britain where real cider and perry are available. Its Web site provides links to many other cider sites, containing much good information on traditional cidermaking and the names and addresses/locations of producers.*

Home Orchard Society

P.O. Box 230192
Tigard, OR 97281
503-639-6250
http://www.wvi.com/~dough/HOS
A nonprofit educational organization whose members can participate in scionwood and rootstock exchanges; the society publishes its newsletter, Pome News, *four times a year.*

New York State Fruit Testing Cooperative Association

P.O. Box 462
Geneva, NY 14456
315-787-2205
A fruit-testing organization founded in 1918 as a nonprofit cooperative fruit nursery.

North American Fruit Explorers (NAFEX)

1716 Apples Road
Chapin, IL 62628
www.nafex.org
NAFEX is a network of more than 3,000 members throughout the United States and Canada devoted to the discovery, cultivation, and appreciation of superior varieties of fruits and nuts. Members receive the quarterly journal Pomona *and can access many old pomological books and other materials from the organization's library. Membership dues are $10 for one year, $19 for two years.*

Seed Savers Exchange

3076 Winn Road
Decorah, IA 52101
319-382-5990
www.seedsavers.org
Seed Savers Exchange is a grassroots organization of more than 8,000 gardeners dedicated to preserving our common plant heritage by growing and sharing heirloom varieties. In addition to growing out vegetables at its Heritage Farm headquarters, SSE also planted its Historic Orchard in 1989, which includes more than 700 different kinds of apples, most of them from nineteenth-century Europe and America. Membership includes an annual Yearbook, where members can find scionwood for numerous apple varieties along with heirloom vegetable seeds.

Slow Food USA

20 Jay Street, Suite M-04
Brooklyn, NY 11201
718-260-8000
www.slowfoodusa.org
The national office for the international Slow Food movement, an organization with more than 80,000 members whose mission is to promote food diversity and local food traditions worldwide. Slow Food's International Ark of Taste has recognized traditional cider producers in the Basque regions, and perry-makers in England's West Country. Slow Food USA promotes artisanal American cider and heritage apples and pears. Regular membership is $60 per year.

Mail-Order and Online Suppliers

A Note on Hard Cider and Perry Producers: Because of differing state alcohol and tax laws, it is currently difficult for cidermakers to sell hard cider to retail consumers by mail. Also, most artisanal hard cider wineries are small in size and rely on local and regional sales. Your best bet is to locate a cidery in your area that sells retail, or to inquire at your local liquor outlet or beer store whether it can find and carry a selection of good-quality regional hard ciders. Some of the sites listed under the Web sites section above offer information and lists of cideries throughout the U.S. and in Europe.

Home Winemaking Equipment and Supplies

The Home Brewery

P.O. Box 730
Ozark, MO 65721
800-321-2739
www.homebrewing.com

E.C. Kraus

P.O. Box 7850
Independence, MO 64054
800-353-1906 (toll-free)
www.eckraus.com

Midwest Homebrewing and Winemaking Supplies

3440 Belt Line Boulevard
Minneapolis, MN 55416
952-925-9835; 888-449-2739 (toll-free)
www.midwestsupplies.com

Yeast Suppliers

White Labs, Inc.
888-5-YEAST-5 (toll-free)
www.whitelabs.com

Wyeast Laboratories

P.O. Box 146
Odell, OR 97044
541-354-1335
www.wyeastlab.com

Apples and Cider Products

Applesource

1716 Apples Road
Chapin, IL 62628
217-245-7589
www.applesource.com

A mail-order company that each fall ships rare, historic, and uncommon apple varieties; customers can order sampler boxes that are custom-packed with any of the varieties they wish to try.

Wood's Cider Mill

1482 Weathersfield Center Road
Springfield, VT 05016
802-263-5547
www.woodscidermill.com
A family farm that has been making boiled cider and cider jelly since 1882.

Festivals and Competitions

CiderDays

Franklin County, Massachusetts
Annual, always the first weekend in November
www.ciderday.org
Founded in 1994, CiderDays has grown into the largest festival of its kind in the U.S. It takes place in many orchards and other venues around Franklin County in western Massachusetts, which is a historic apple-growing and cider-producing regions dotted with farms and scenic hill towns. Features lots of workshops, speakers, orchard and cider mill tours, and apple and cider tastings; many family activities as well.

Great Lakes Olde World Syder Competiton (GLOWS)

Sponsored by the Michigan Beer Guide
www.michiganbeerguide.com
GLOWS is one of several cider competitions that have cropped up in the U.S. over the past few years, and it has judging for various categories/styles of cider and perry, separated into commercial and noncommercial entries. Judges are all BJCP-certified, and it can be very instructive to get comments on your own ciders from such an event.

Mail-Order Sources for Apple and Pear Trees

Adams County Nursery

P.O. Box 108, 26 Nursery Road
Aspers, PA 17304
717-677-8105
www.acnursery.com
Established in 1905; Web site offers good apple-growing information.

Bay Laurel Nursery

2500 El Camino Real
Atascadero, CA 93422
805-466-3406
www.baylaurelnursery.com

Big Horse Creek Farm

P.O. Box 70
Lansing, NC 28643
www.bighorsecreekfarm.com
Large selection of apples, with a focus on those varieties that originated or grow well in the southern Appalachian region.

Boyer Nurseries & Orchard

405 Boyer Nursery Road
Biglerville, PA 17307
717-677-8558
www.boyernurseries.com

Cloud Mountain Farm

6906 Goodwin Road
Everson, WA 98247
360-966-5859
www.cloudmountainfarm.com

Cummins Nursery

18 Glass Factory Bay
Geneva, NY 14456
865-681-8423; 607-227-6147
www.cumminsnursery.com

Offers one of the best selections of bareroot cider apple varieties, and one of the few sources for European perry pears.

Edible Forest Nursery

653 S. Segoe Road, Apt. 4
Madison, WI 53711
608-663-0840
www.edibleforestnursery.com

Fedco Trees

P.O. Box 520
Waterville, ME 04903
207-873-7333
www.fedcoseeds.com/trees.htm
Good selection of rare and classic Maine apples, as well as other varieties.

Greenmantle Nursery

3010 Ettersburg Road
Garberville, CA 95542
707-986-7504
www.greenmantlenursery.com

Lawson's Nursery

2730 Yellow Creek Road
Ball Ground, GA 30107
770-893-2141
A selection of old and new apples, specializing in varieties for the Southern U.S.

Henry Leuthardt Nurseries Inc.

Montauk Highway, Box 666
East Moriches, Long Island, NY 11940
631-878-1387
www.henryleuthardtnurseries.com
Specializes in espalier-trained fruit trees, but also offers other dwarf and semidwarf trees.

Miller Nurseries

5060 West Lake Road
Canandaigua, NY 14424-8904
800-836-9630
www.millernurseries.com

One Green World

28696 South Cramer Road
Molalla, OR 97038-8576
503-651-3005; 877-353-4028 (toll-free)
www.onegreenworld.com

Raintree Nursery

391 Butts Road
Morton, WA 98356
360-496-6400
www.raintreenursery.com

St. Lawrence Nurseries

325 State Highway 345
Potsdam, NY 13676
315-265-6739
www.sln.potsdam.ny.us
A good selection of organically grown, cold-hardy apples for northern climates, grafted on standard Antonovka rootstock; including some good old cider varieties like Ashmead's Kernel, Bullock, and several russets.

Trees of Antiquity

20 Wellsona Road
Paso Robles, CA 93446
805-467-9907
www.treesofantiquity.com

Vintage Virginia Apples

P.O. Box 210
North Garden, VA 22959
434-295-5382
www.vintagevirginiaapples.com
Offers an excellent variety of heritage apple varieties, including many old Southern varieties and ones that are good for cider-making (Harrison, Hewes Crab, etc.). Also sells gift boxes of apples, apple rootstocks, and scionwood for grafting.

NOTES

Chapter 1—A History of Cider

1. Barrie E. Juniper and David J. Mabberley. *The Story of the Apple* (Portland, Ore.: Timber Press, 2006).

2. Henry David Thoreau, "Wild Apples," in *The Works of Thoreau,* ed. Henry S. Canby (Boston: Houghton Mifflin, 1937), 730.

3. Joan Morgan and Alison Richards, *The New Book of Apples* (London: Ebury Press, 2002), 186.

4. Spencer A. Beach, *The Apples of New York,* vol. 1 (Albany, N.Y.: J. B. Lyon Co., 1905), 10.

5. John Hull Brown, *Early American Beverages* (New York: Bonanza Books, 1966), 17–18.

6. Ibid., 15–16.

7. Morgan and Richards, 153-54.

8. William Coxe, *A View of the Cultivation of Fruit Trees, and the Management of Orchards and Cider,* facsimile of 1817 ed. (Rockton, ON: Pomona Books, 1976), 93.

9. J. C. Folger and S. M. Thomson, *The Commercial Apple Industry of North America* (New York: Macmillan, 1923), 10.

10. J. M. Trowbridge, *The Cider Maker's Handbook: A Complete Guide for Making and Keeping Pure Cider* (New York: Orange Judd Co., 1917), 8–9.

Chapter 2—Apple Varieties for Cider

1. Leonard Mascall, from Robert Hogg, *The Fruit Manual,* 5th ed. (London, 1884), quoted in Beach, 263.

Chapter 3—Sweet Cider: From Tree to Juice

1. Vrest Orton, *The American Cider Book,* rev. ed. (New York: North Point Press, 1995), 28–29.

2. Source: US Apple Association

3. Dianne Onstad, *The Whole Foods Companion* (White River Junction, Vt.: Chelsea Green, 1996), 20, 25.

4. H. V. Taylor, *The Apples of England* (London: Crosby Lockwood & Son, Ltd., 1936), 35.

5. For more detailed information and a recipe for making your own iodine solution, go to http://www.umass.edu/fruitadvisor/clements/articles/sitest.htm.

6. Georges Warcollier, *The Principles and Practice of Cider-Making,* trans. Vernon L. S. Charley and Pamela M. Mumford (London: Leonard Hill Ltd., 1949), 70–71.

7. Sally Fallon, *Nourishing Traditions,* 2nd edition (Washington, D.C.: New Trends Publishing, 2001), 587.

Chapter 4—Hard Cider: From Juice to Bottle

1. Gene Logsdon, *Good Spirits: A New Look at Ol' Demon Alcohol* (White River Junction, Vt.: Chelsea Green Publishing, 1999), 16–17.

Chapter 5—Cider Styles and Traditions

1. Orton, 9.

2. Beach, *The Apples of New York,* vol. 1, 10.

3. Mrs. Boyle Bernard, *Our Common Fruits* (London: Frederick Warne & Co., 1866), 8.

4. Coxe, 93.

5. Source: National Association of Cider Makers (UK), cited in Peter Mitchell, *Out of the Orchard into the Glass* (London/Pershore, England: NACM and Mitchell F&D Ltd., 2005), 20.

6. Cézanne and Morgan Miller, "Cider Styles," Cider Space Web site, http://www.teleport.com/~incider/ciderstyles.html (Jan. 11, 1999).

Chapter 6—Tasting and Evaluating Cider

1. Trowbridge, 8–9.

Chapter 7—Perry, or Pear Cider

1. For more historical facts on pear-growing and perry in England, see Gillian Grafton, "Pears and Perry in the UK" (http://homepage.ntlworld.com/scrumpy/cider/history2.htm) and Bob Capshew, "Pear Cider," in *Michigan Beer Guide,* 12:96 (May-June 2008).

2. Dave Matthews, "Mantilly—World Pear Capital," in *CAMRA's Good Cider Guide* (St. Albans, England: Campaign for Real Ale, 2005), 107-09.

3. For additional information on English perry pear culti-vars, see *HortScience,* vol. 37:2 (April 2002). 261-62, and L.C. Luckwill and A. Pollard, *Perry Pears* (Bristol: University of Bristol, 1963).

Chapter 8—Stronger Waters: Cider Vinegar and Spirits

1. Orton, 126.

2. R. W. Apple, "Seductive Brandy of Normandy's Eden," New York Times, 16. September 1998, see F, p. 1.

3. A. J. Liebling, *Normandy Revisited* (New York: Simon & Schuster, 1958), quoted in Apple.

4. Coxe, 75.

5. Marialisa Calta, "Where Cider Gets a French Kick," New York Times, 11 November 2007 (http://travel.nytimes .com/2007/11/11/travel/11journeys.html).

6. Coxe, 98–99.

BIBLIOGRAPHY

Alwood, William B. *A Study of Cider Making in France, Germany, and England*. Washington, DC: US Government Printing Office, 1903.

American Pomological Society. *History of Fruit Growing and Handling in the United States of America and Canada, 1860–1972*. Kelowna, B.C.: Regatta City Press Ltd., 1976.

Bailey, Liberty Hyde. *The Principles of Fruit Growing*. New York: Macmillan, 1916.

Beach, Spencer A. *The Apples of New York*. Albany, N.Y.: J. B. Lyon Co., 1905.

Bernard, Mrs. Boyle. *Our Common Fruits*. London: Frederick Warne & Co., 1866.

Brown, John Hull. *Early American Beverages*. New York: Bonanza Books, 1966.

Brown, Sanborn C. *Wines and Beers of Old New England*. Hanover, N.H.: University Press of New England, 1978.

Browning, Frank. *Apples*. New York: North Point Press, 1998.

Browning, Frank, and Sharon Silva. *An Apple Harvest: Recipes and Orchard Lore*. Berkeley, Ca.: Ten Speed Press, 1999.

Buell, J. S. *The Cider Maker's Manual*. Buffalo: Haas, Nauert & Co., 1874.

Bultitude, John. *Apples: A Guide to the Identification of International Varieties*. Seattle: University of Washington Press, 1983.

Bunker, John P. Jr. *Not Far from the Tree: A Brief History of the Apples and the Orchards of Palermo, Maine, 1804–2004*. Palermo, Me.: Self-published, 2007.

Burford, Tom. *Apples: A Catalog of International Varieties*. Revised and expanded edition. Monroe, Va.: Self-published, 2004.

Calhoun, Creighton Lee Jr. *Old Southern Apples*. Blacksburg, Va.: McDonald & Woodward, 1995.

Campaign for Real Ale. *CAMRA's Good Cider Guide*. Revised edition. St. Albans, Herts., UK: CAMRA, 2005.

Copas, Liz. *A Somerset Pomona: The Cider Apples of Somerset*. Wimborne, Dorset, UK: Dovecote Press, 2001.

Correnty, Paul. *The Art of Cidermaking*. Boulder, Colo.: Brewers Publications, 1995.

Coxe, William. *A View of the Cultivation of Fruit Trees, and the Management of Orchards and Cider*. Rockton, ON: Pomona Books, 1976. Facsimile reprint of 1817 edition published by M. Carey & Son, Philadelphia, Pa.

Downing, A. J. *The Fruit and Fruit Trees of America*. New York: Wiley and Putnam, 1845.

Drouin, Beatrice, and Christian Drouin. *Au Coeur de la Cuisine Normande: Cidre, Calvados et Pommeau*. Conde-sur-Noireau, France: Editions Charles Corlet, 2001.

Folger, J. C., and S. M. Thomson. *The Commercial Apple Industry of North America*. New York: Macmillan, 1923.

Graves, Robert. *The White Goddess*. New York: Farrar, Straus & Giroux, 1966.

Hanson, Beth, ed. *The Best Apples to Grow and Buy*. (Brooklyn Botanic Garden All-Region Guides, Handbook #181). Brooklyn, NY: Brooklyn Botanic Garden, 2005.

Hedrick, U. P. *Systematic Pomology*. New York: Macmillan, 1925.

Hogg, Robert. *The Apple and Its Varieties*. London: Groombridge & Sons, 1851.

Hogg, Robert, and H. G. Bull. *Apples and Pears as Vintage Fruits*. Hereford, UK: Jakeman & Carver, 1886.

Janson, H. Frederic. *Pomona's Harvest: An Illustrated Chronicle of Antiquarian Fruit Literature*. Portland, Ore.: Timber Press, 1996.

Juniper, Barrie, and David J. Mabberley. *The Story of the Apple*. Portland, Ore.: Timber Press, 2006.

Kenrick, William. *The New American Orchardist*. Boston: Otis, Broaders and Co., 1846.

Logsdon, Gene. *Good Spirits: A New Look at Ol' Demon Alcohol*. White River Junction, Vt: Chelsea Green Publishing, 1999.

Luckwill, L.C., and A. Pollard, eds. *Perry Pears*. Bristol, UK: University of Bristol, 1963.

Manhart, Warren. *Apples for the Twenty-First Century*. Portland, Ore.: North American Tree Co., 1996.

Marshall, John, and Rick Steigmeyer. *Washington Apple Country*. Portland, Ore.: Graphic Arts Center Publishing Co., 1995.

Mattsson, Henrik. *Calvados: The Word's Premier Apple Brandy*. Malmo, Sweden: Flavourrider.com, 2004.

Maynard, Harold H. *Marketing Northwestern Apples*. New York: Ronald Press, 1923.

Mitchell, Peter. *Out of the Orchard into the Glass: An Appreciation of Cider and Perry*. London and Pershore, Worcs., UK: National Association of Cider Makers/Mitchell F&D Ltd., 2005.

Morgan, Joan, and Alison Richards. *The New Book of Apples*. London: Ebury Press, 2002.

Onstad, Dianne. *The Whole Foods Companion*. White River Junction, Vt.: Chelsea Green Publishing, 1996.

Orton, Vrest. *The American Cider Book*. New York: North Point Press, 1995.

Phillips, Michael. *The Apple Grower: A Guide for the Organic Orchardist*. Revised and expanded edition. White River Junction, Vt.: Chelsea Green Publishing, 2005.

Proulx, Annie, and Lew Nichols. *Cider: Making, Using & Enjoying Sweet & Hard Cider. 3rd edition*. North Adams, Mass.: Storey Publishing, 2003.

Smith, Muriel W. G. *National Apple Register of the United Kingdom*. Pinner, UK: Ministry of Agriculture, Fisheries and Food, 1971.

Stilphen, George Albert. *The Apples of Maine*. Bolster's Mills/Harrison, Maine: Stilphen's Crooked River Farm, 1993.

Tannahill, Reay. *Food in History*. New York: Stein and Day, 1973.

Taylor, H. V. *The Apples of England*. London: Crosby Lockwood & Son, Ltd., 1936.

Thomine, Jean-Paul, and Christian Drouin. *Normandy Cocktails: A Guide for 138 Recipes*. Conde-sur-Noireau, France: Editions Charles Corlet, 2005.

Thompson, C. J. S. *The Hand of Destiny: Folklore and Superstition in Everyday Life*. New York: Bell Publishing, 1989.

Thoreau, Henry David. *Journal*. ("The Writings of Henry David Thoreau"). Princeton, NJ: Princeton University Press, 1990.

———. *The Works of Thoreau*, Henry S. Canby, ed. Boston: Houghton Mifflin, 1937.

Trowbridge, J. M. *The Cider Maker's Handbook: A Complete Guide for Making and Keeping Pure Cider*. New York: Orange Judd Co., 1917.

Warcollier, Georges. *The Principles and Practice of Cider-Making,* translated by V. L. S. Charley, with Pamela M. Mumford. London: Leonard Hill Ltd., 1949. Translation of 3rd edition of *La Cidrerie* (Paris: Baillière et Fils, 1928).

Westwood, Melvin N. *Temperate-Zone Pomology*. San Francisco: W. H. Freeman, 1978.

Whealy, Kent, ed. *Fruit, Berry and Nut Inventory*. 3rd edition. Decorah, Iowa: Seed Savers Exchange, 2001.

Williams, R. R. *An Introduction to Modern Cider Apple Production*. Bristol, UK: Long Ashton Research Station, 1975.

Wilkinson, Albert E. *The Apple: A Practical Treatise Dealing with the Latest Modern Practices of Apple Culture*. Boston: Ginn and Co., 1915.

Wynne, Peter. *Apples: History, Folklore, Horticulture, and Gastronomy*. New York: Hawthorn Books, 1975.

Yepsen, Roger. *Apples*. New York: W. W. Norton, 1994.

INDEX